T

SIMP

SEASONS

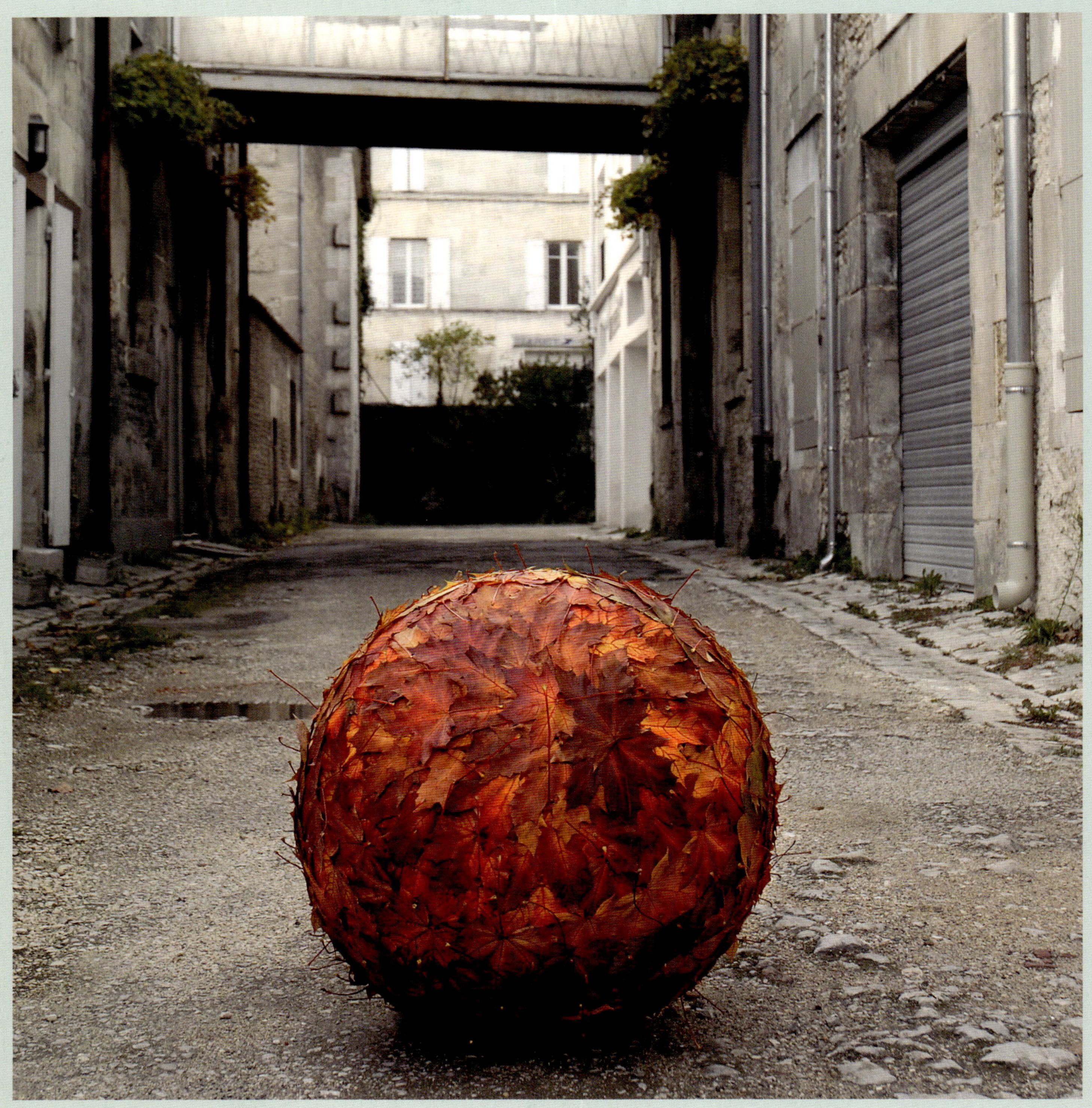

LAND ART
IN TOWN

SIMPLE INSPIRATION THROUGH THE SEASONS

MARC POUYET

Translation by Roland Glasser

F

FRANCES LINCOLN LIMITED
PUBLISHERS

Land Art in Town

Originally published in French as *Artistes de Nature en Ville*

First published in the English language by
Frances Lincoln Ltd
www.franceslincoln.com

Translation by Roland Glasser

A catalogue record for this book is available from the British Library.

ISBN: 978-0-7112-3477--2

Printed and bound in China

1 3 5 7 9 8 6 4 2

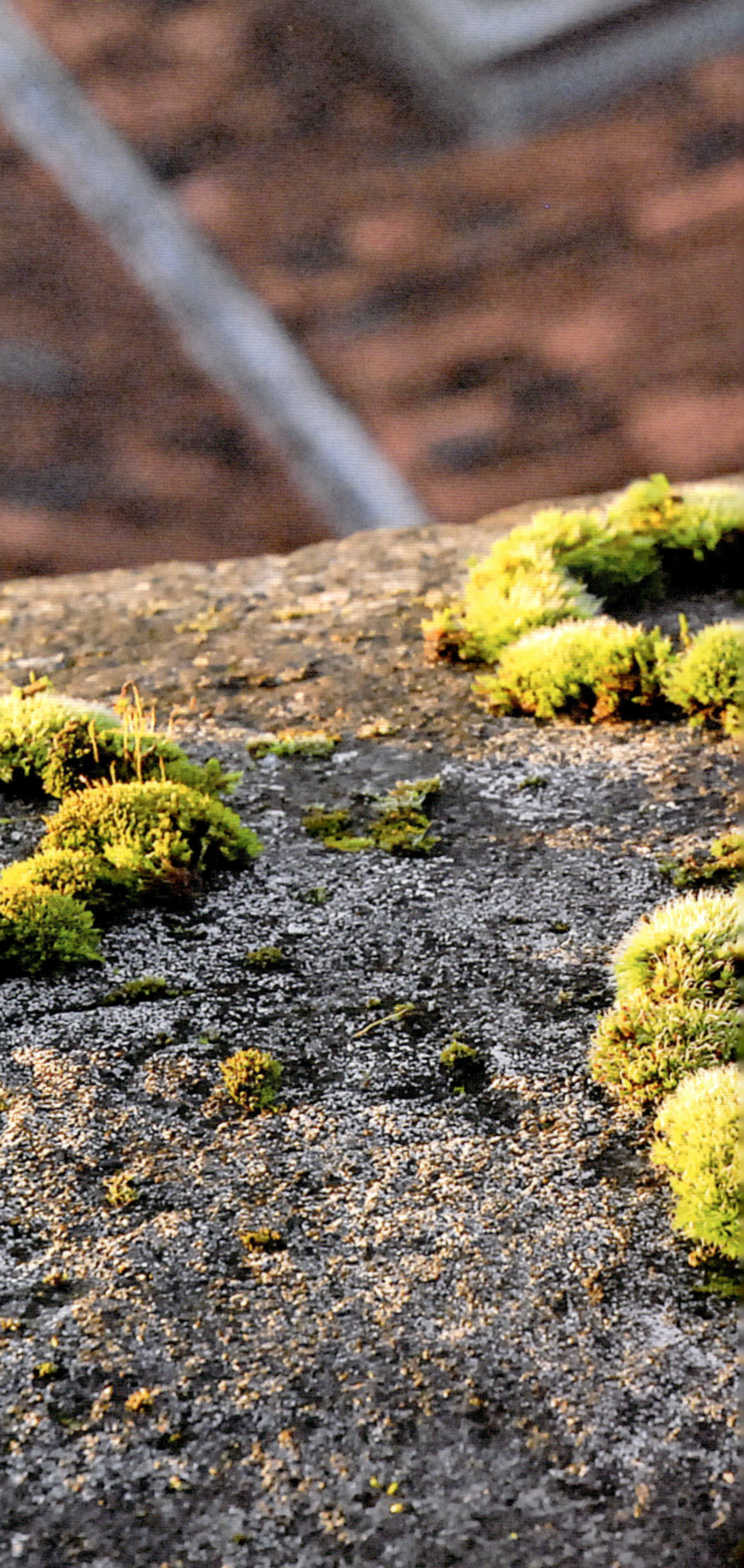

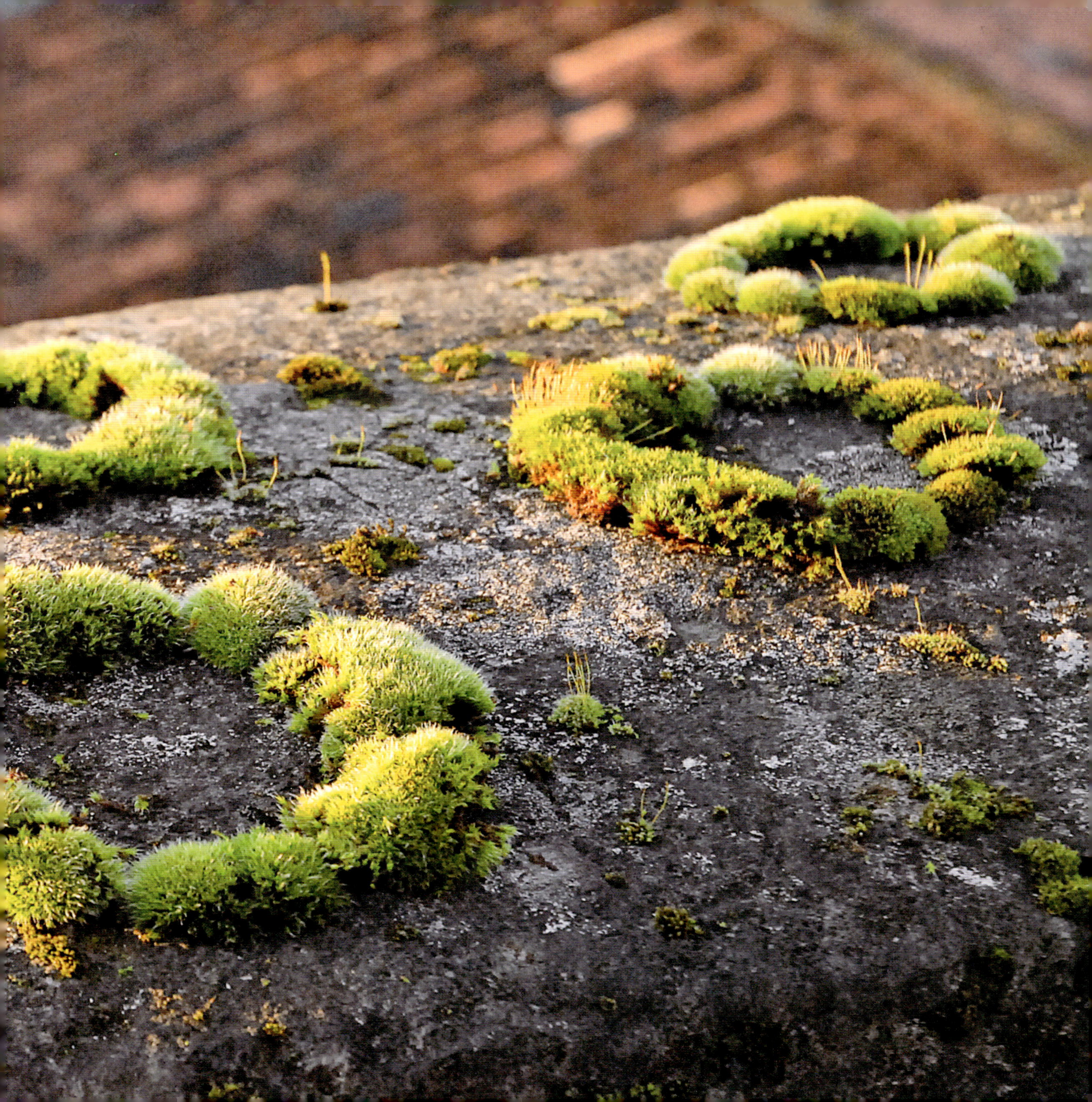

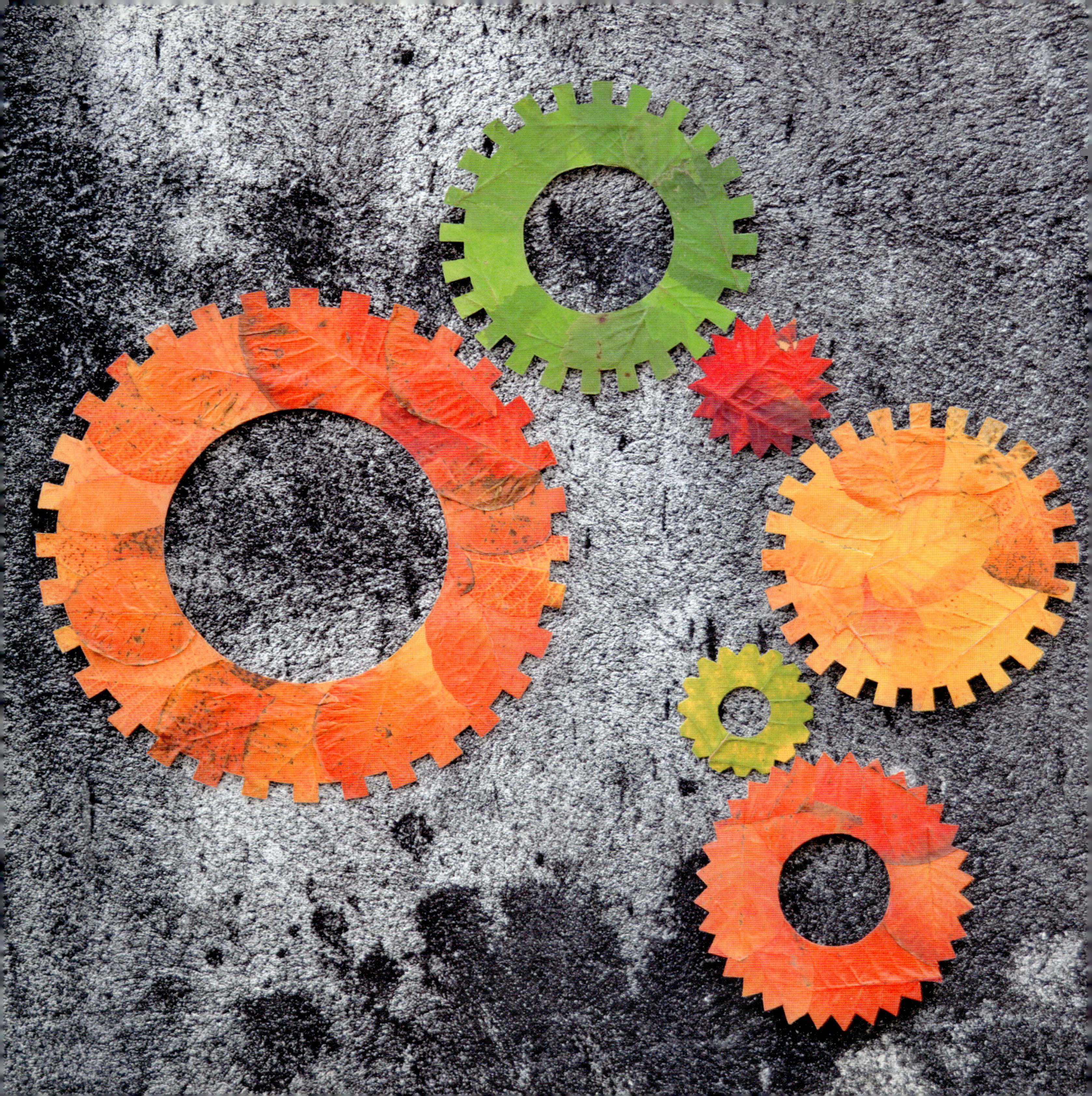

INTRODUCTION

"What can you do when you live in a town?
There's no nature!" Silence.
The little boy's interjection left me speechless.
But nature is everywhere! "Look around you,
there are lots of things you can collect and use."
Phew, got out of that one!

A group of schoolchildren had come to view my exhibition and take part in a land art workshop in a park pavilion in the Paris suburb of Saint-Denis one afternoon. Out in the park, there were plenty of natural elements to collect and use to make installations.

The workshop over, I headed back into Paris, but as I walked to the metro, sat in the train, changed lines, then walked some more, that kid's remark kept going round and round in my head. We were lucky today, but what do you do if there's no lovely green space close by? I reflected on this as I walked, and the truth of my blurted out response became clear as I looked around me: nature really is everywhere.

From flowers to grass to berries to leaves to twigs to stones. Nature is there on the wall of that building, in this car park, at the pavement's edge, on the train platform, in that crack between two paving stones and pushing up through the tarmac. You need to be observant here in town, perhaps more than elsewhere, keep your eyes open, your ears pricked and your nose keen.

You'll have no shortage of installation ideas if you keep the right mindset. The urban landscape offers an infinite variety of different media, unexpected, original, poetic and strange: a public bench, a street sign, a direction arrow marked on the ground.

That very evening I received an email from Jean-Sébastien Griffaton, a "playful gardening" specialist, in which he mentioned the guerrilla gardening movement, seed bombs and clandestine gardens. Then followed some discussions with Fred Lisak, my French publisher, and the theme of a new book was born: Land Art in Town. Very close to street art, it's true, but I for one will continue to use natural materials.

Here we are two years later, and you can see the results of my work, made all over France and in a few other countries too, from cities to suburbs to provincial towns. It is yet more proof that you can really make land art anywhere. Not only is it a magnificent educational tool but a pleasant, creative and poetic way of learning about your urban environment.

Now it's up to you.
Maybe catch up with you on the corner of Green Street?

Marc Pouyet

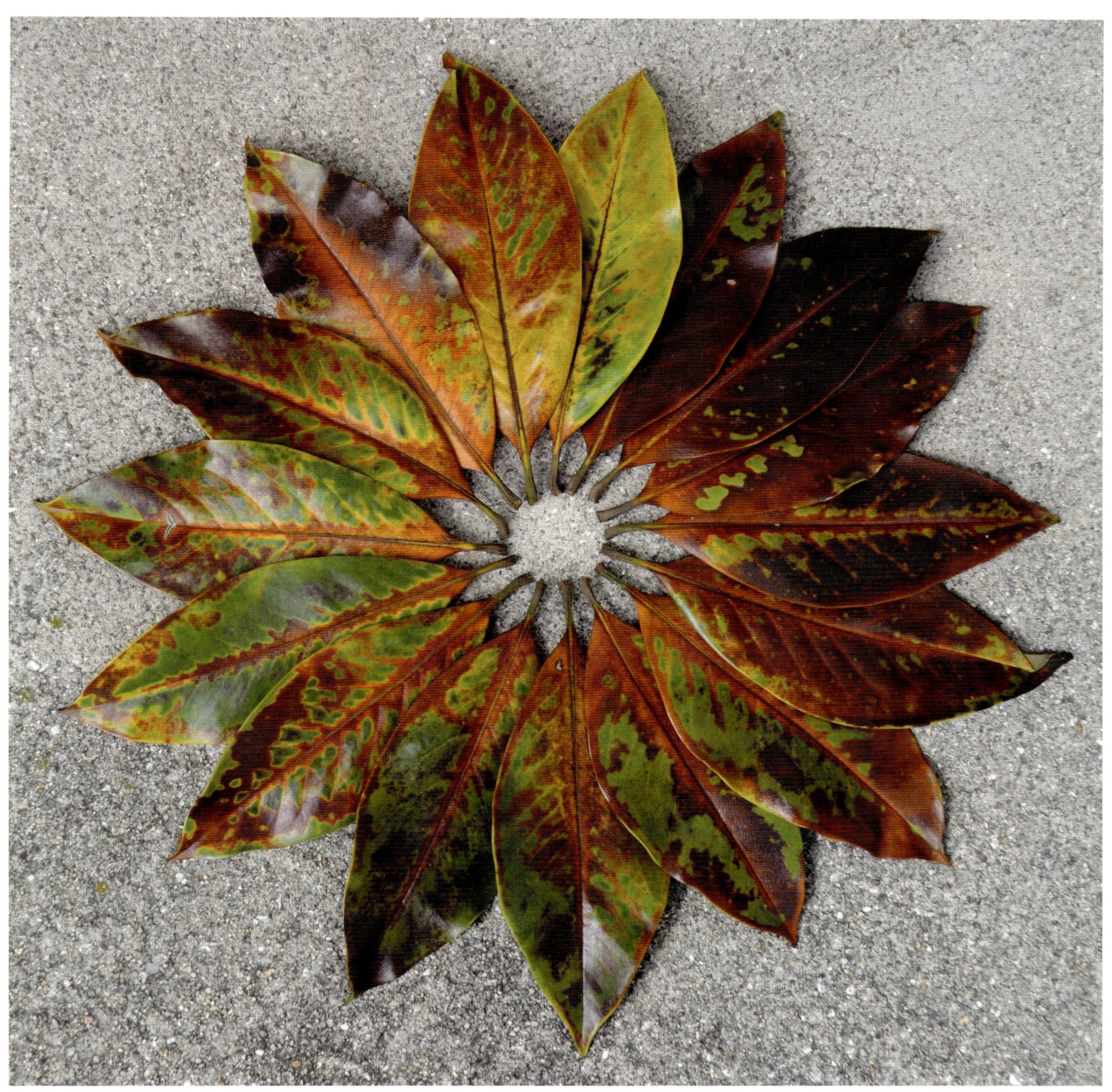

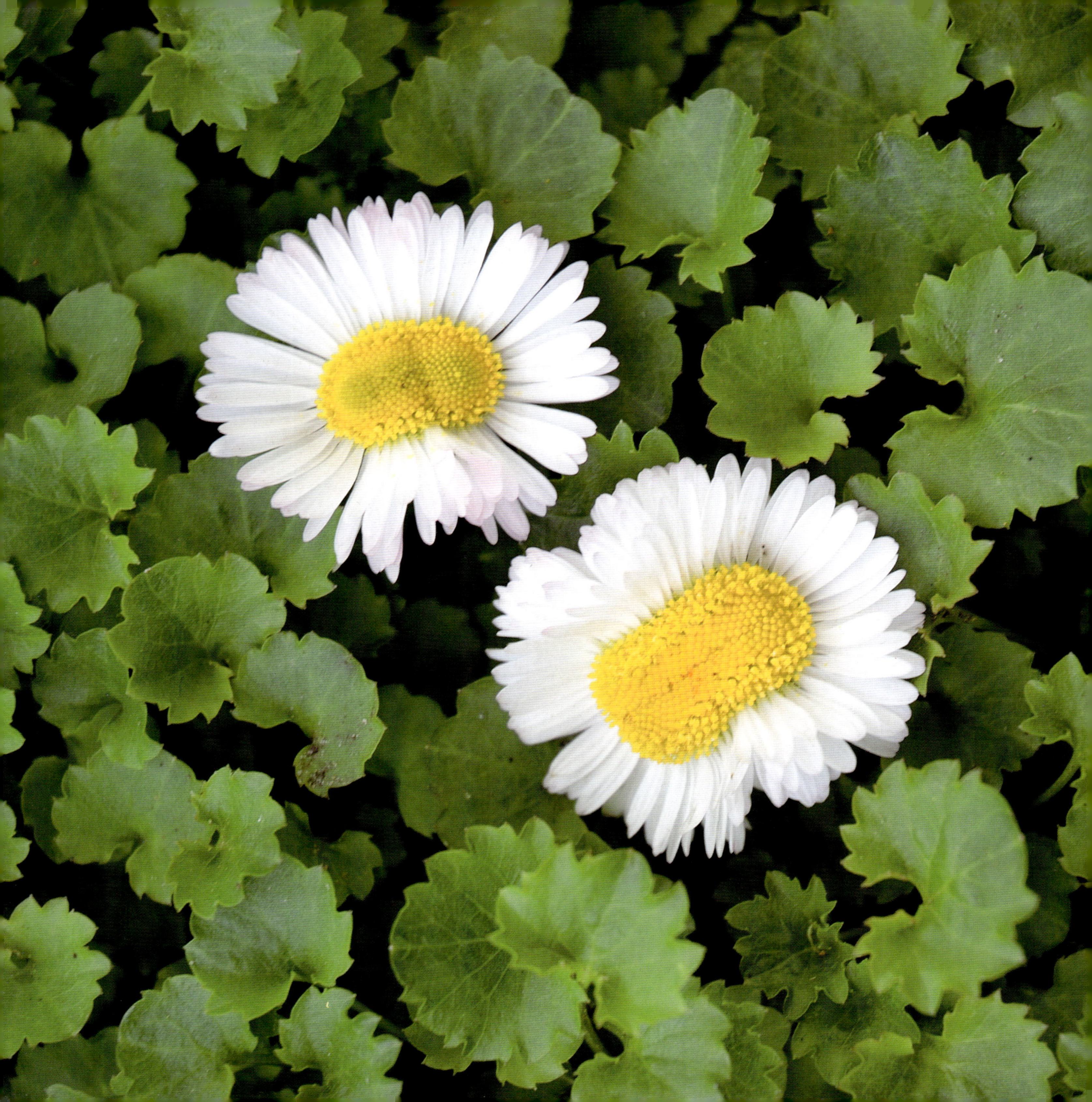

SPRING

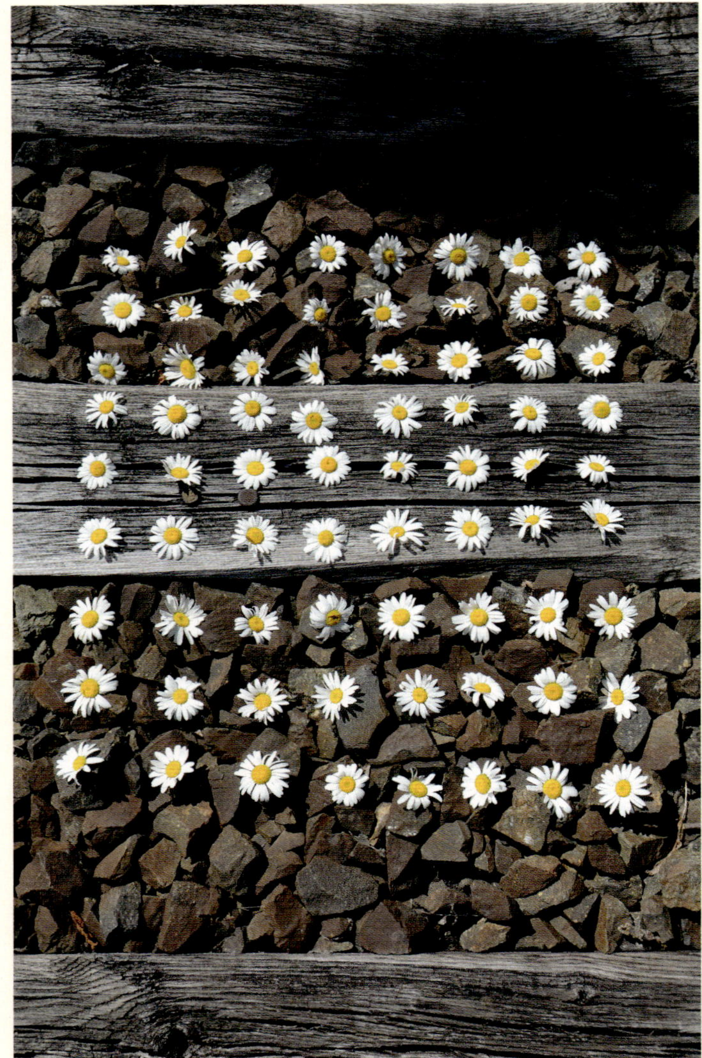

Wake up the sleepers with a sunny square.

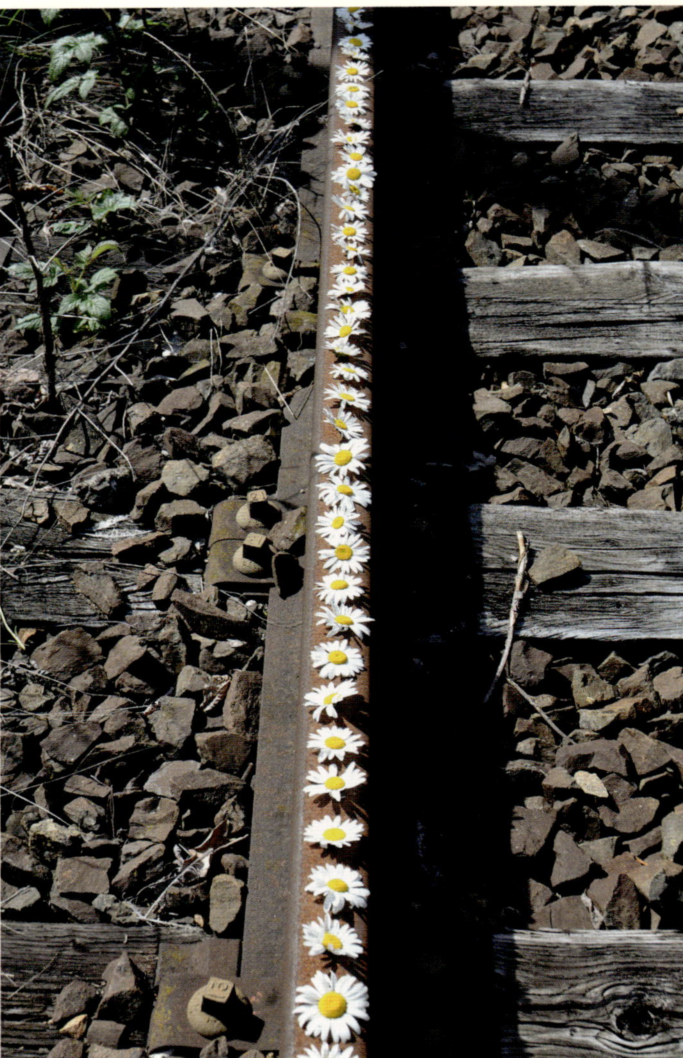

Get your daisies on the right track.

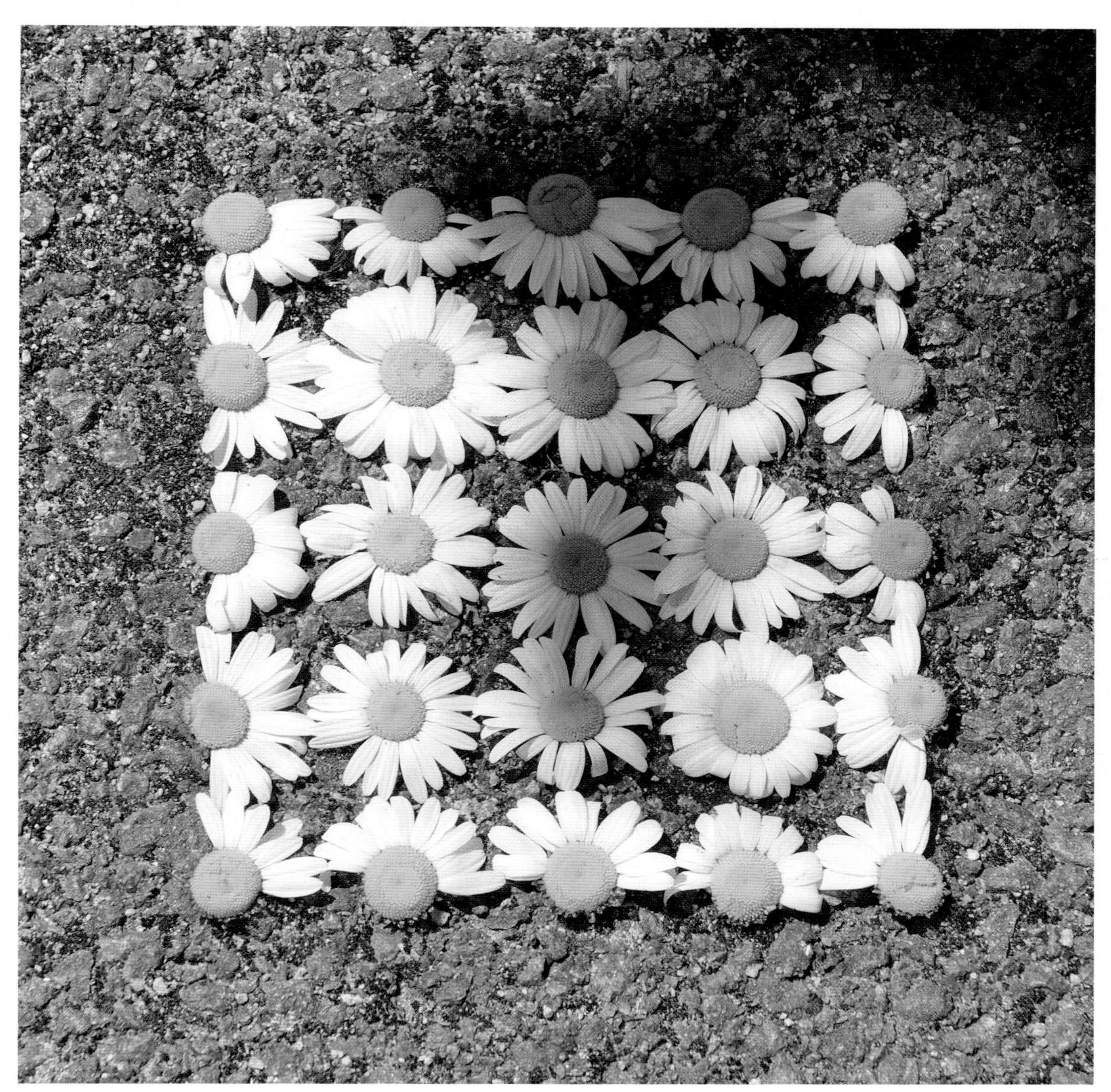

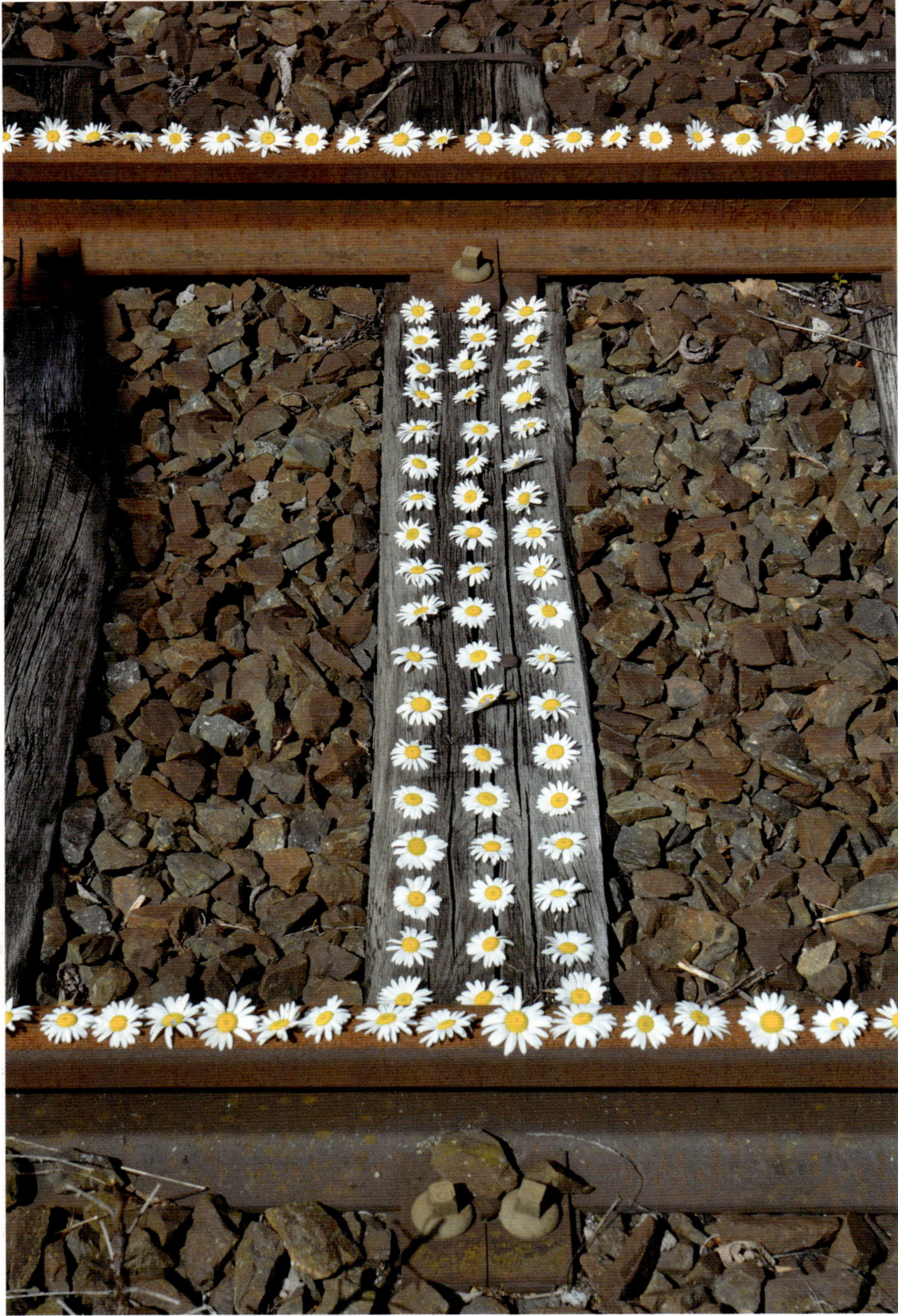

Rusty steel and old cracked wood smile again with a fresh spring makeover.

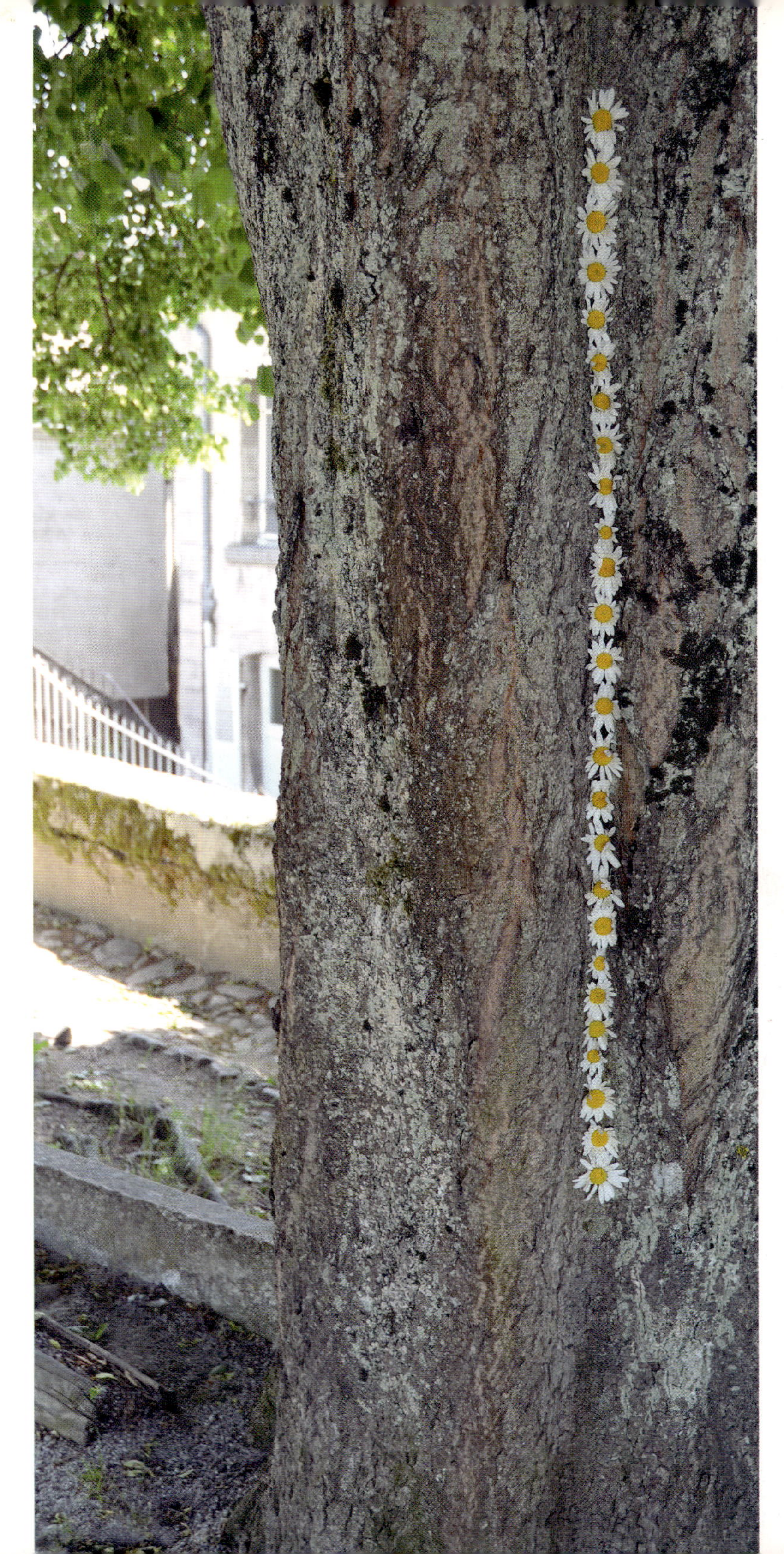

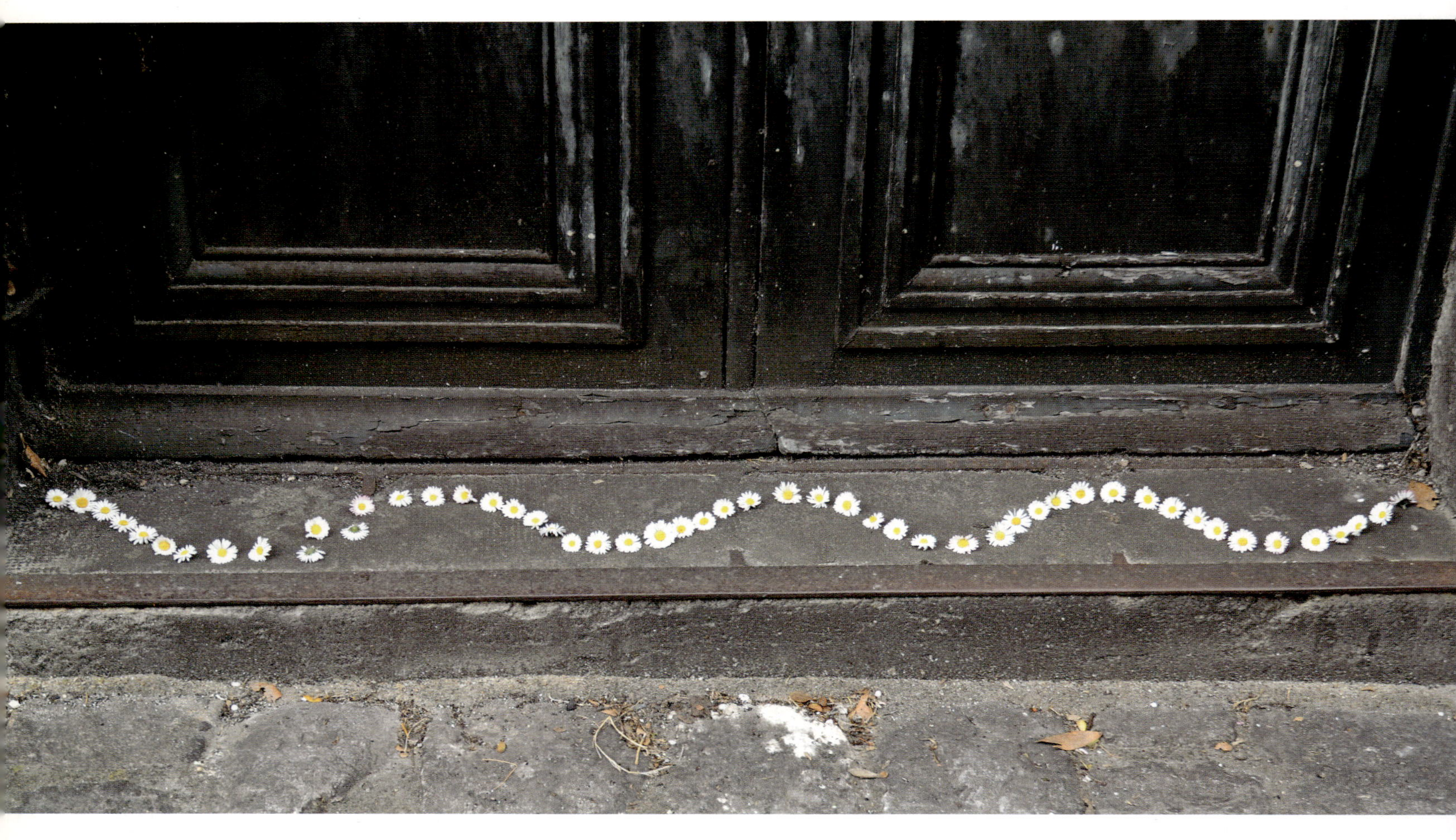

Springtime smiles at your door.

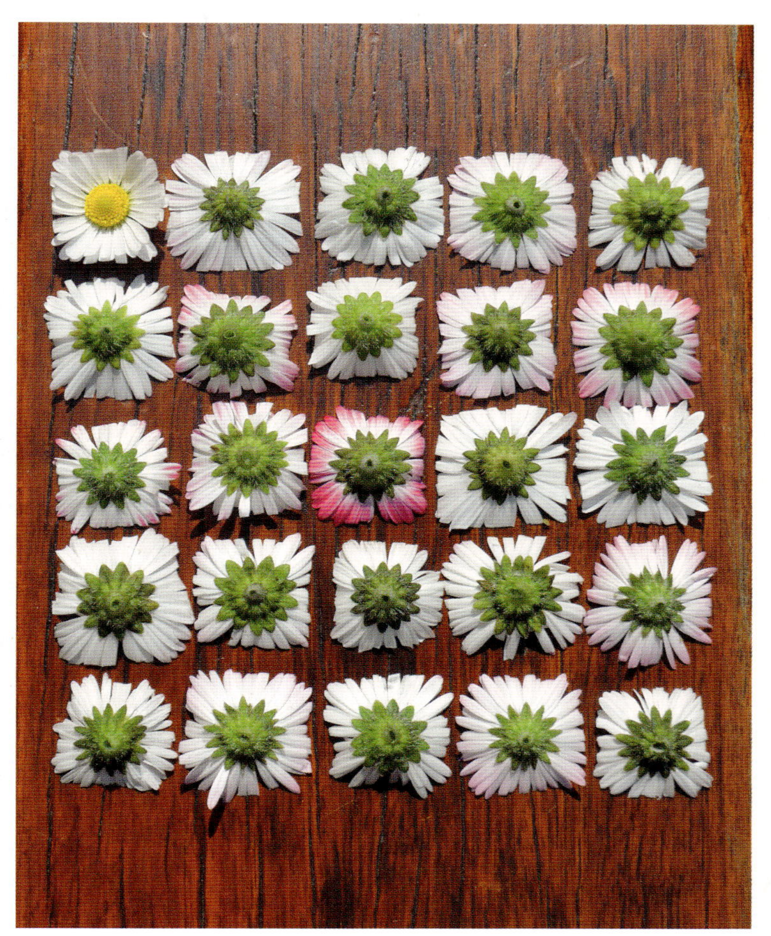

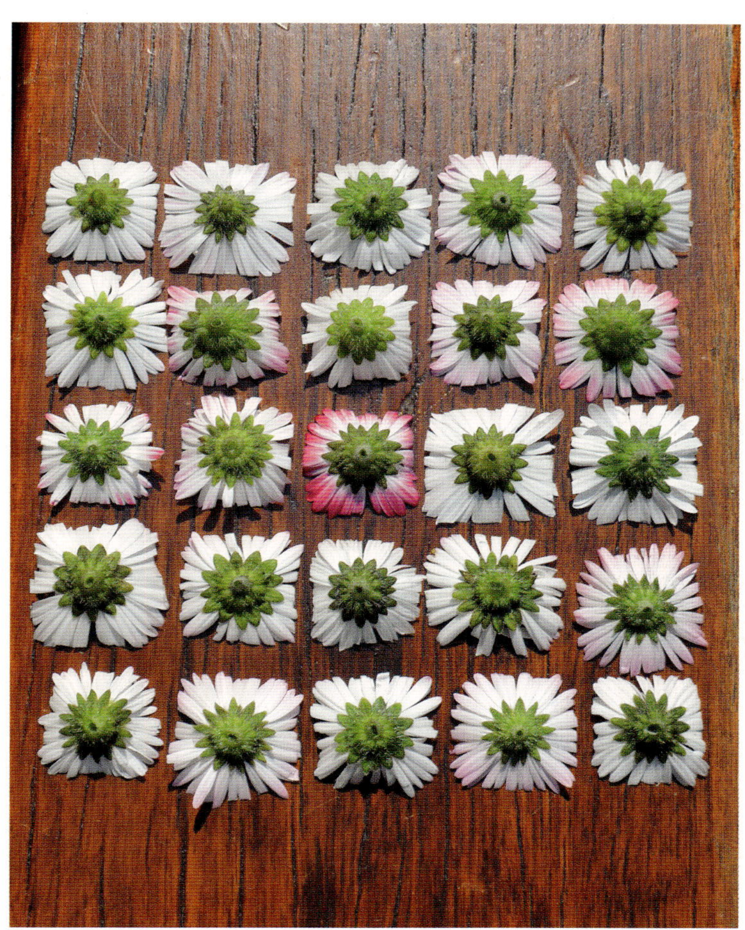

Trimmed daisies gather in neat 5 x 5 squares to make the biggest impact in the most compact space.

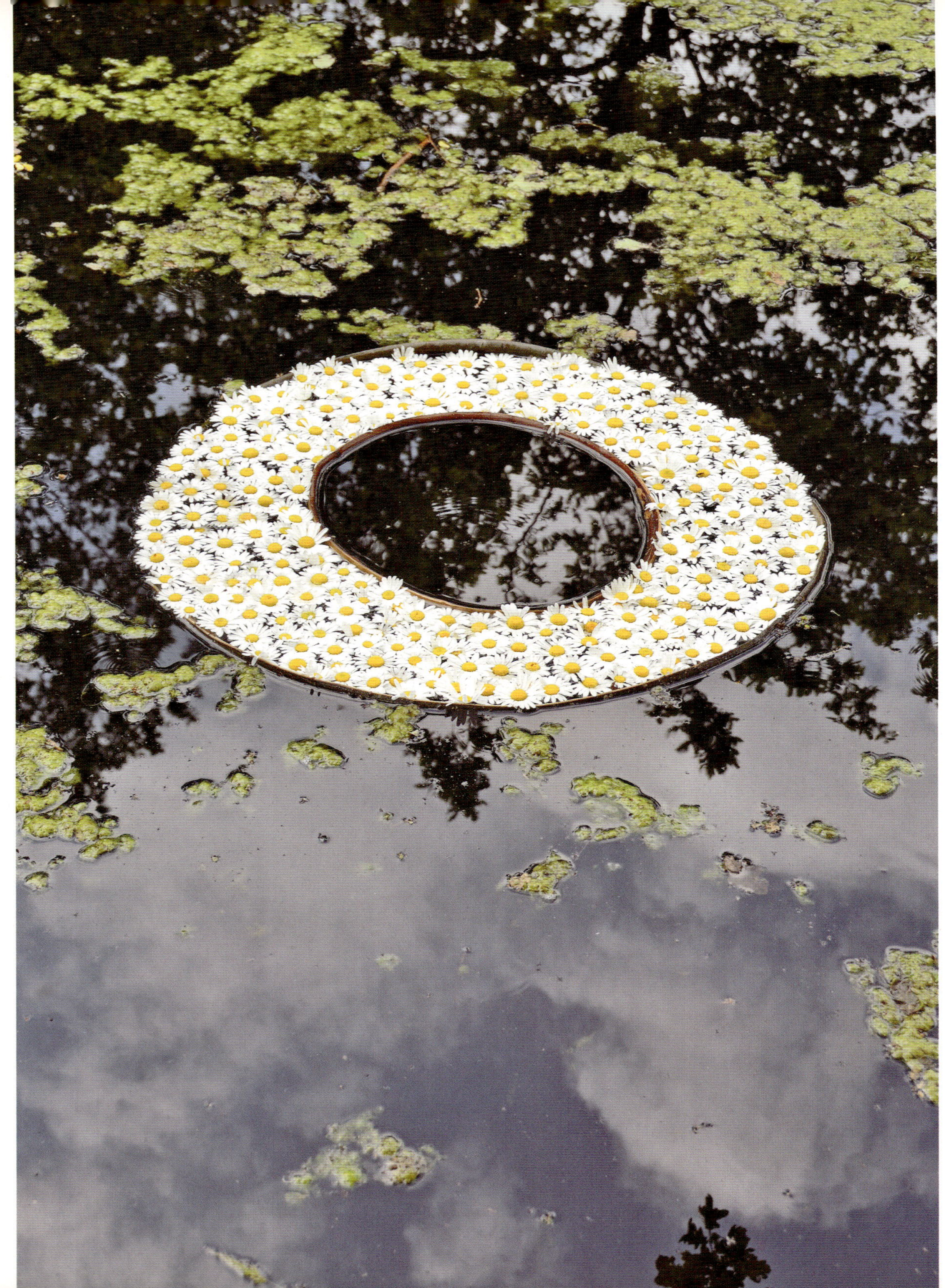

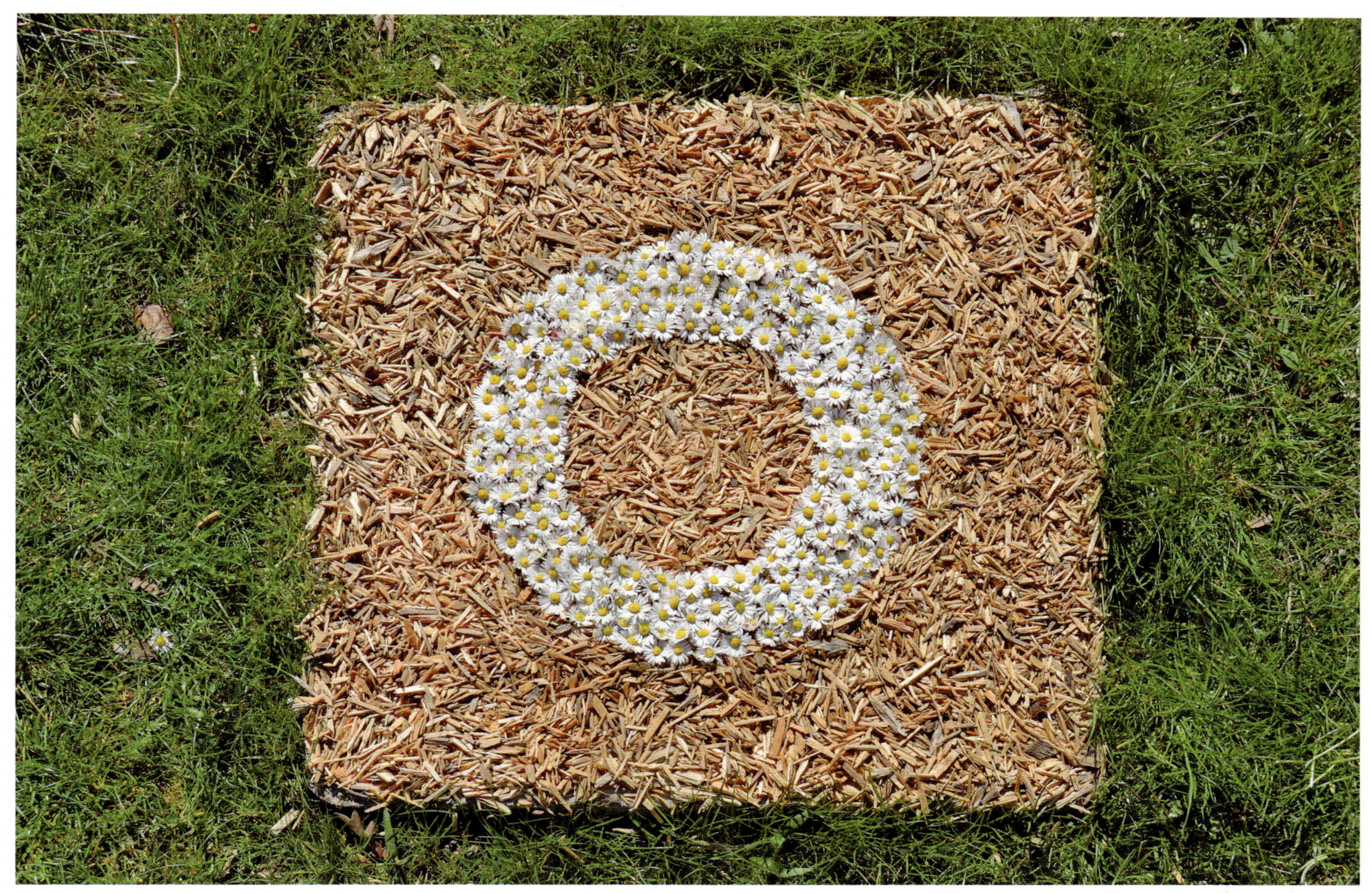

A daisy circle on a flax straw square framed by grass.
An installation by Isabelle and Marie-Claire, made during
a land-art workshop.

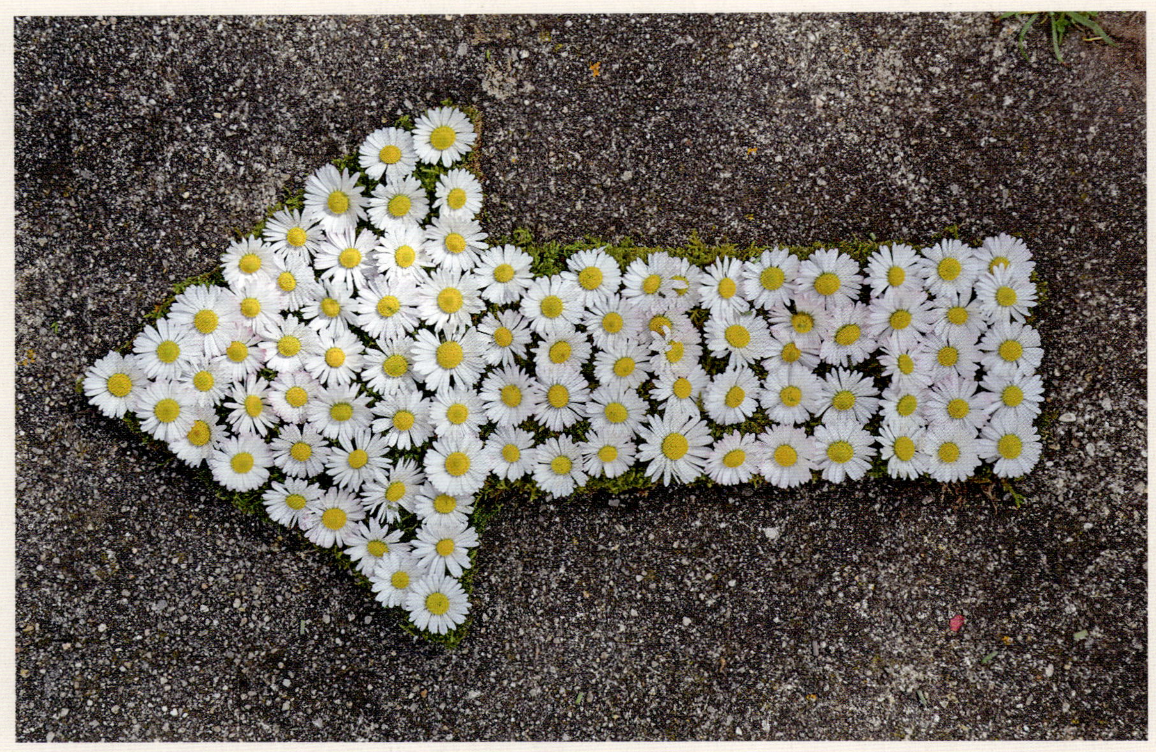

Spring is here, just follow the signs!

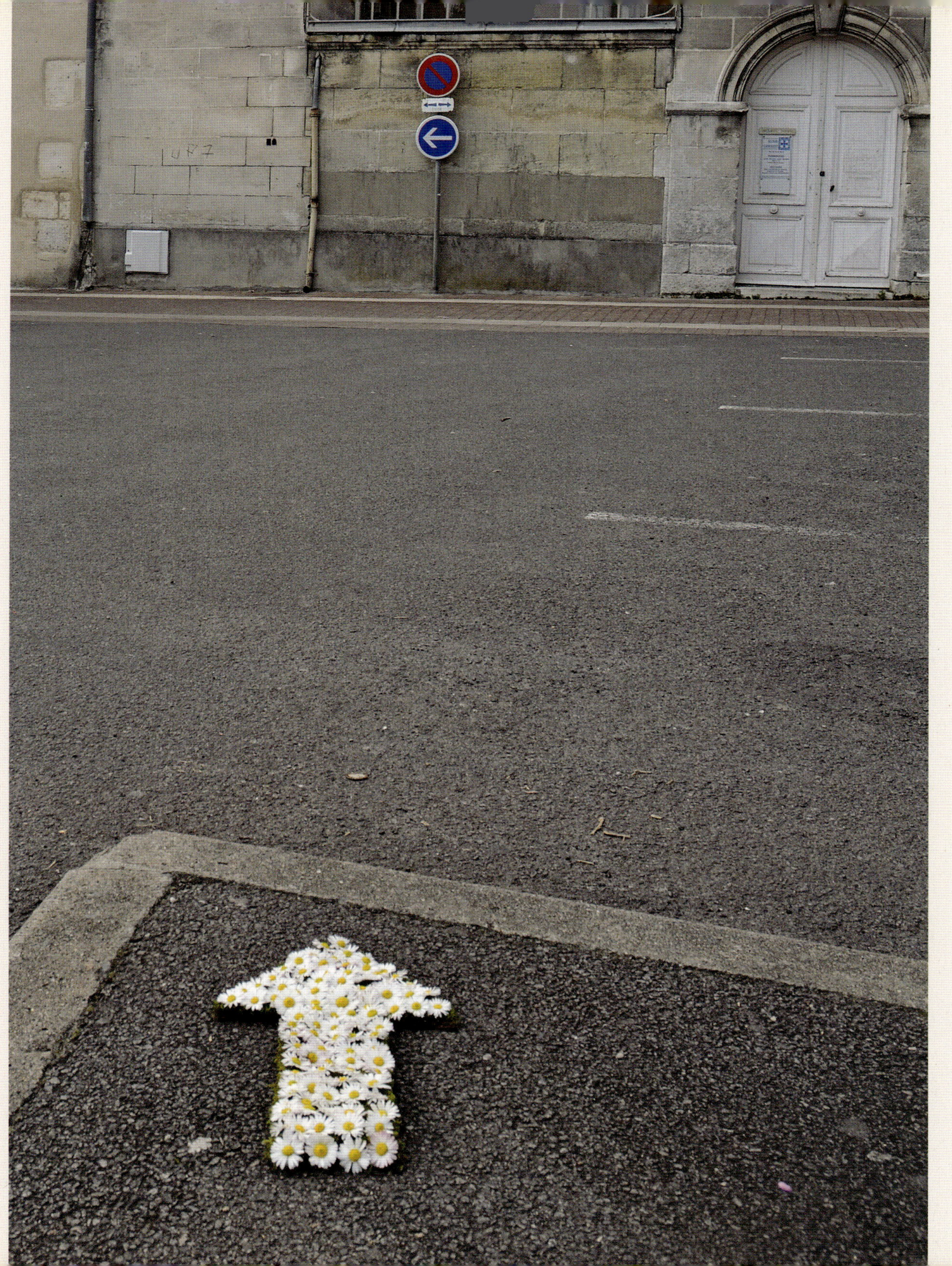

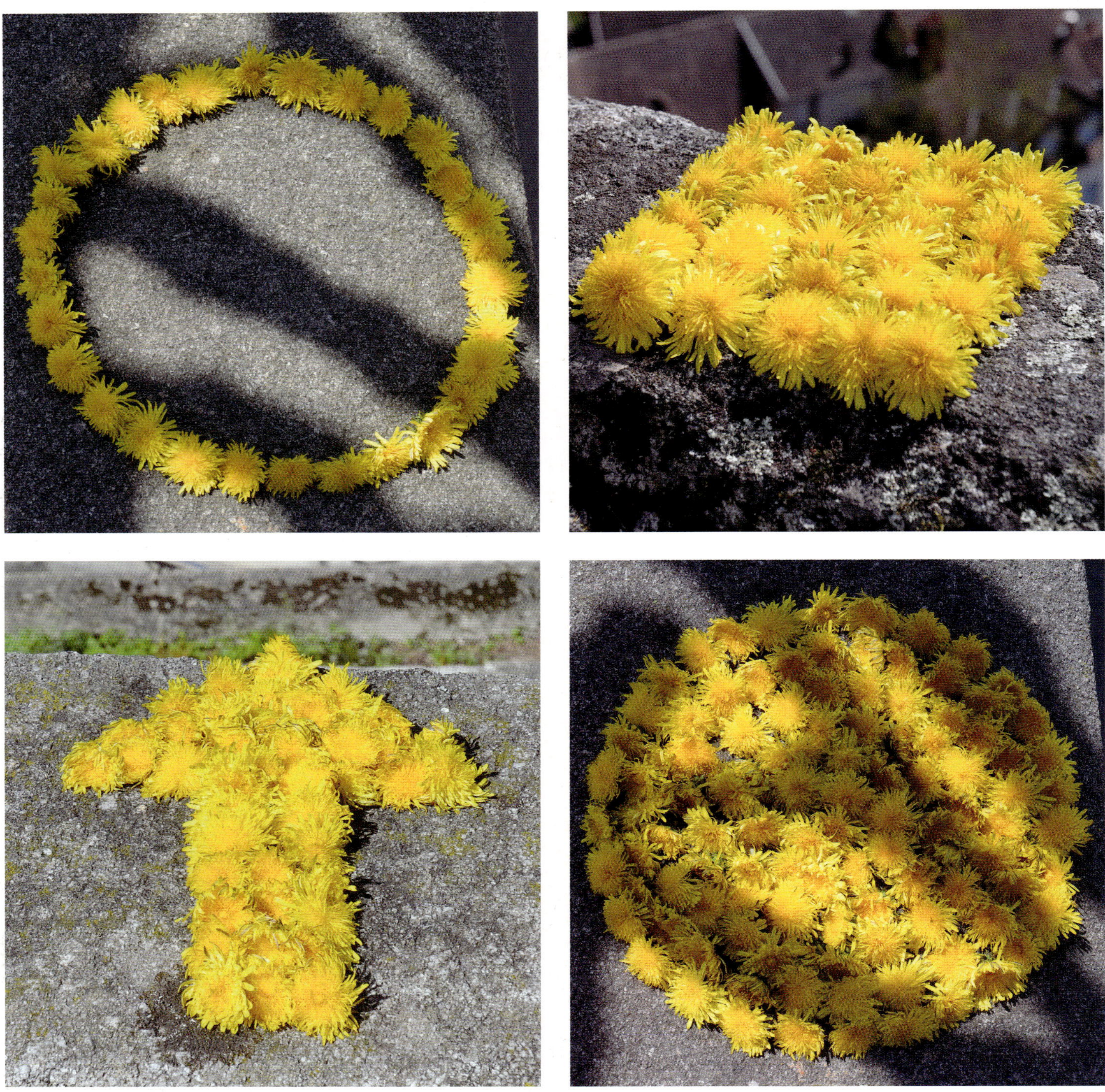

Dandelions lead the way
to sunnier times.

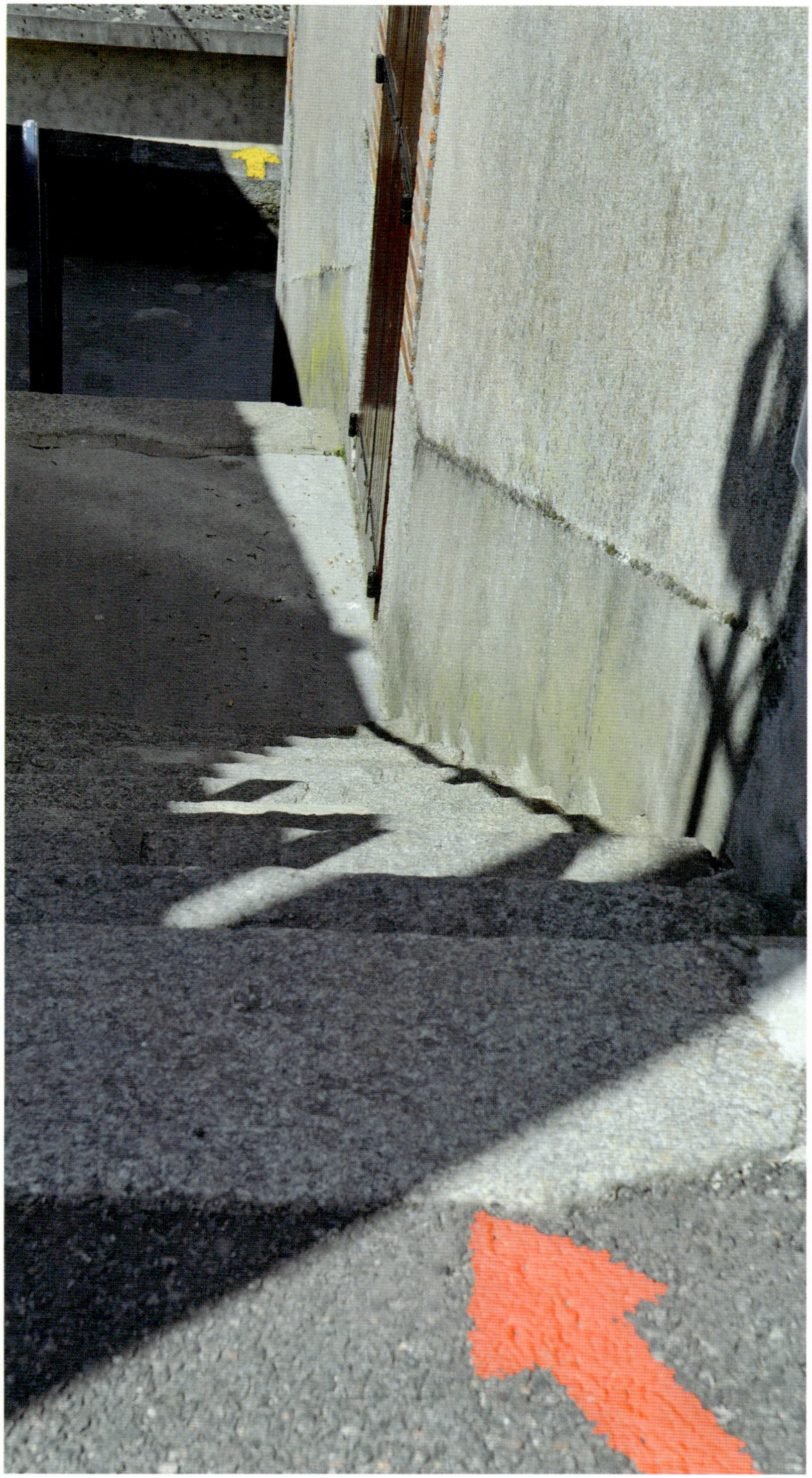

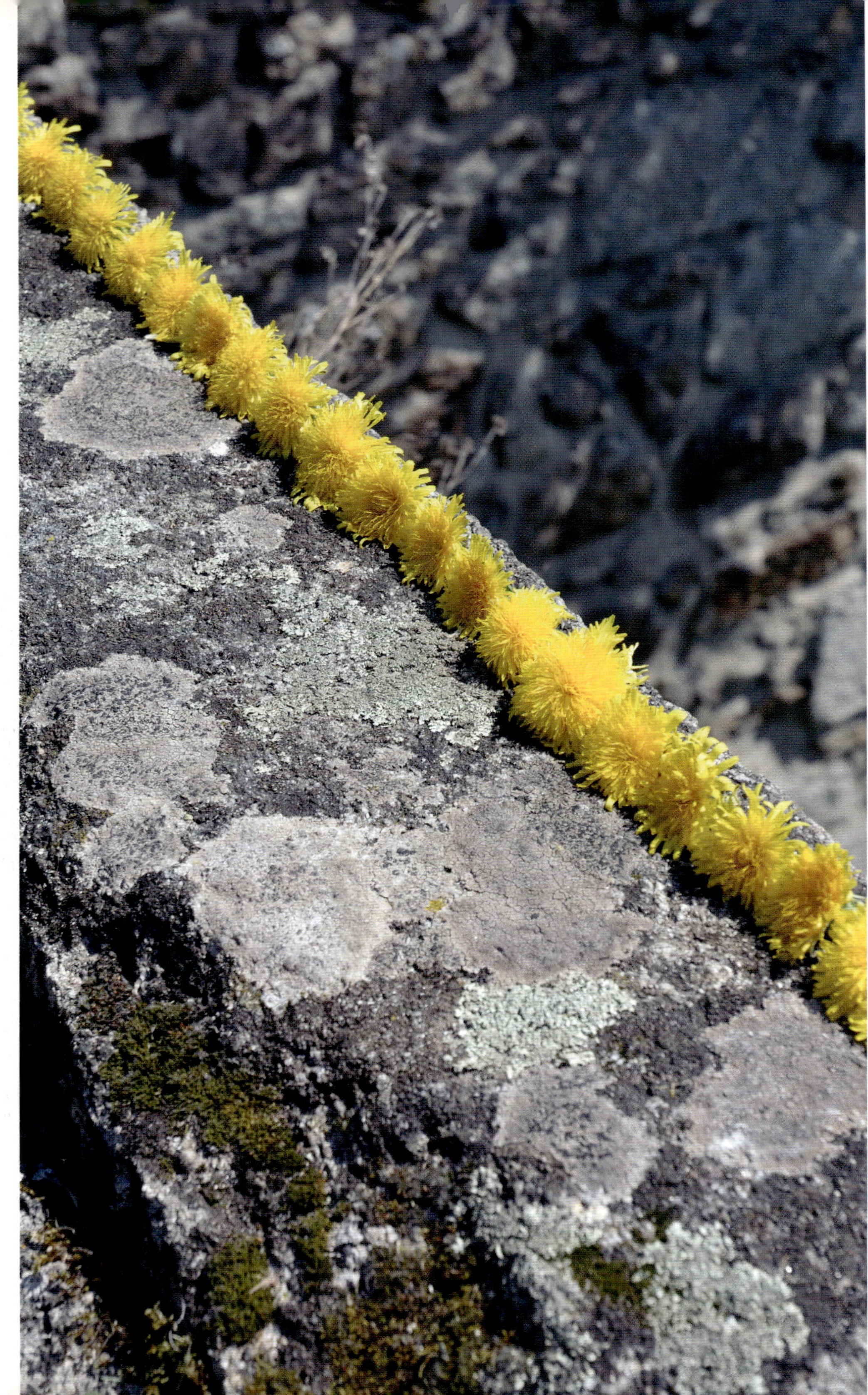

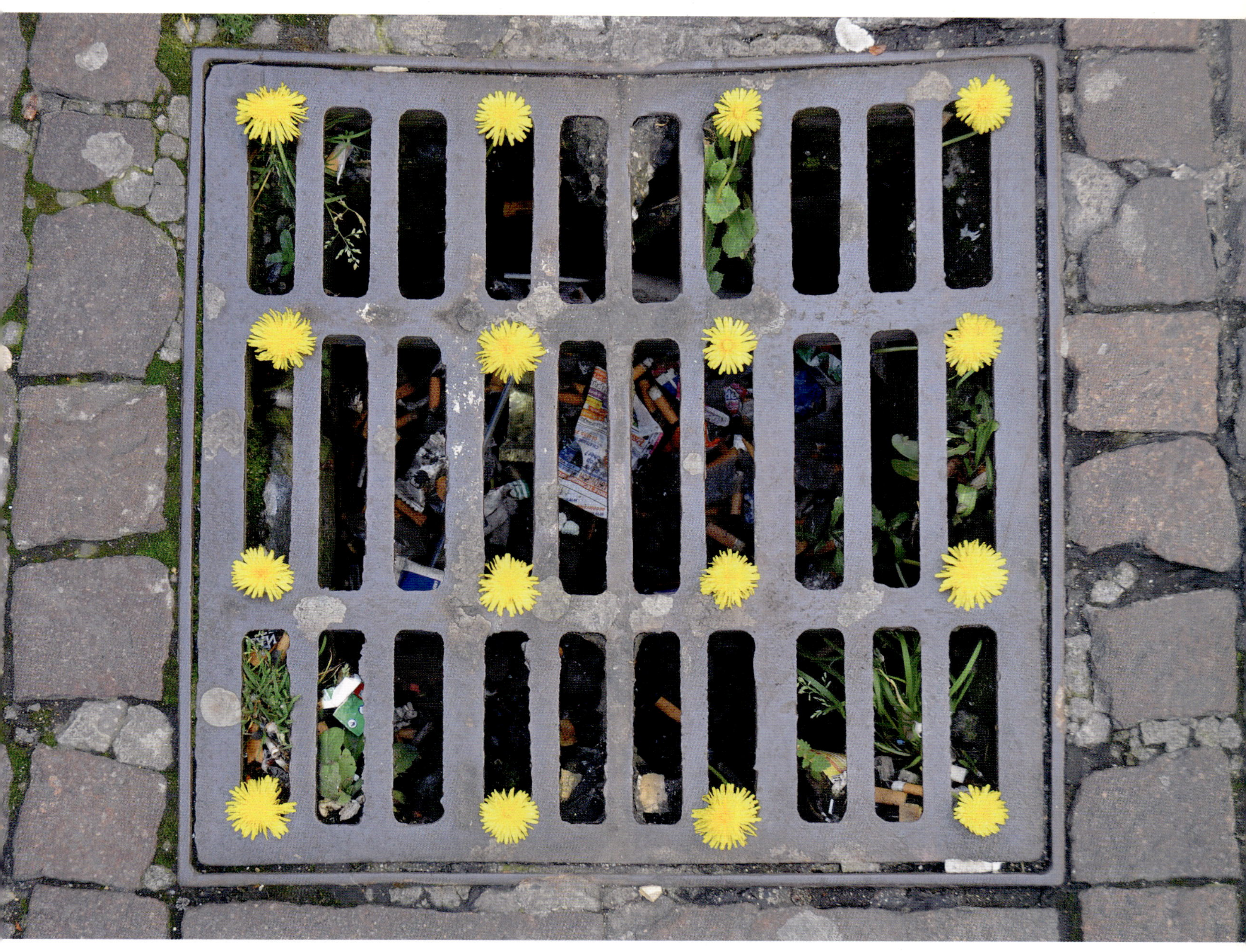

Minimalist monument at your feet.

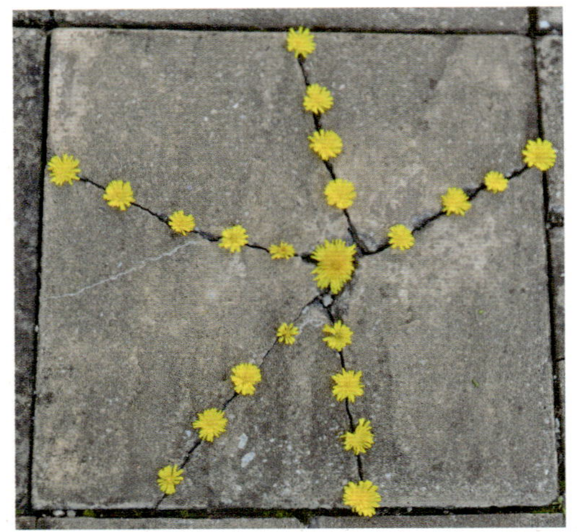

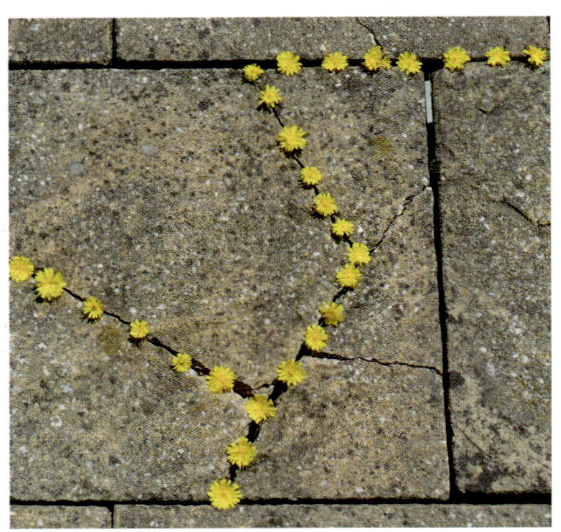

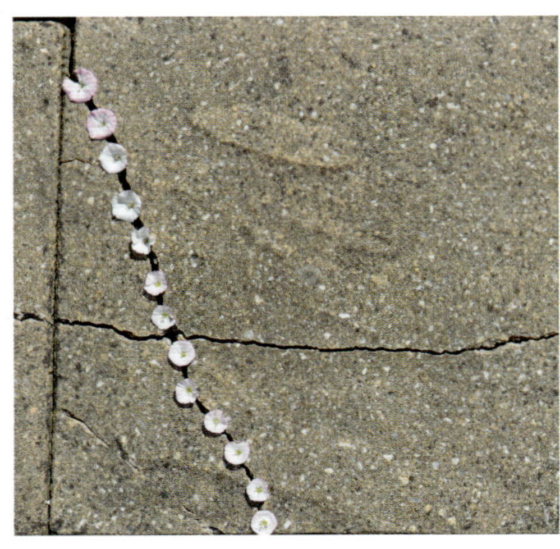

I spent a pleasant Saturday afternoon restoring these cracked paving stones with some carefully selected flowerheads. It was a busy street, but not a single passerby walked on them. All took special care to avoid my handiwork, even at the last moment, and there were many happy smiles!

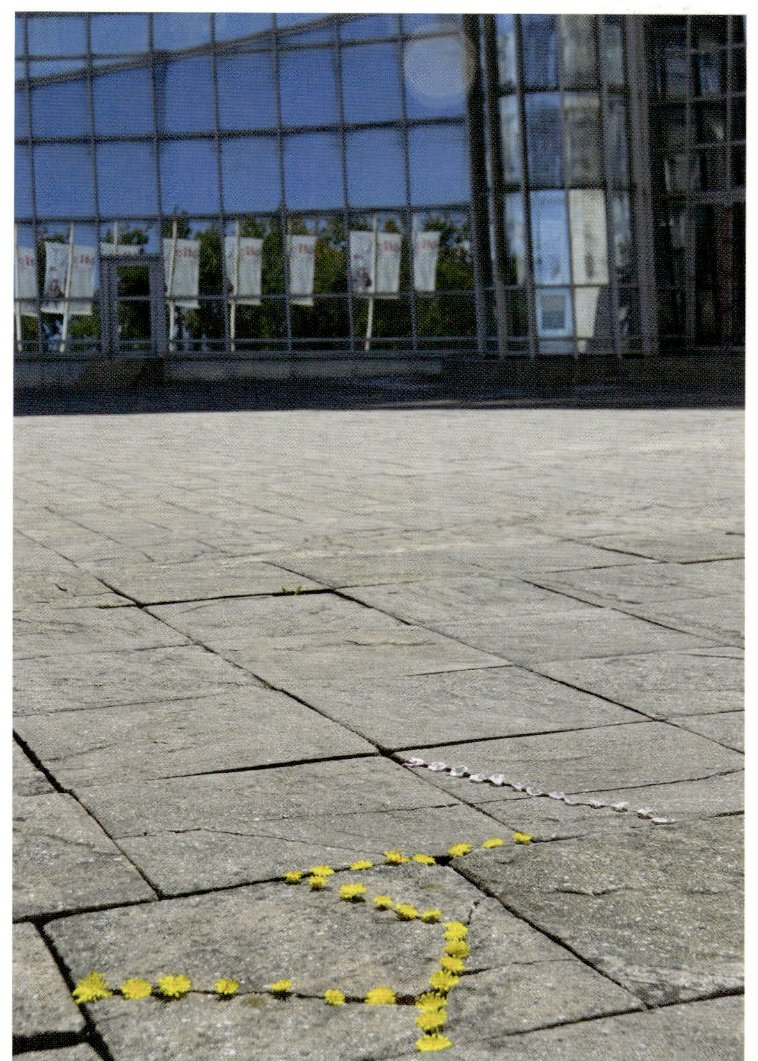

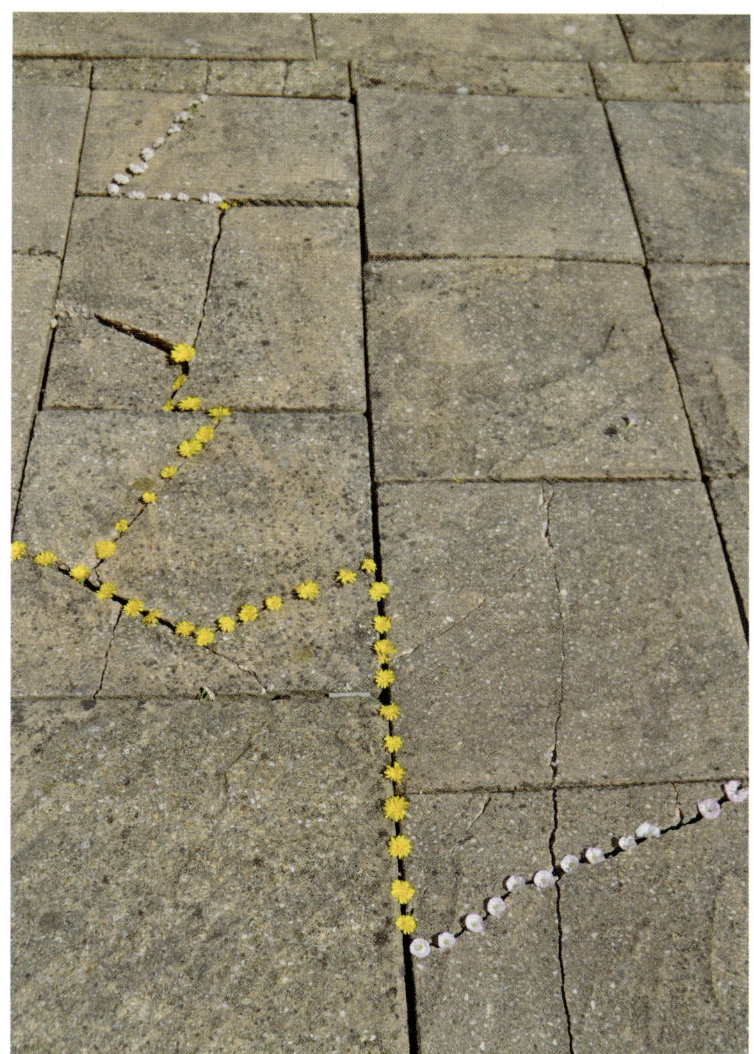

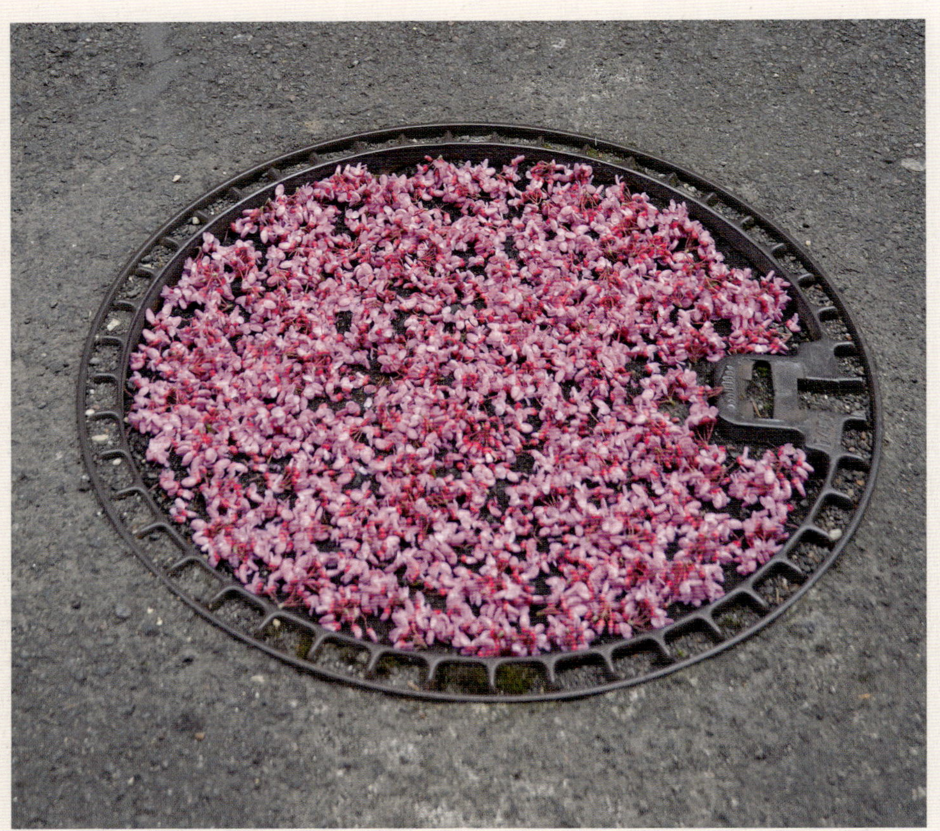

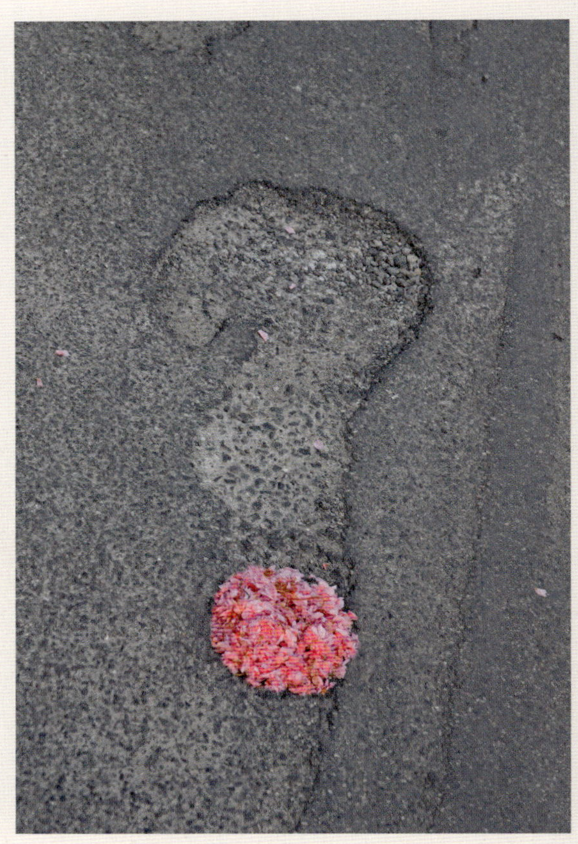

Can there be a prettier way of marking out pedestrian hazards than with these lovely spring blossoms?

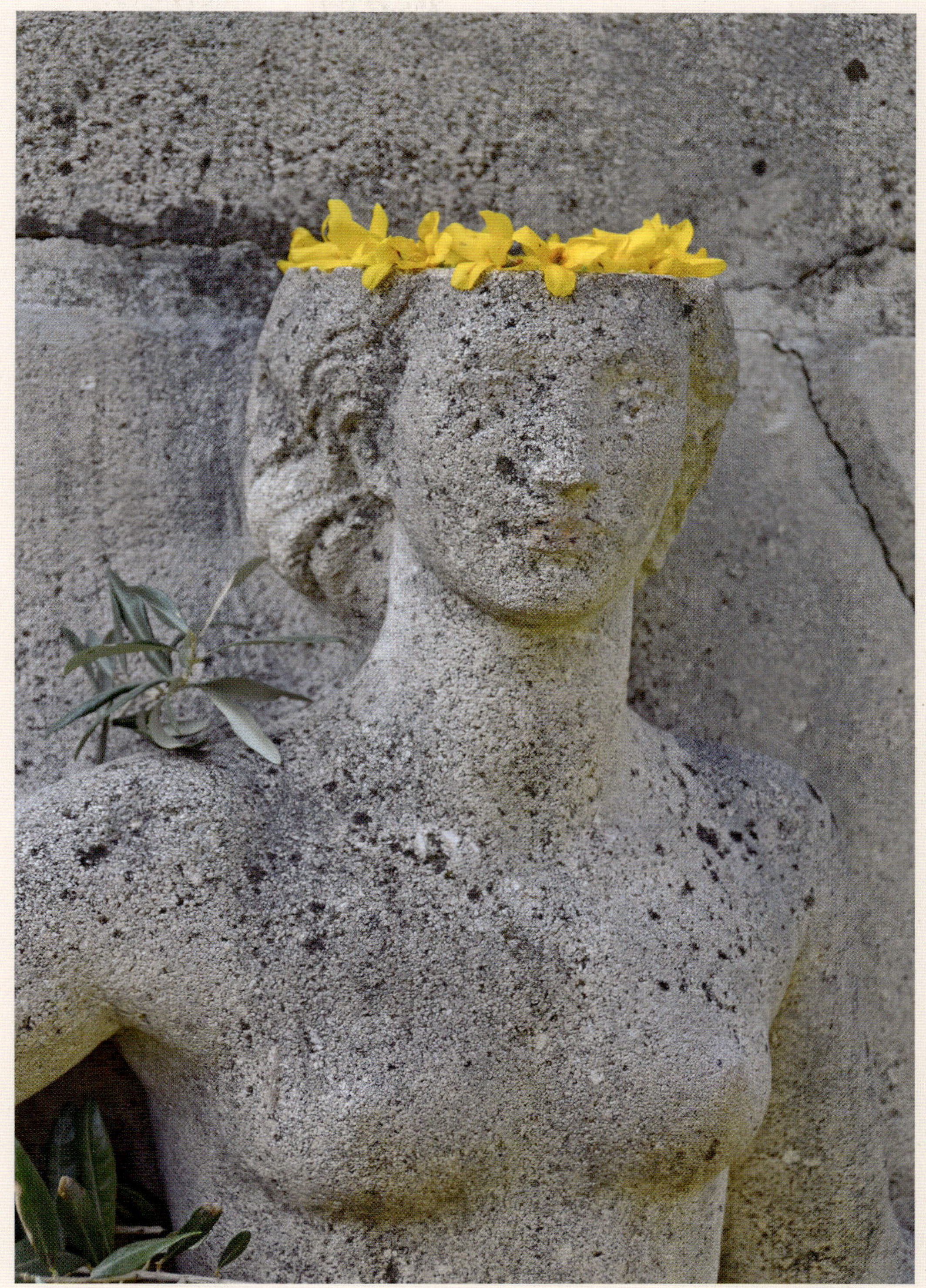

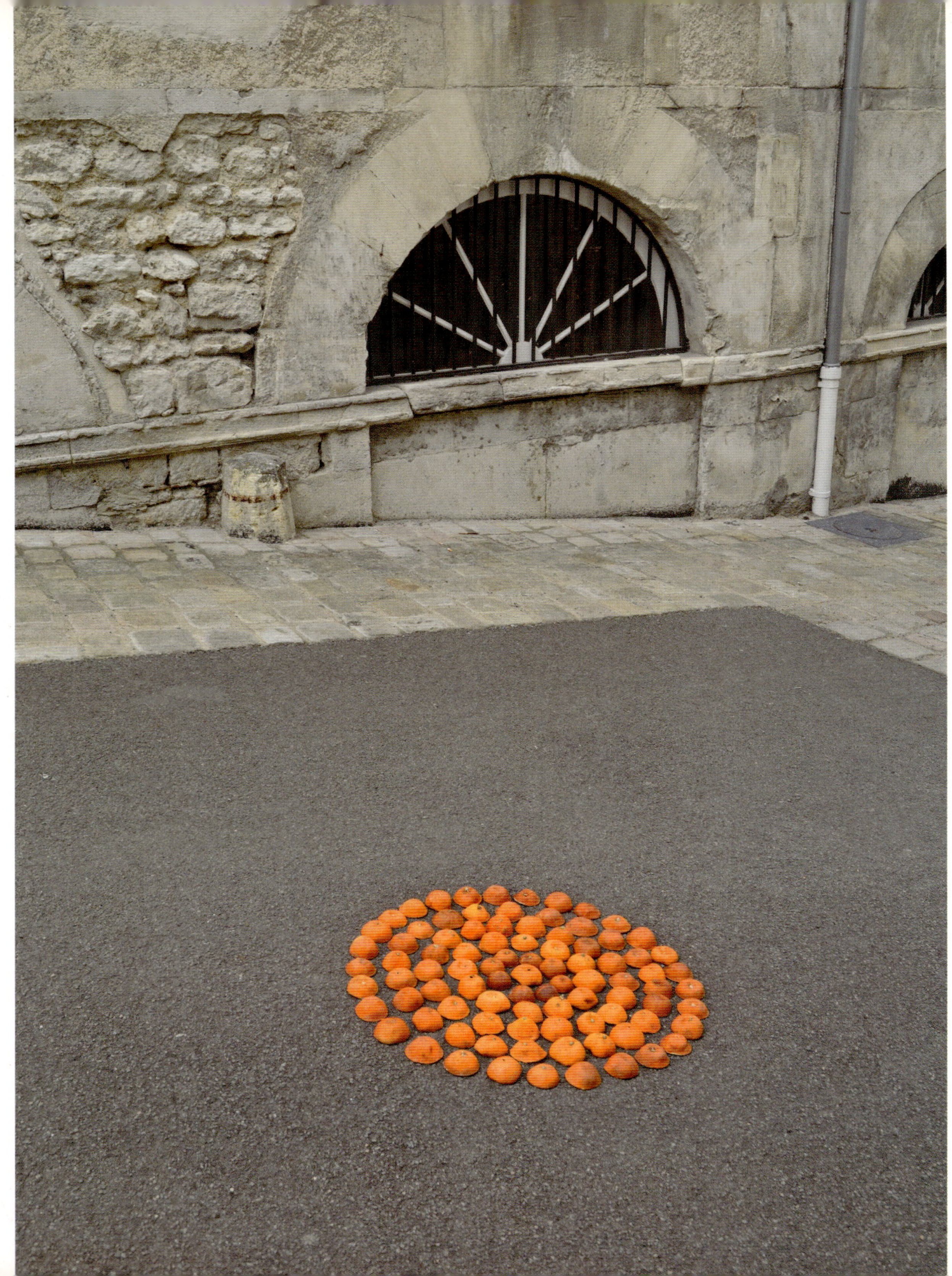

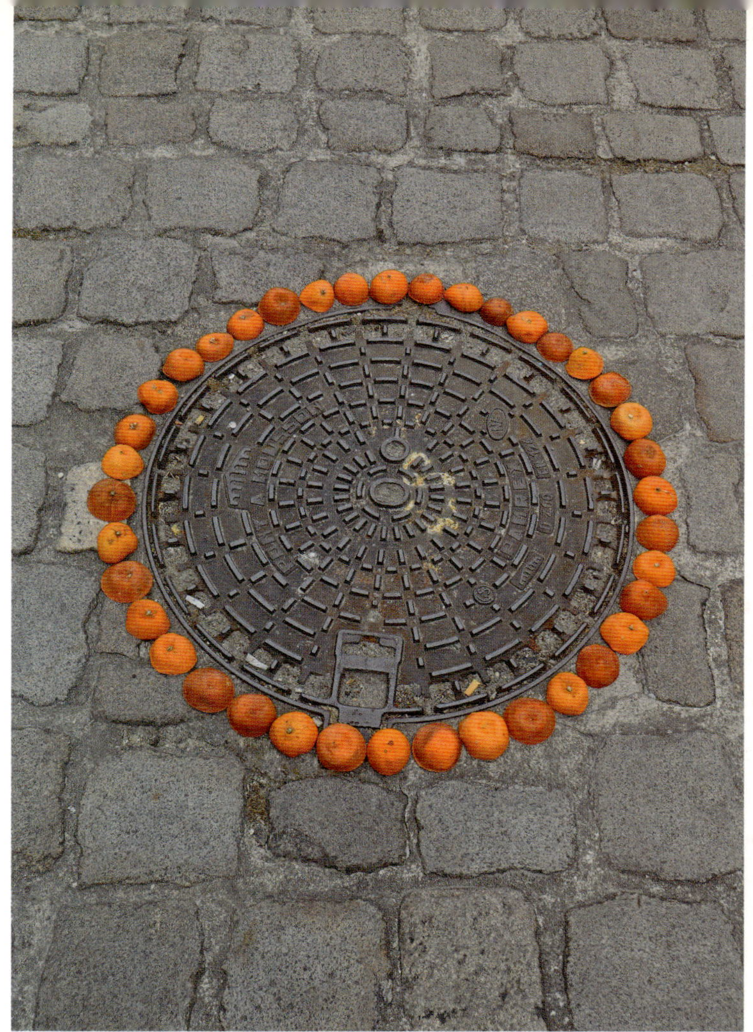

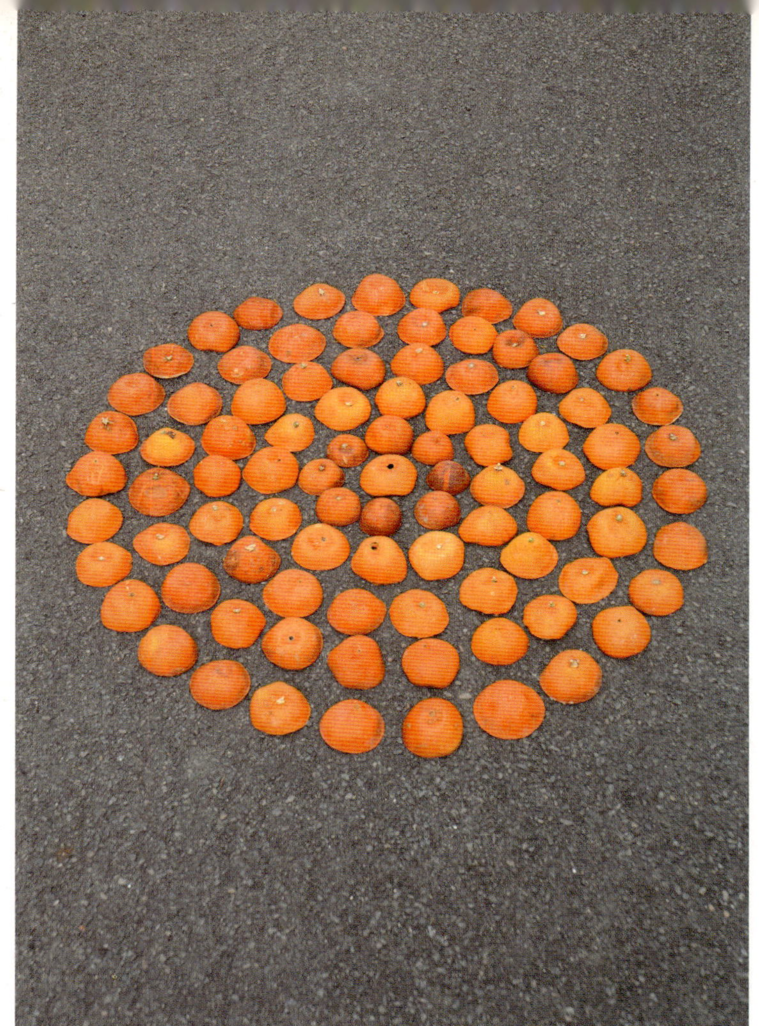

Banish greyness with some artfully placed orange halves.

Make use of the different shades to create a more complex composition.

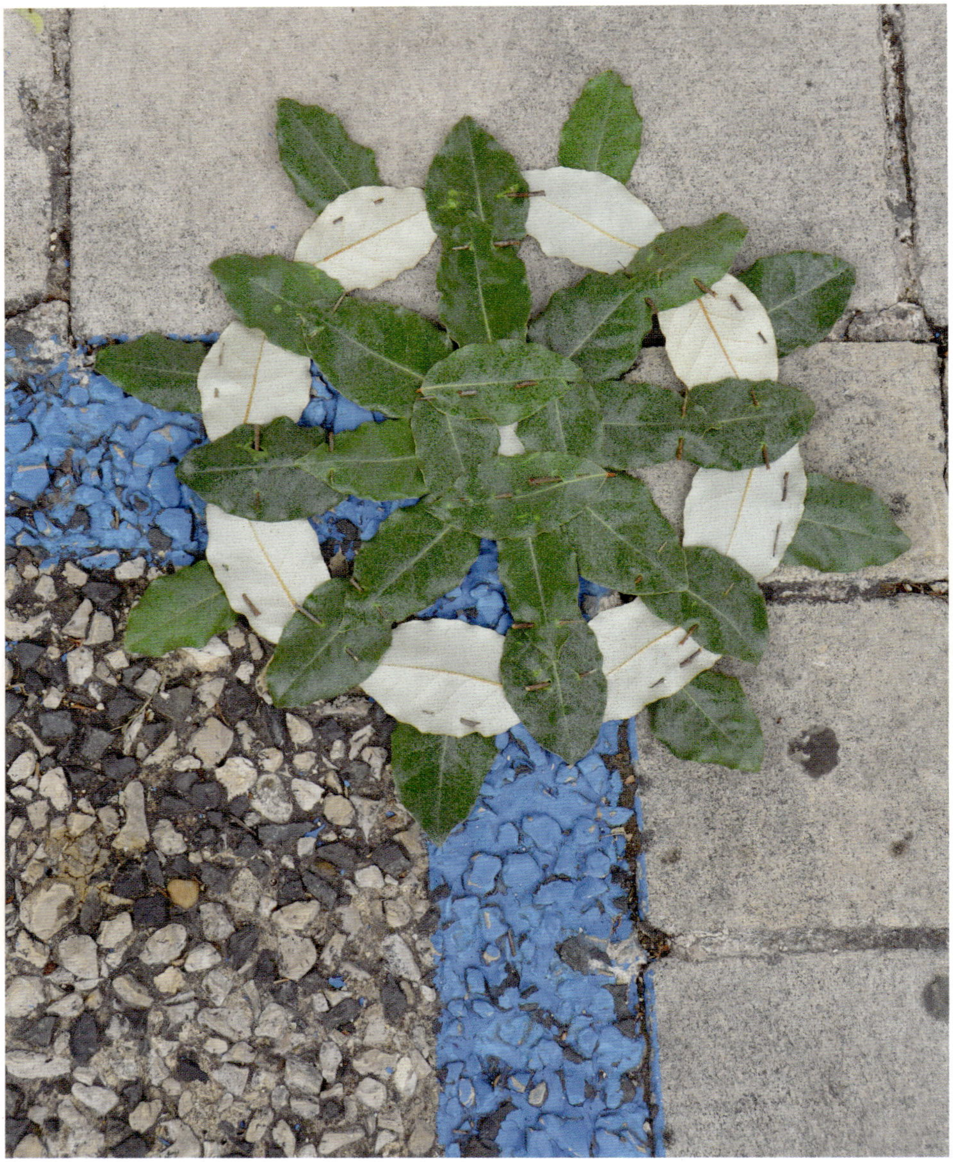

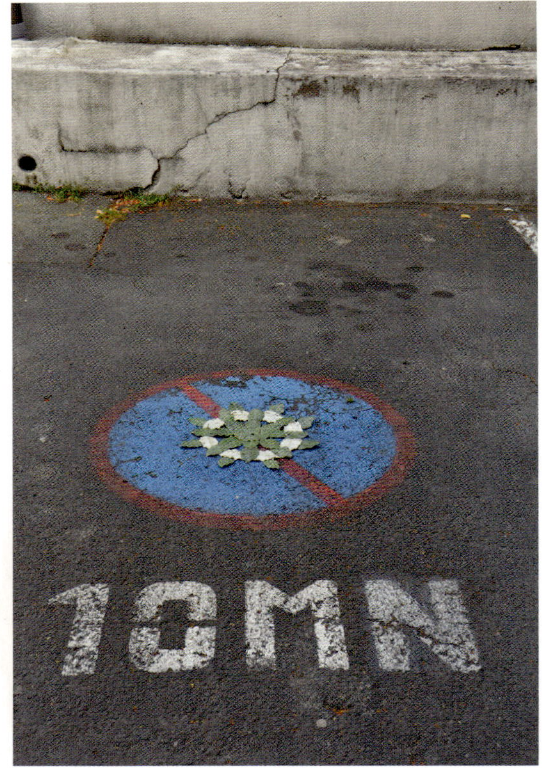

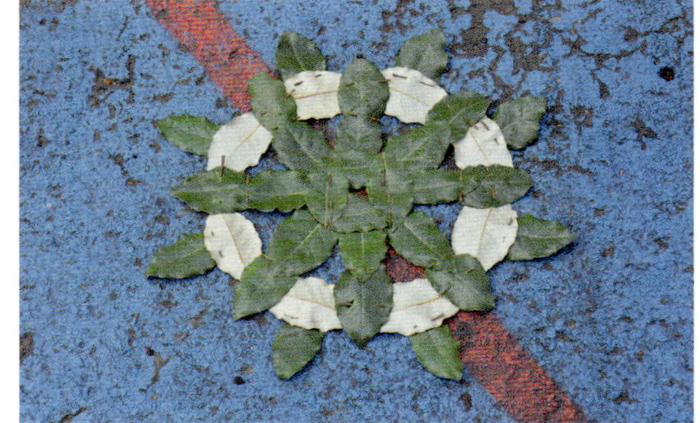

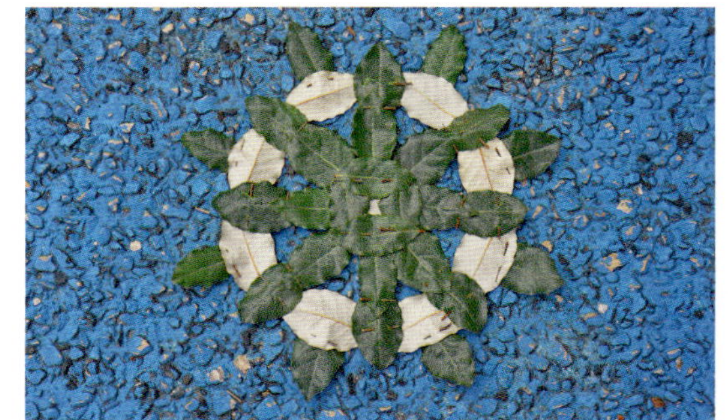

A spiky circle of oleaster leaves and sloe thorns break up the straight lines all around.

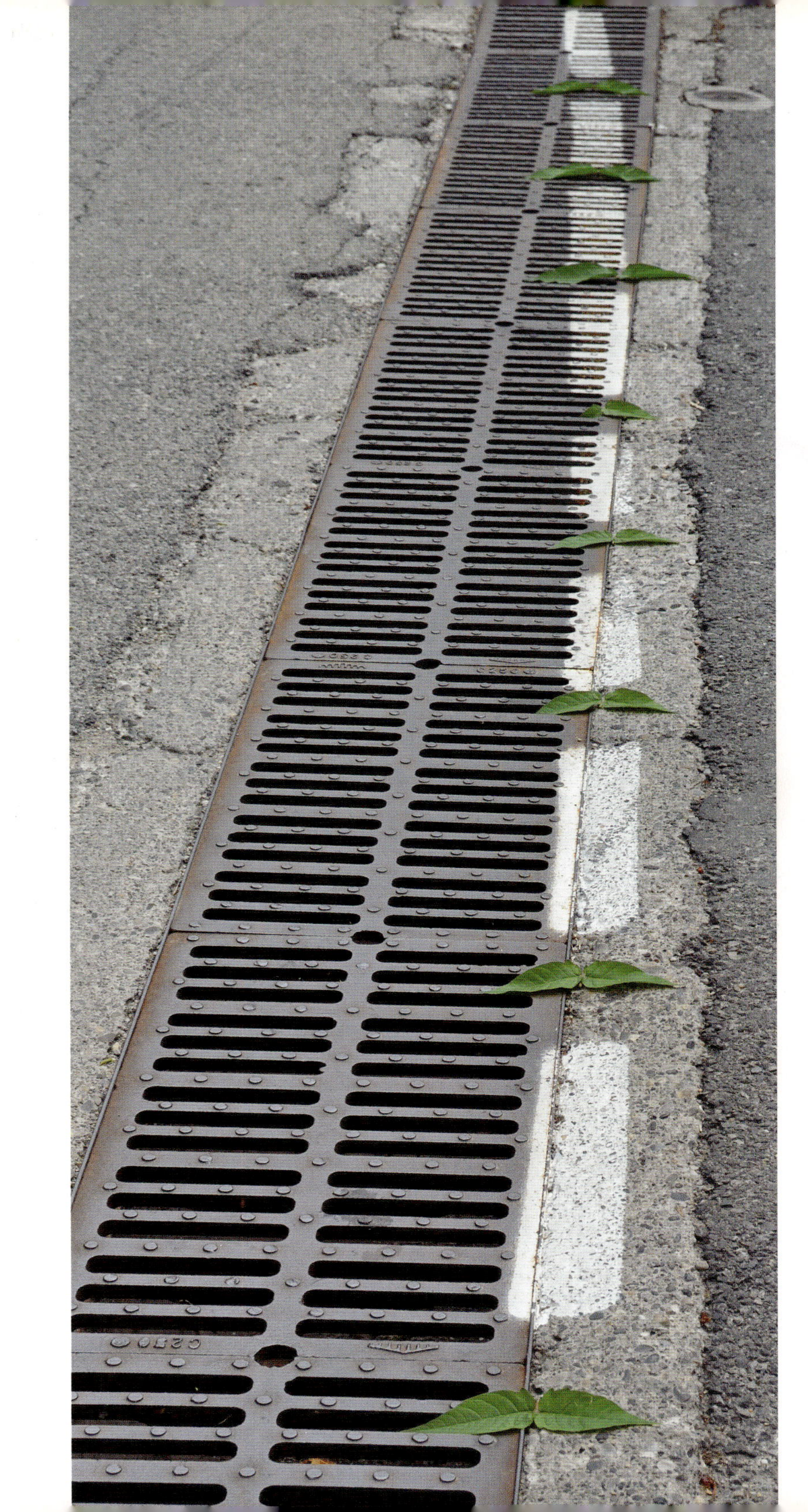

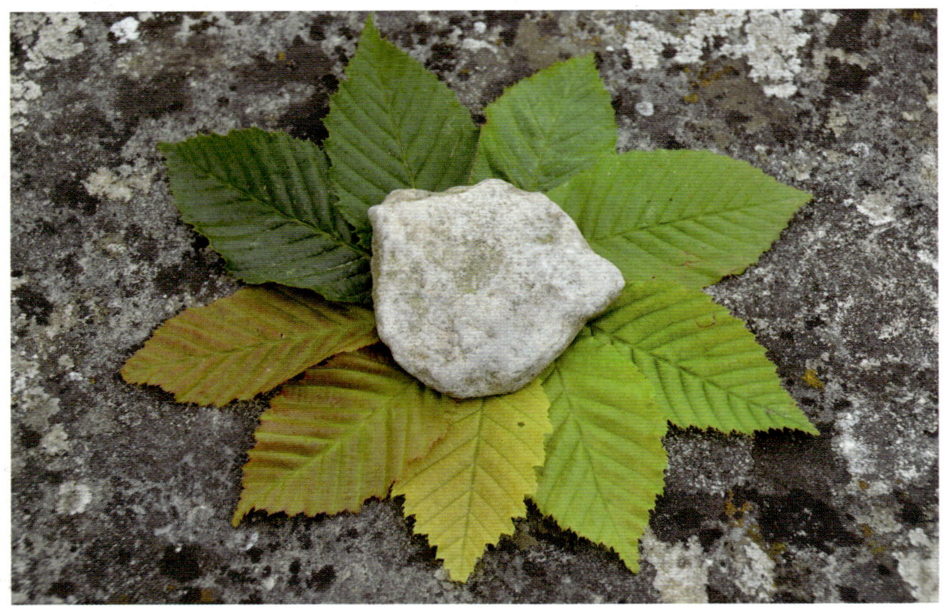

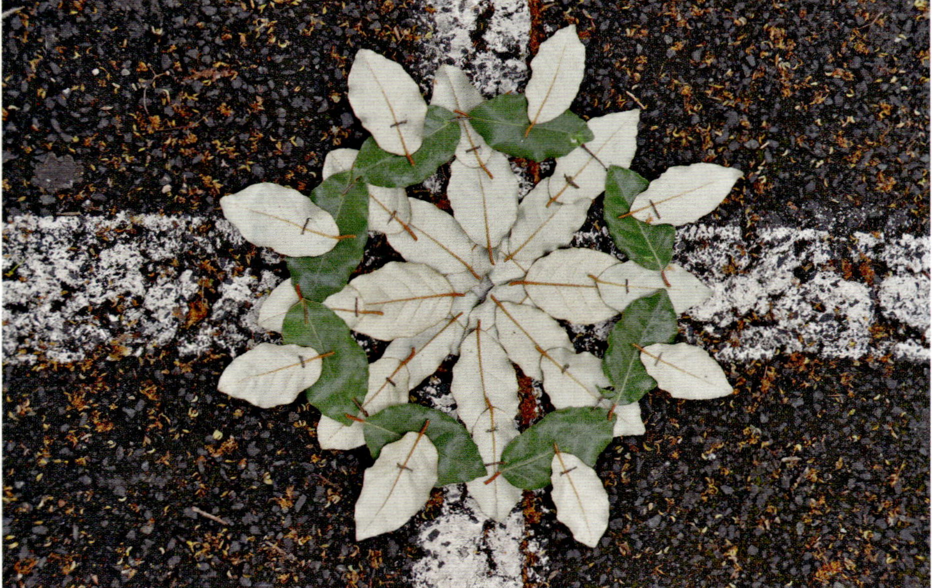

Turn leaves into flower arrangements across the town.

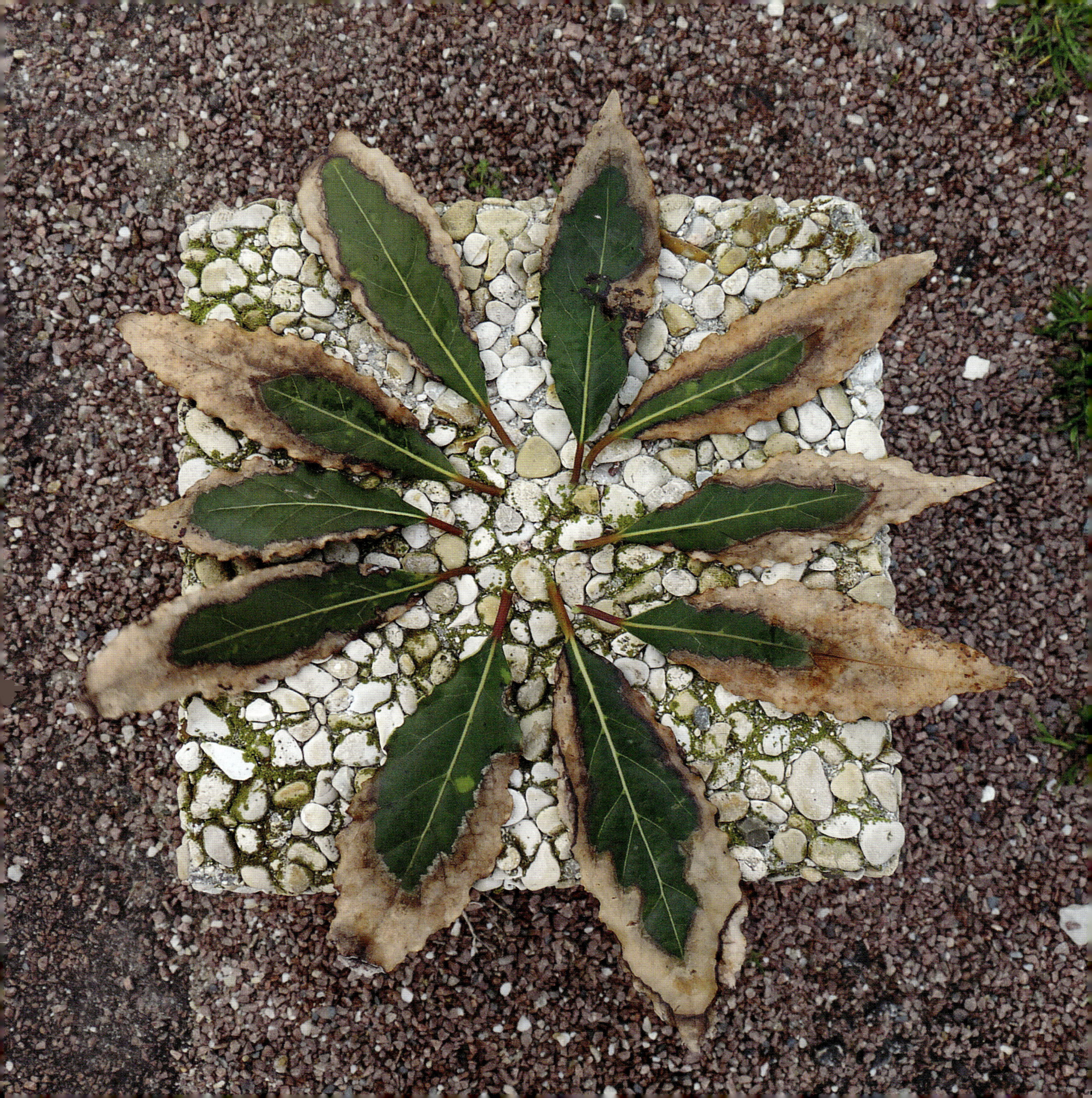

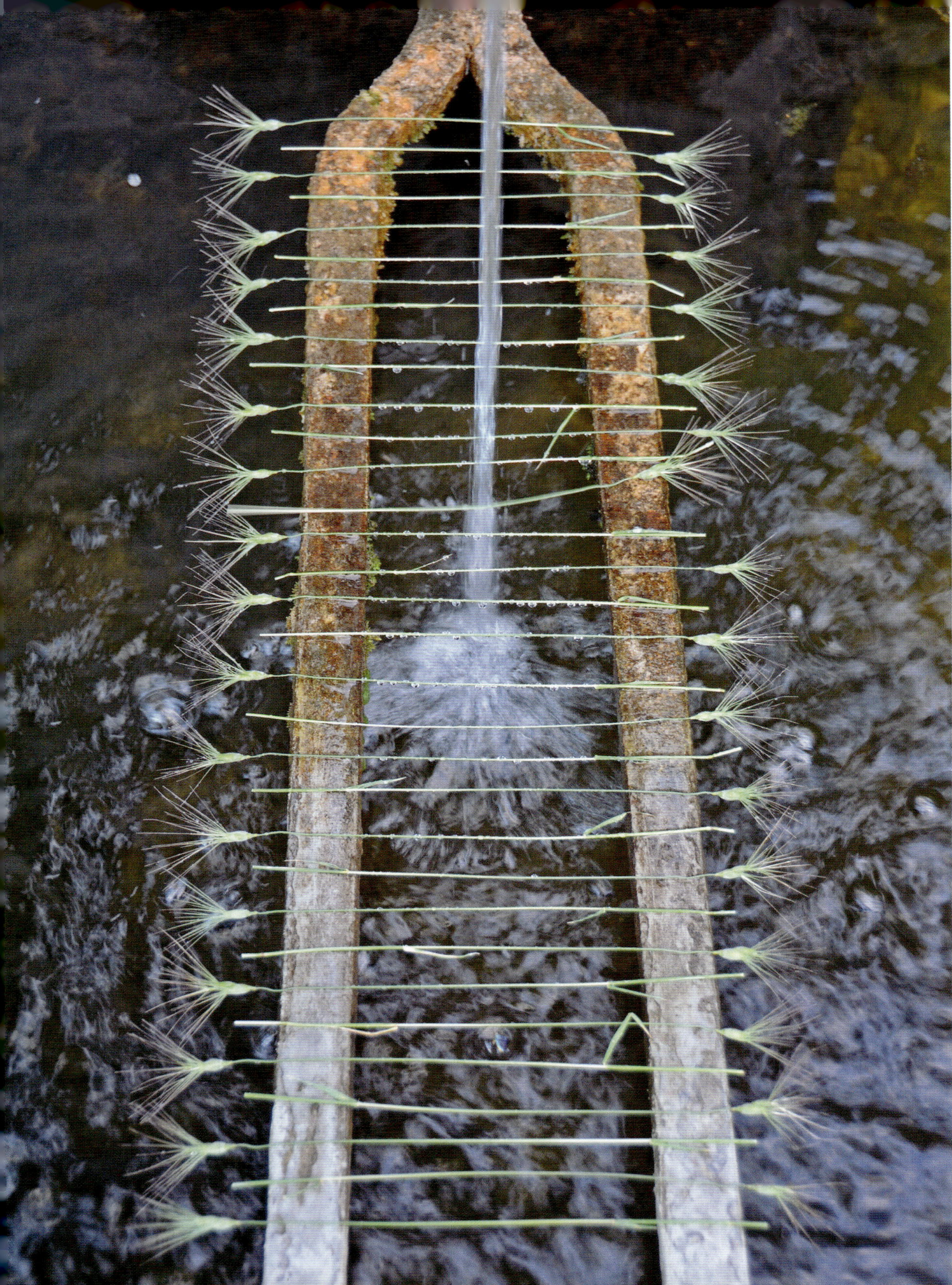

Ponds, fountains and other water features make great canvases for land art! Collect a few natural objects, think about lighting and movement, then create your installation.

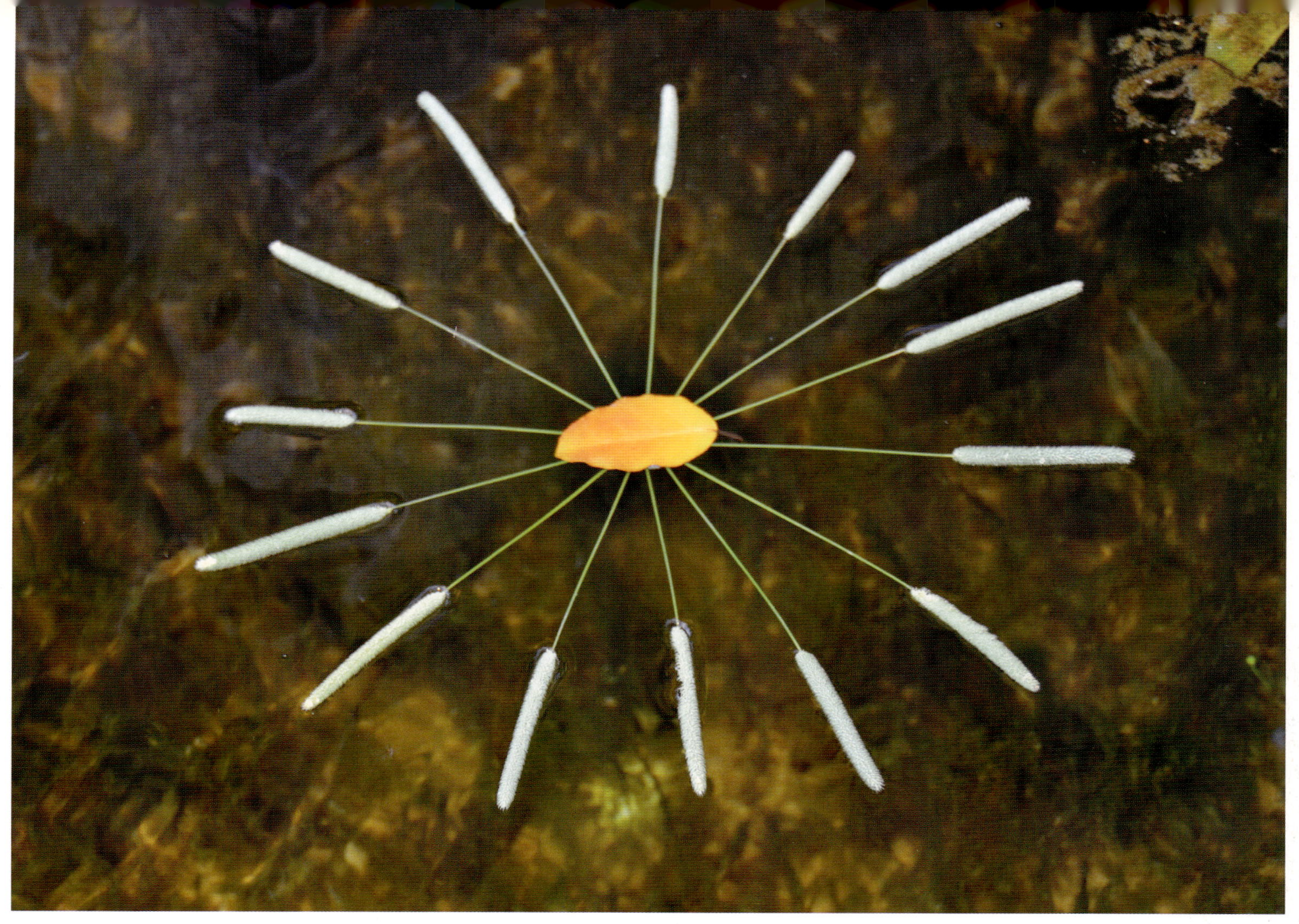

Do take a photograph. Just remember that when working with water it can be hard to predict the result. But you will often be pleasantly surprised.

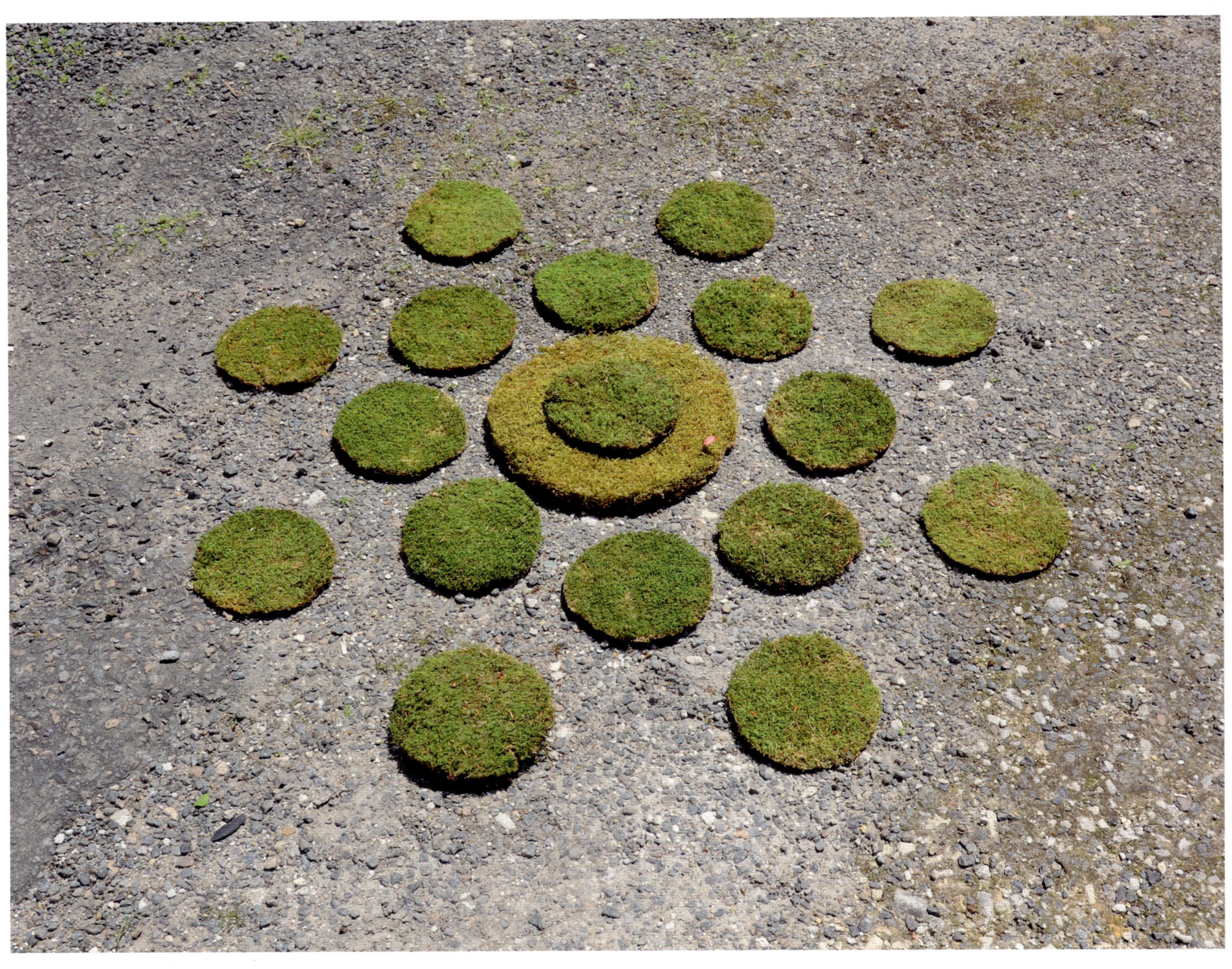

Even as humble a material as grass or moss can be shaped and arranged in attractive ways.

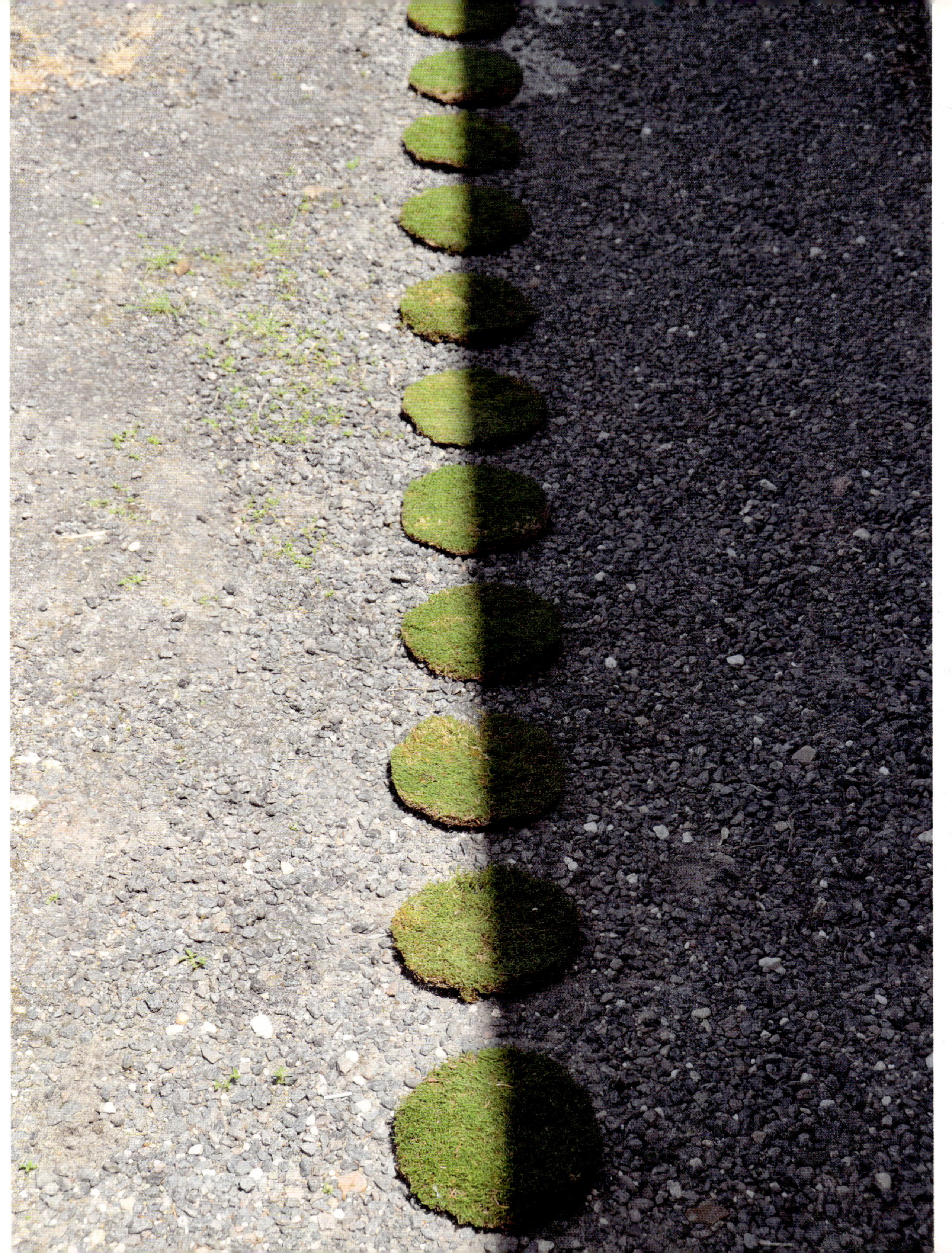

A twig circle around a patch of lichen beside the river evokes boats' moooring rings.

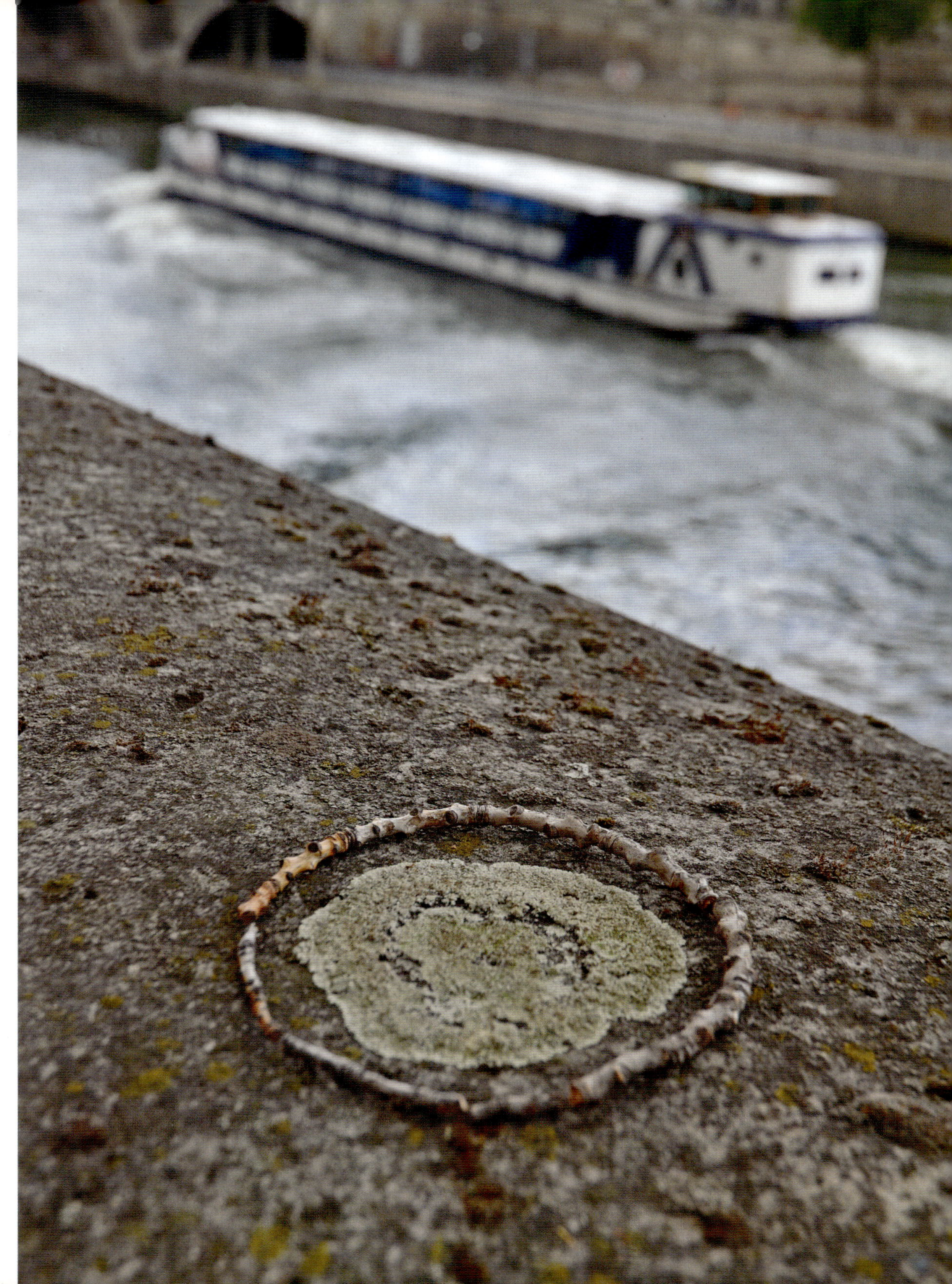

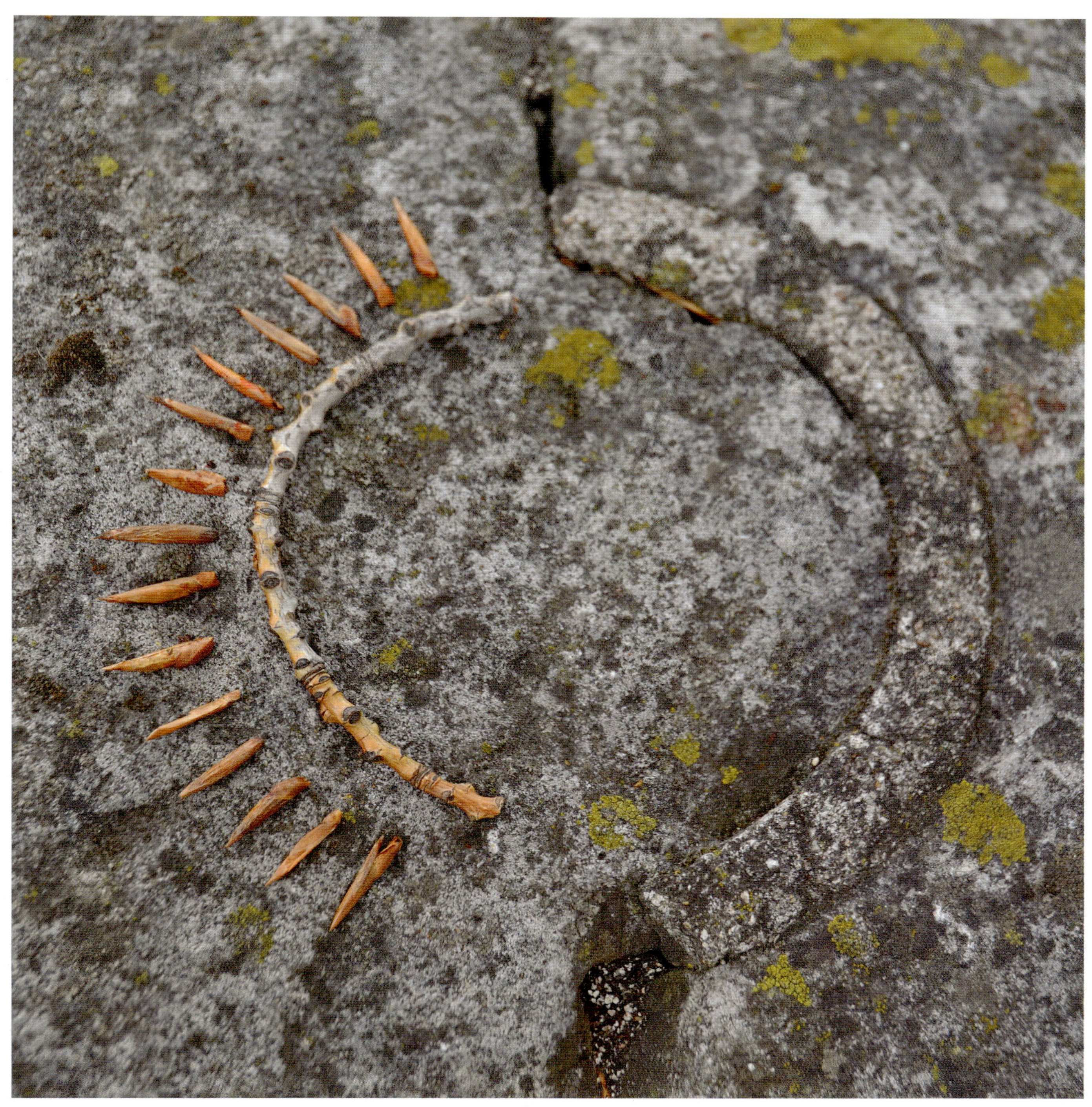

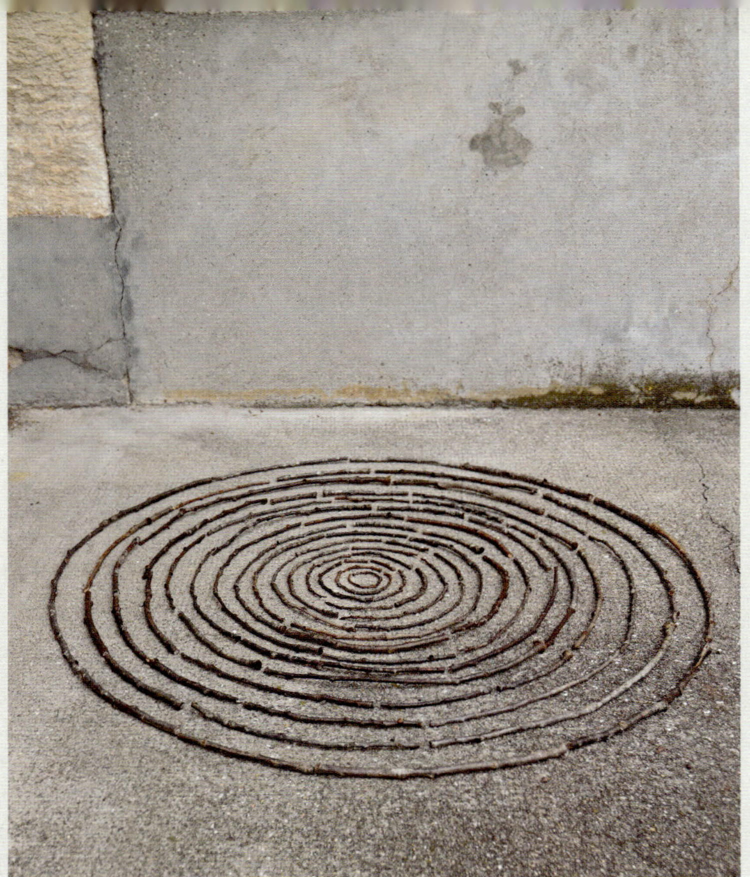

The simplest, most commonly found materials can be used to make stunning patterns.

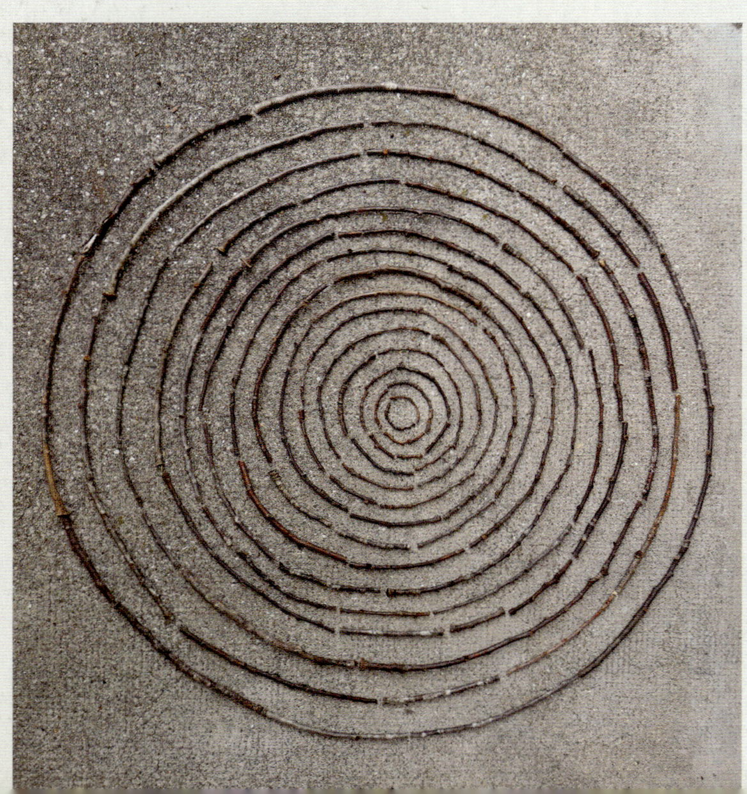

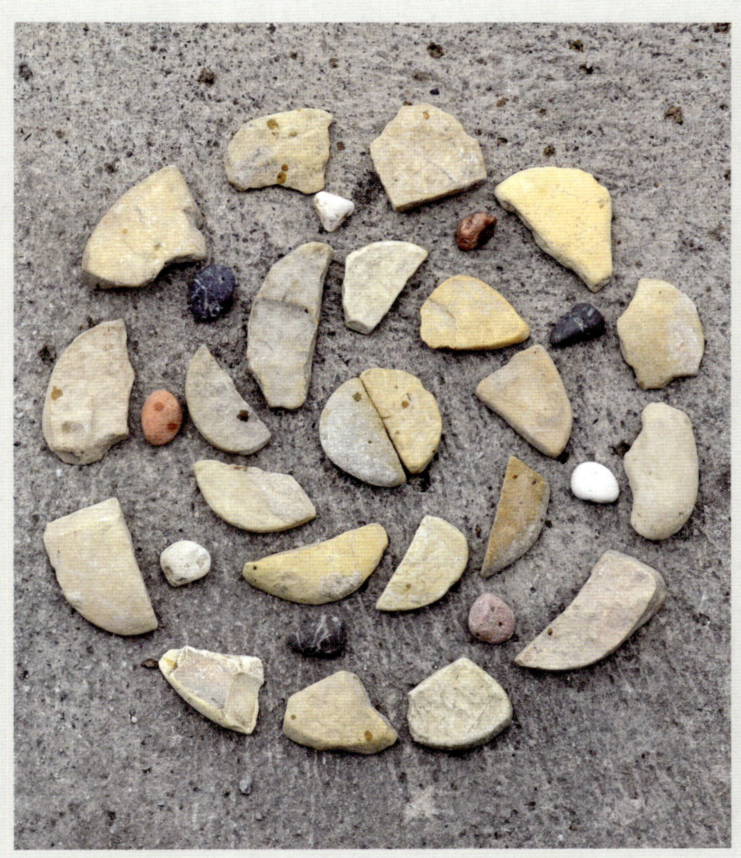

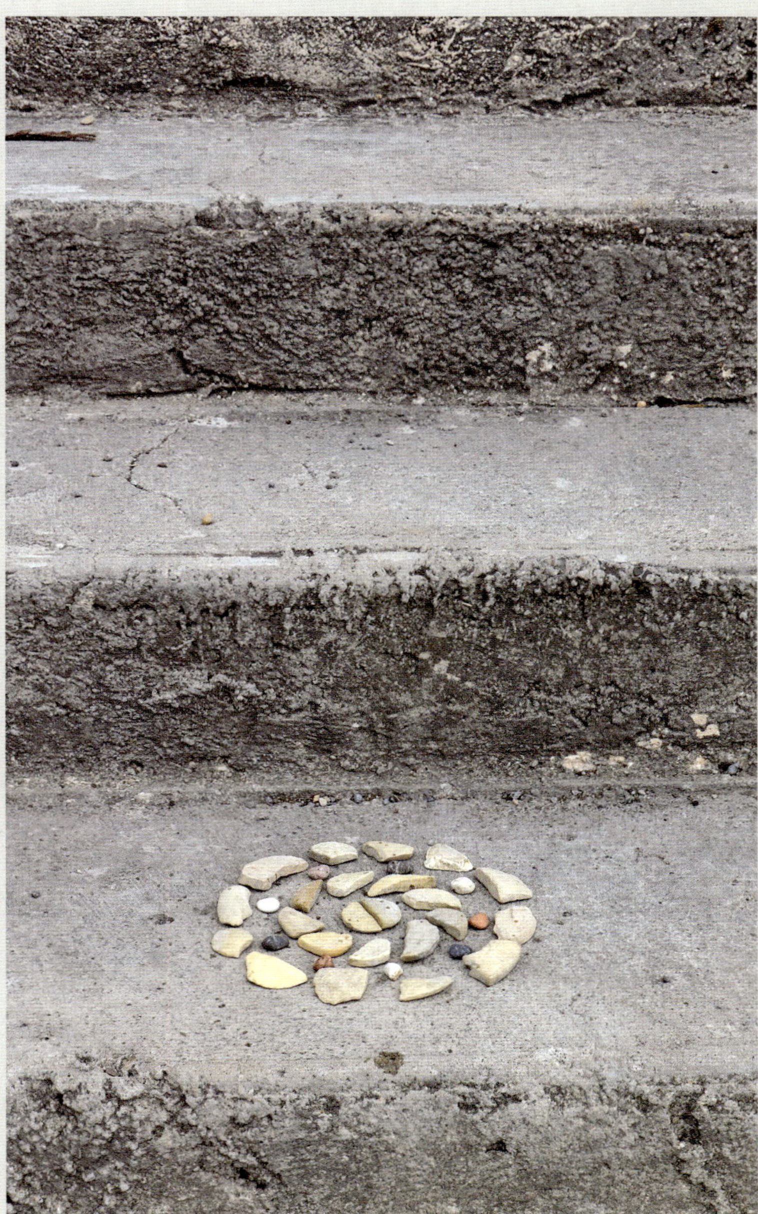

We walk over them every day, yet stones and pebbles present an infinite variety of shape and colour. There is no better place to start for the budding land artist.

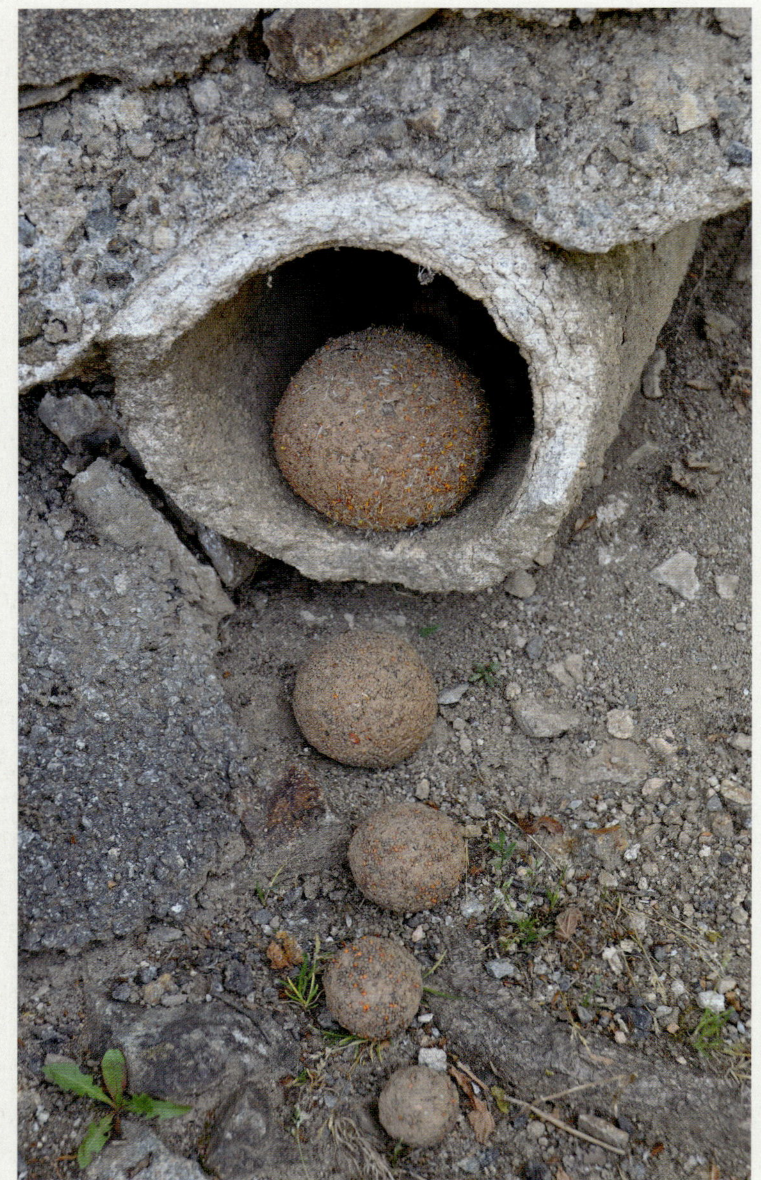

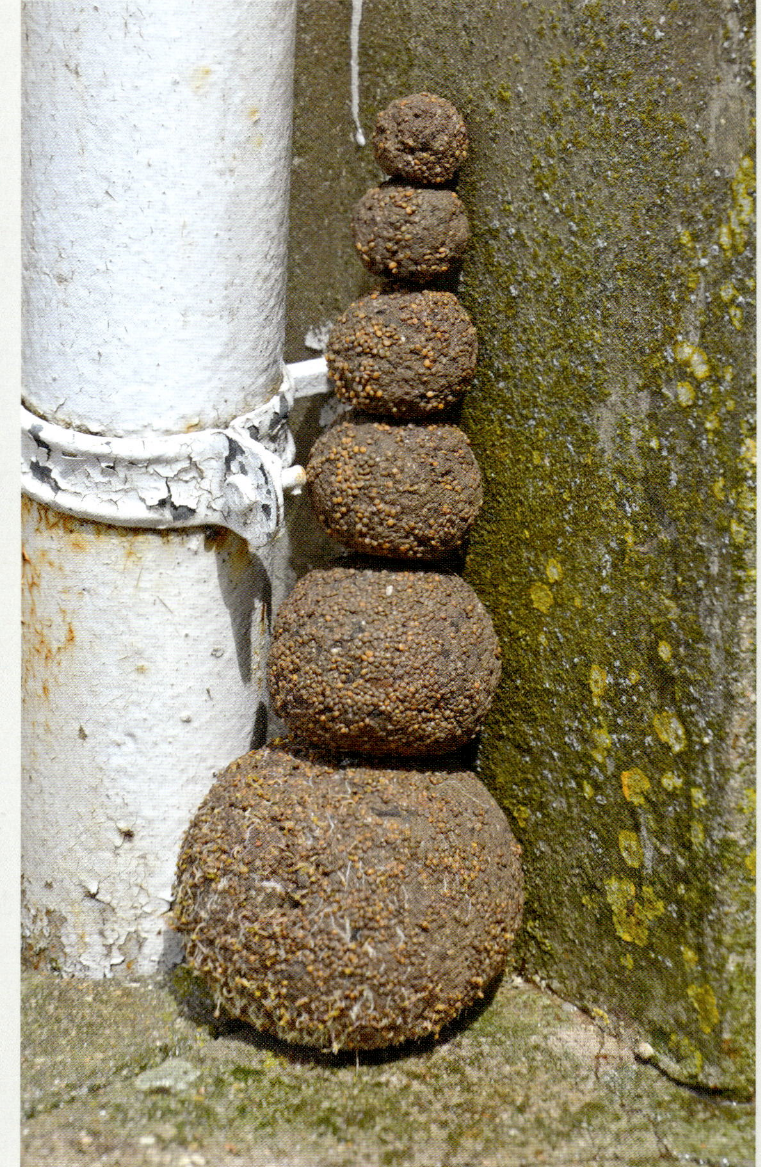

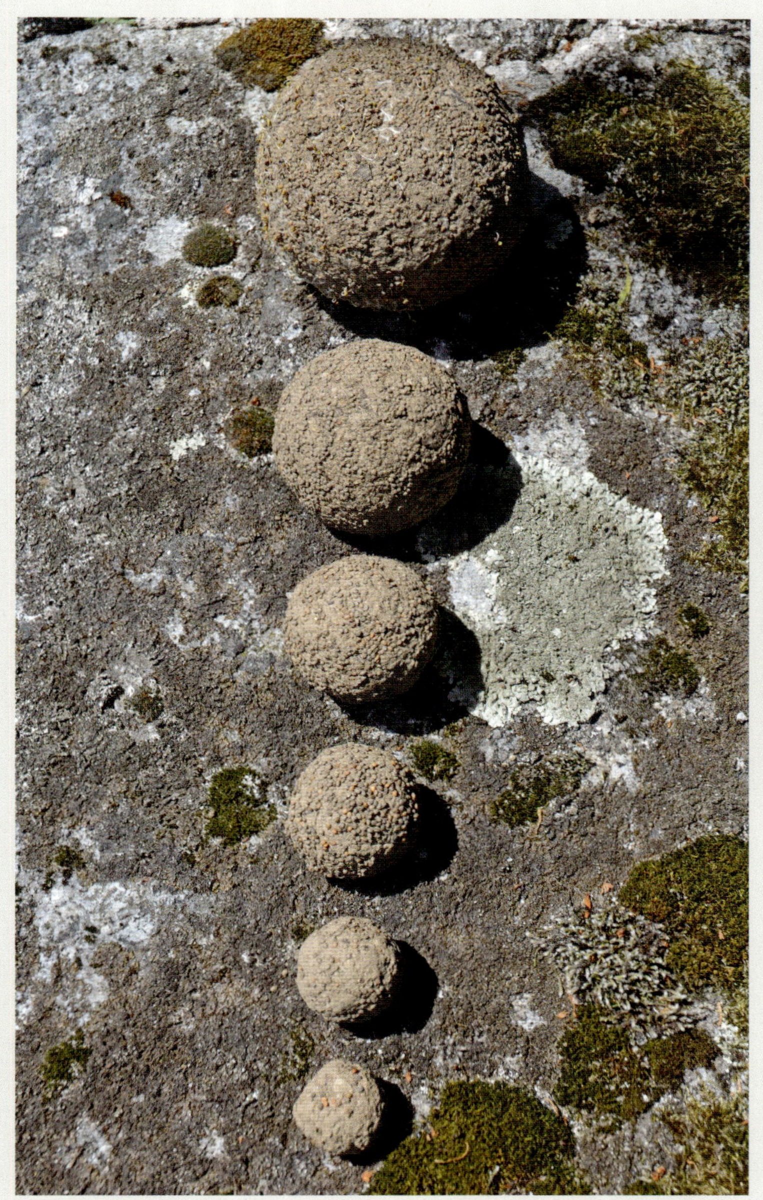

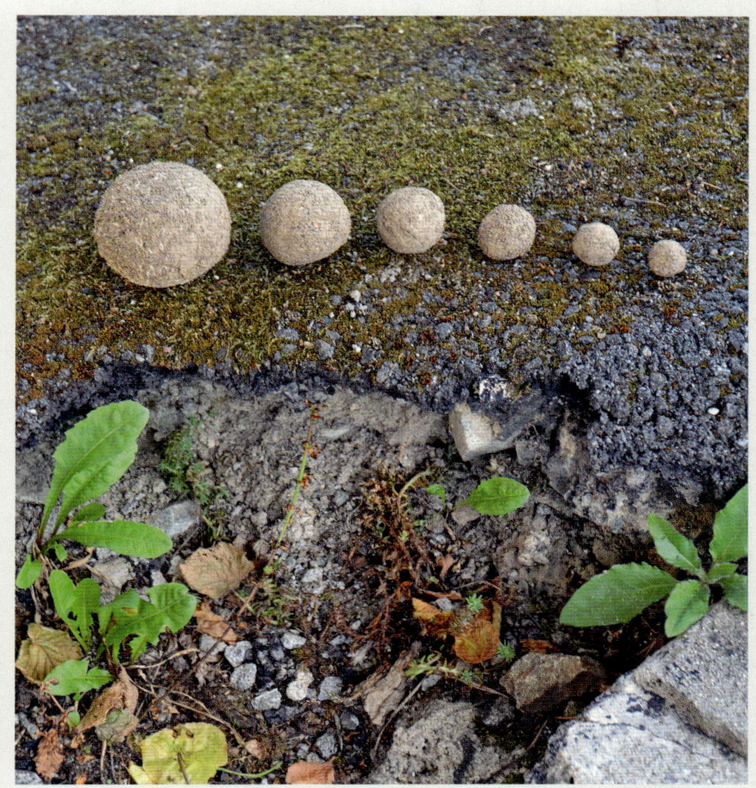

Why not combine art with guerilla gardening? Take some seeds, mix them with 1/3 earth for nourishment and 2/3 clay to make a solid ball. Then scout a suitable site. Vacant lots, roadsides and those empty stretches along railway lines are perfect. Remember that this is quite the opposite of vandalism, so proceed with care. Ideally choose a wet time of year to encourage germination.

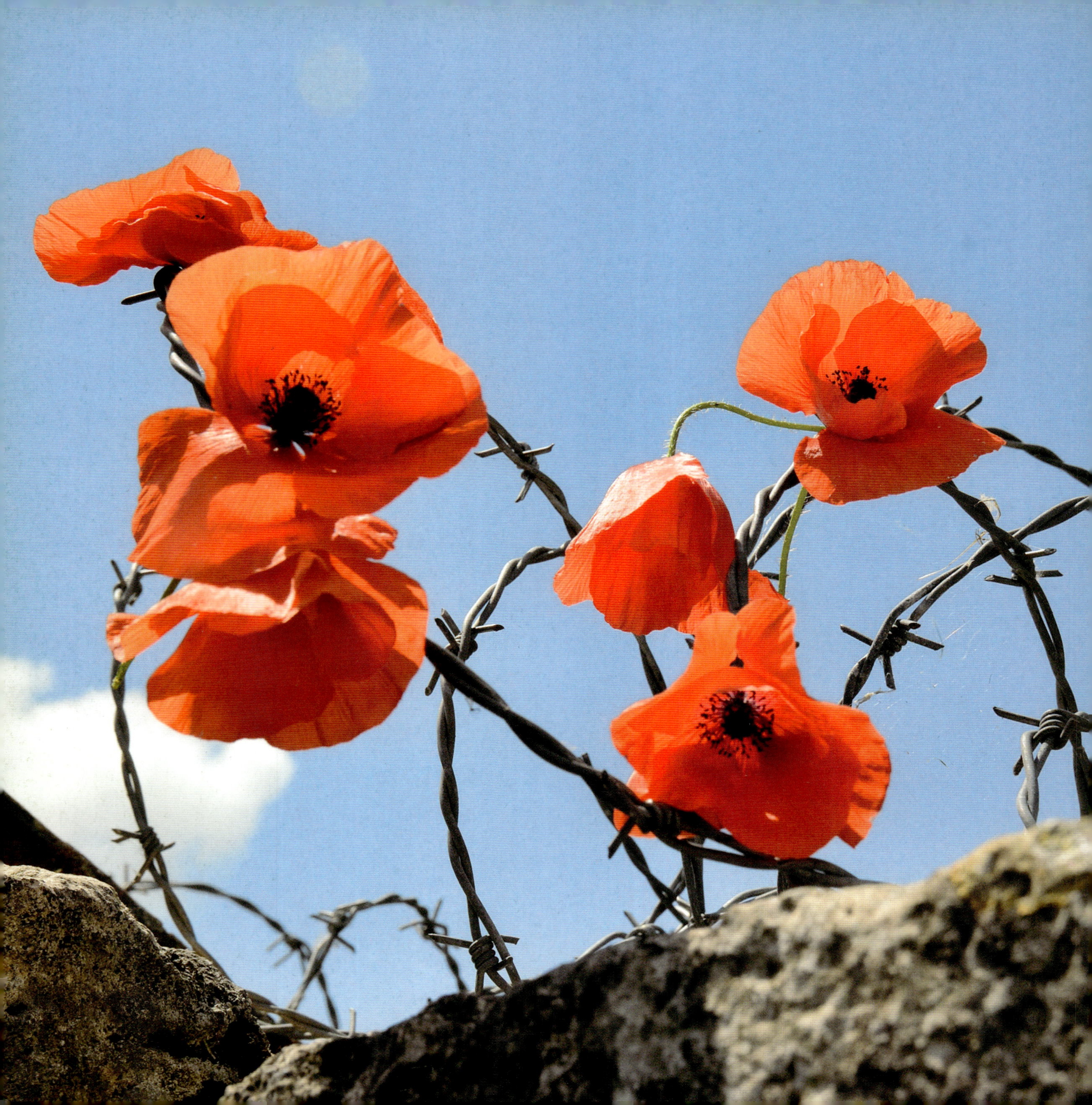

SUMMER

Magnolia leaves are very well suited to making a range of compositions, since they offer a certain rigidity, a pleasing shape and a lovely range of colours.

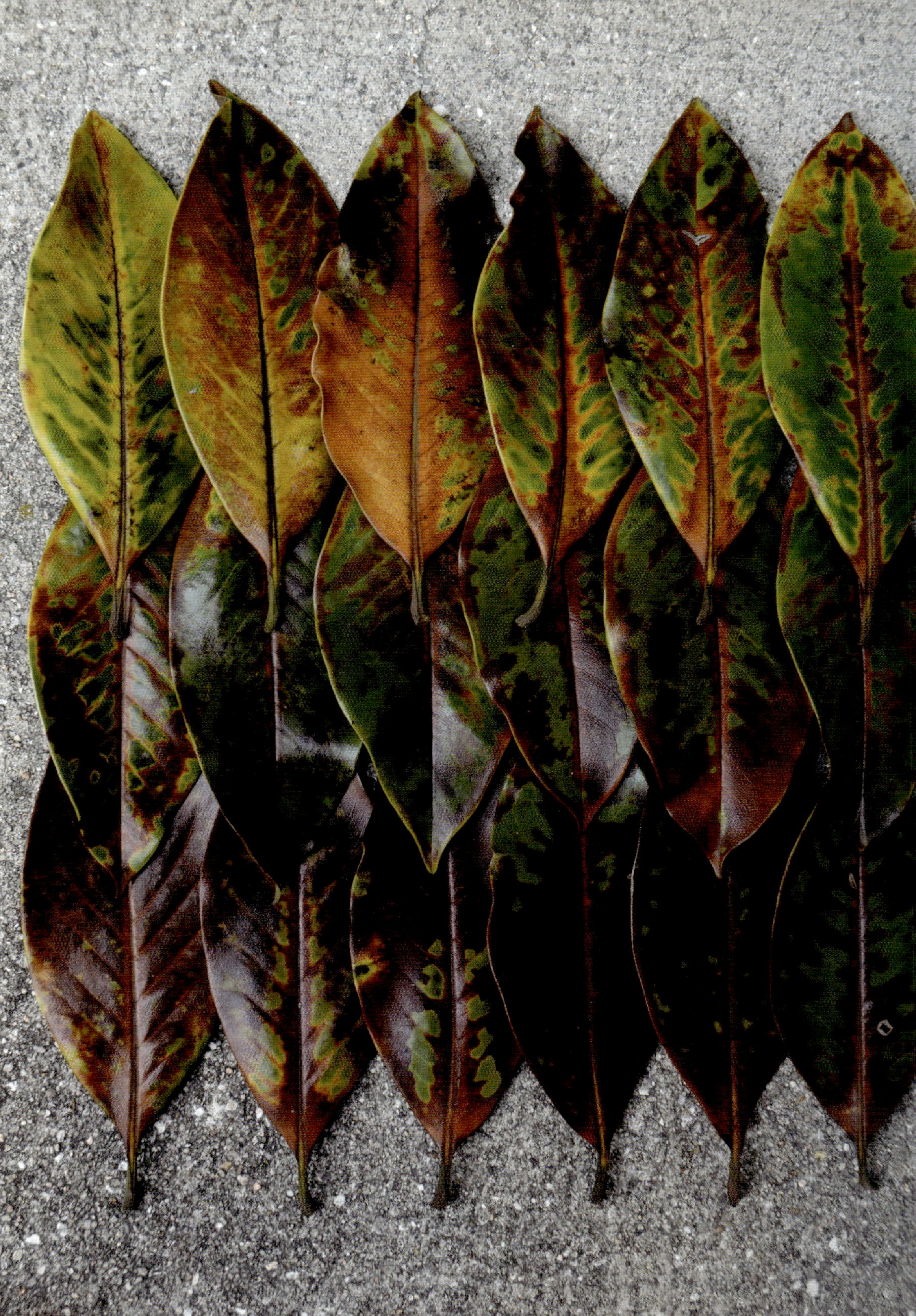

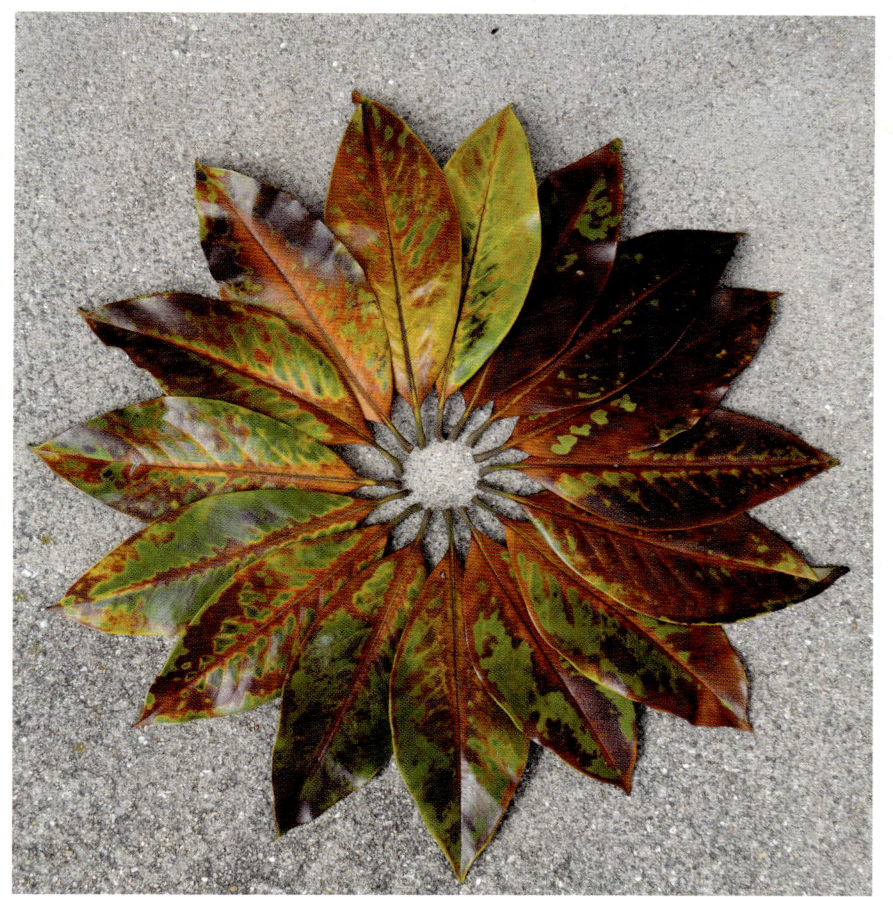

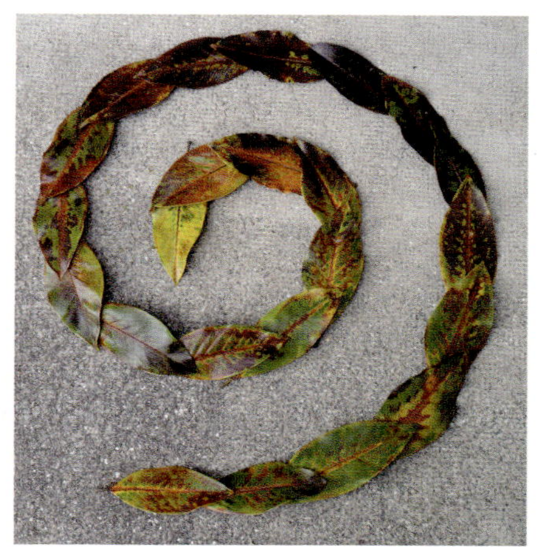

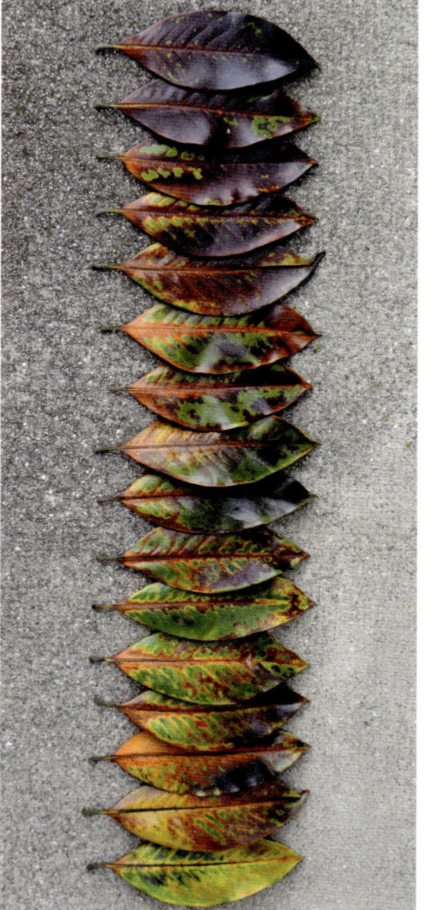

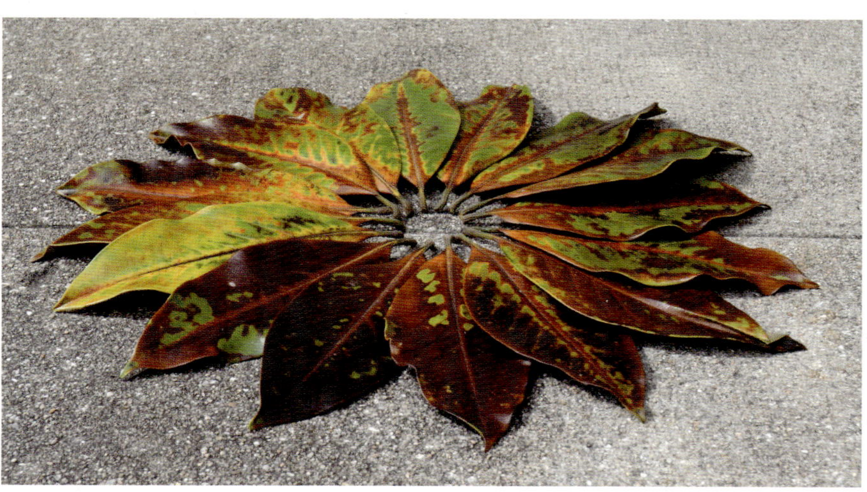

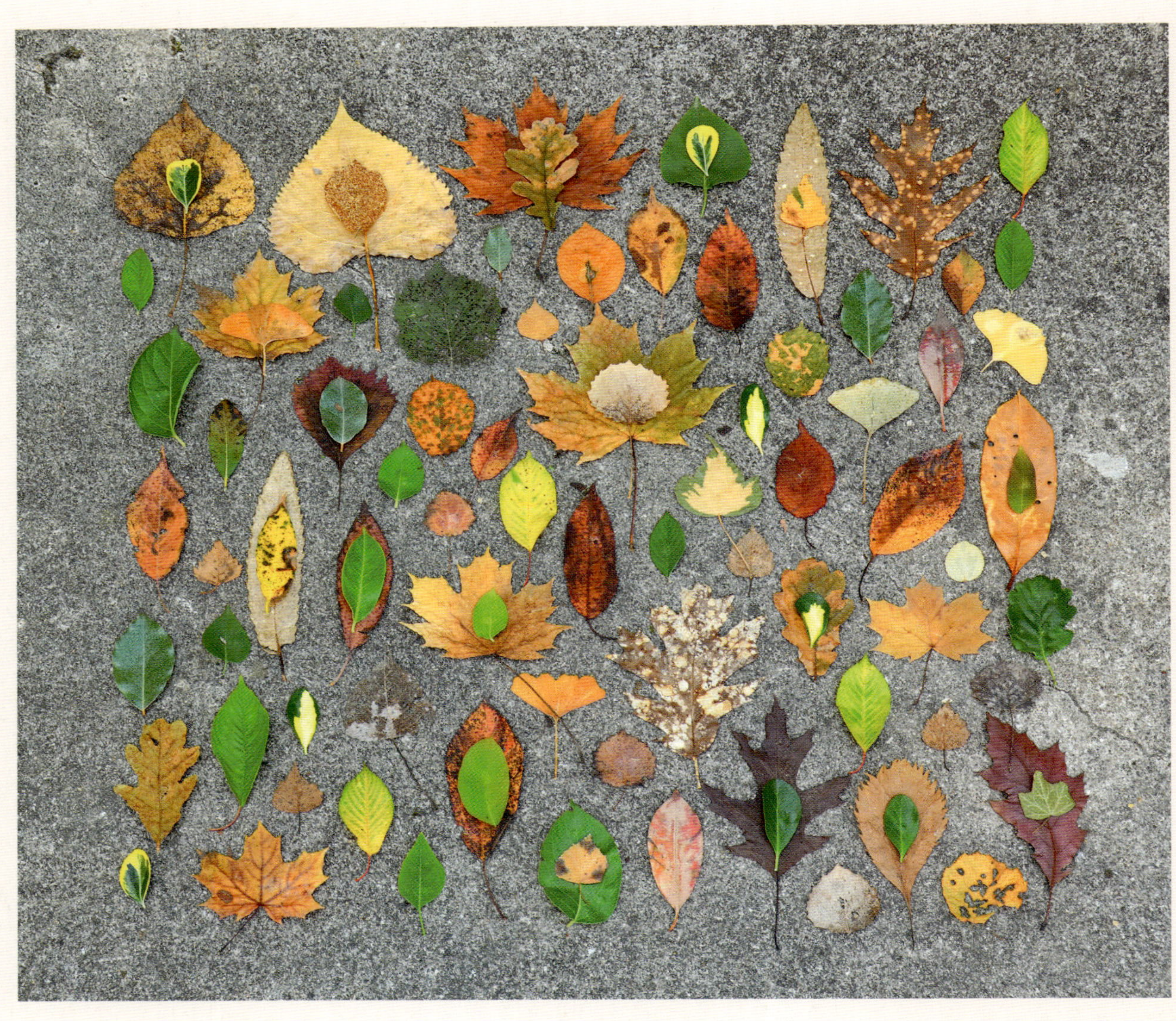

What a beautiful collection of shapes, textures and hues!

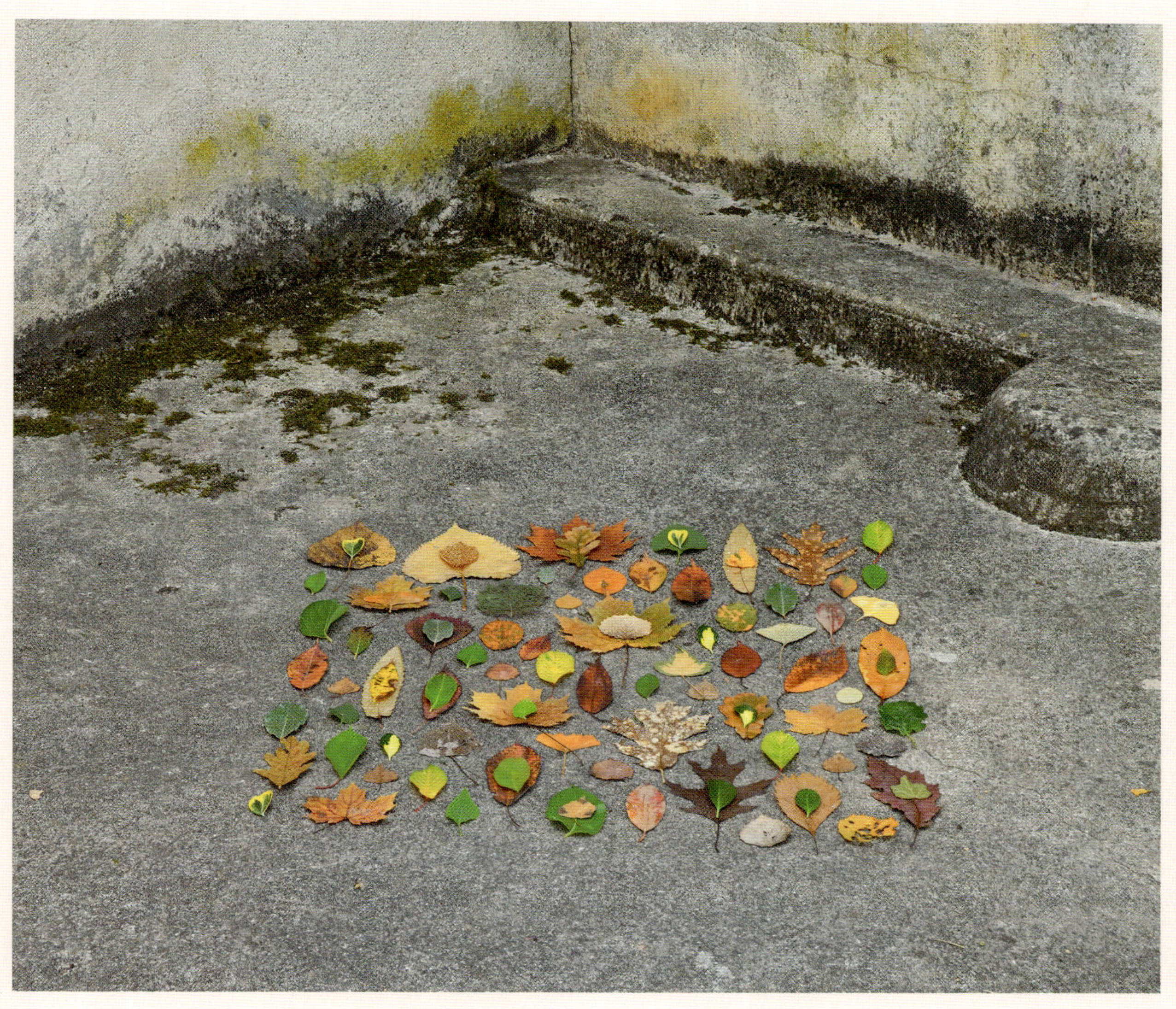

Bring a miniature forest into a corner of town.

A rigid tree of Japanese laurel.

I pushed the stalks of the leaves behind the metal bar, and used a mixture of earth and water to stick them to the wall, opposite.

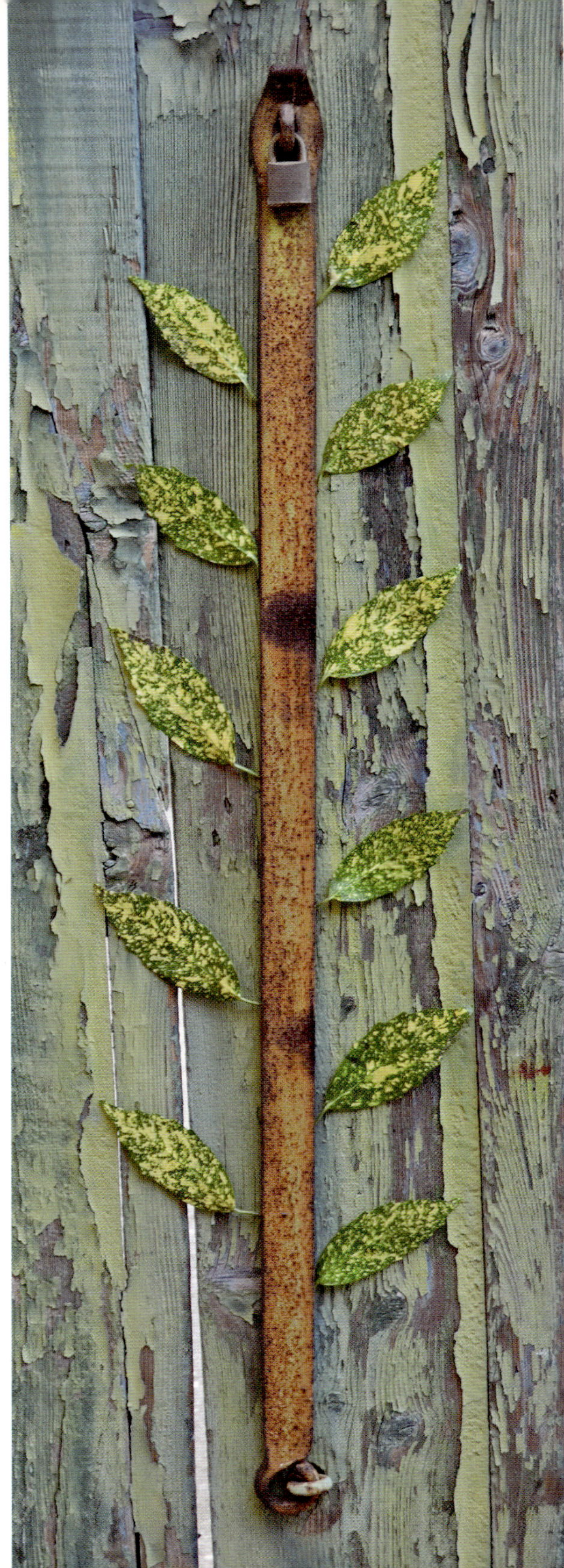

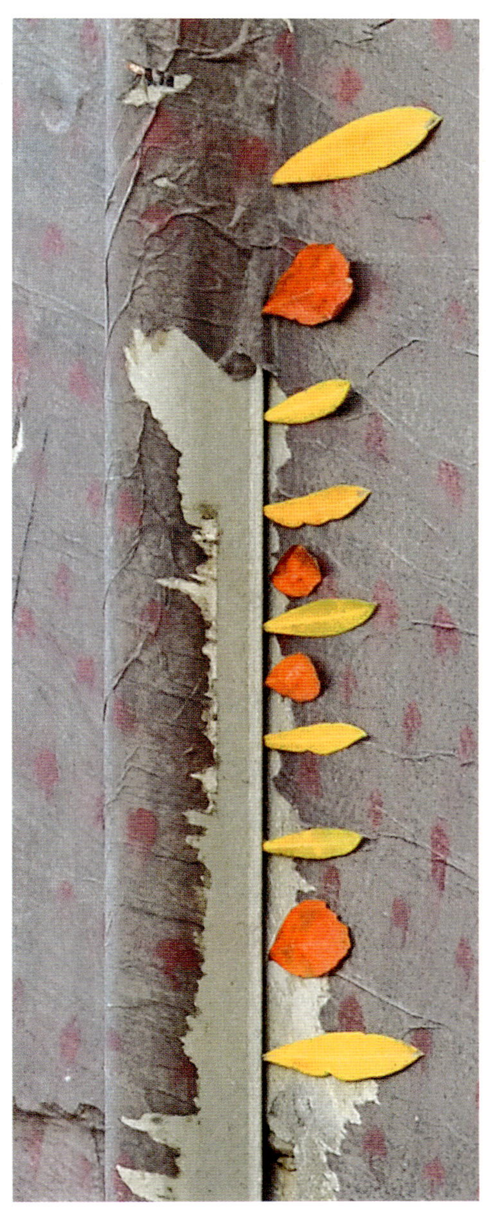

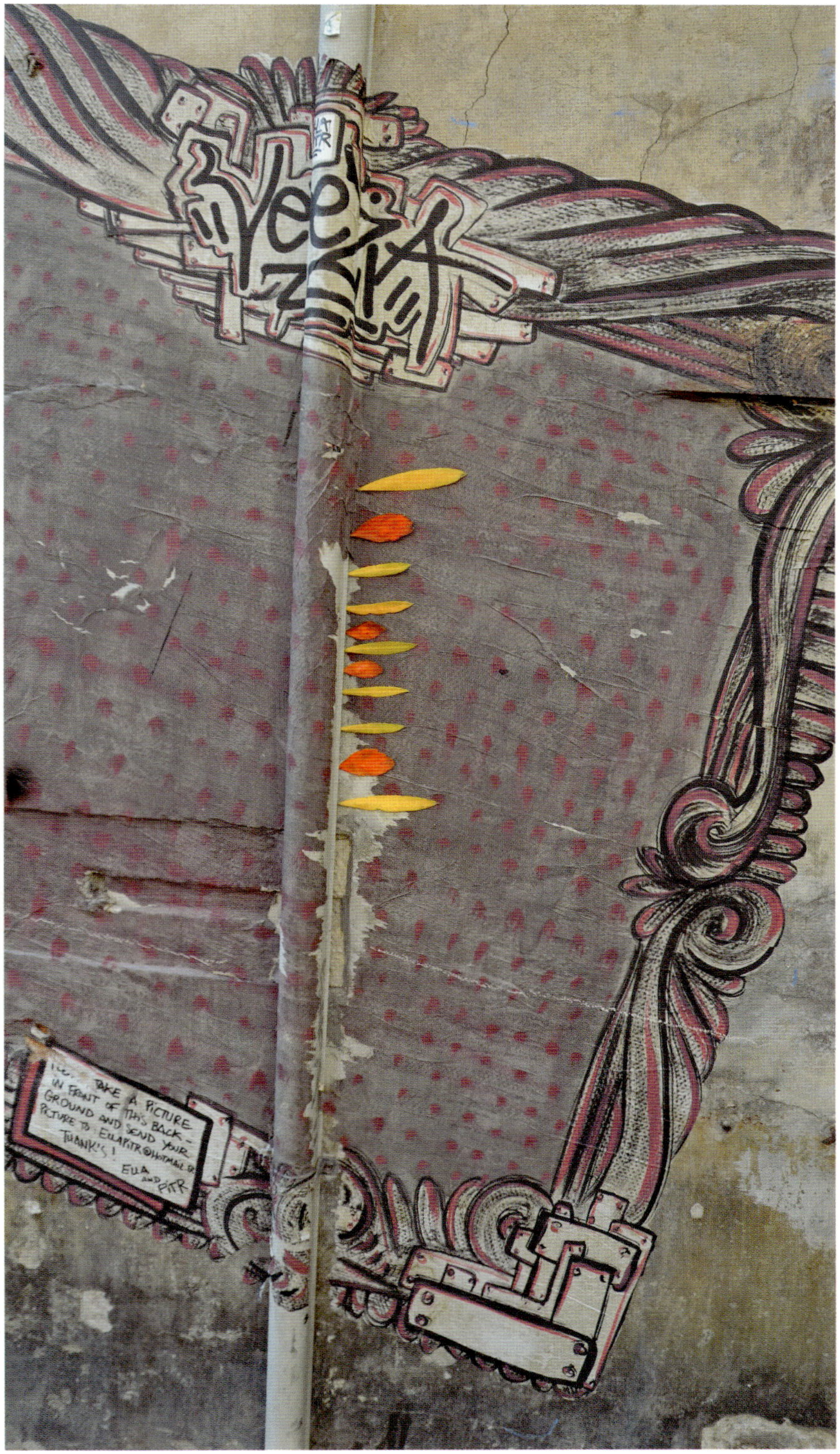

Willow and quaking aspen leaves.

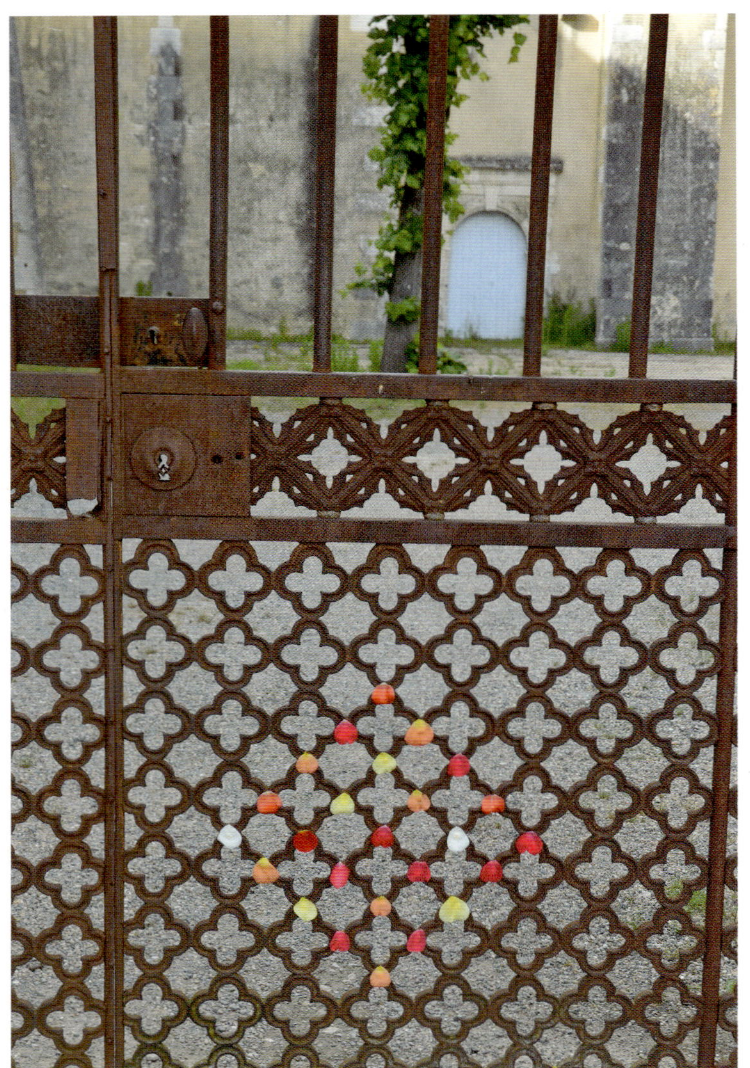

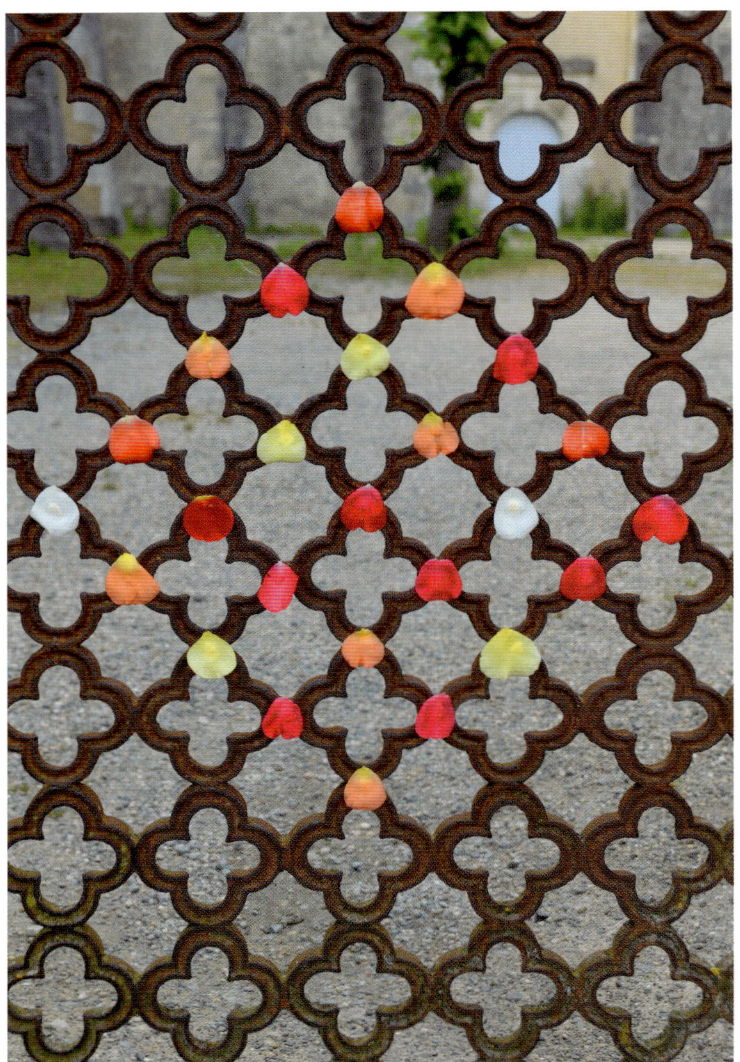

Bright petals transform a tired old gate with a splash of summer colour.

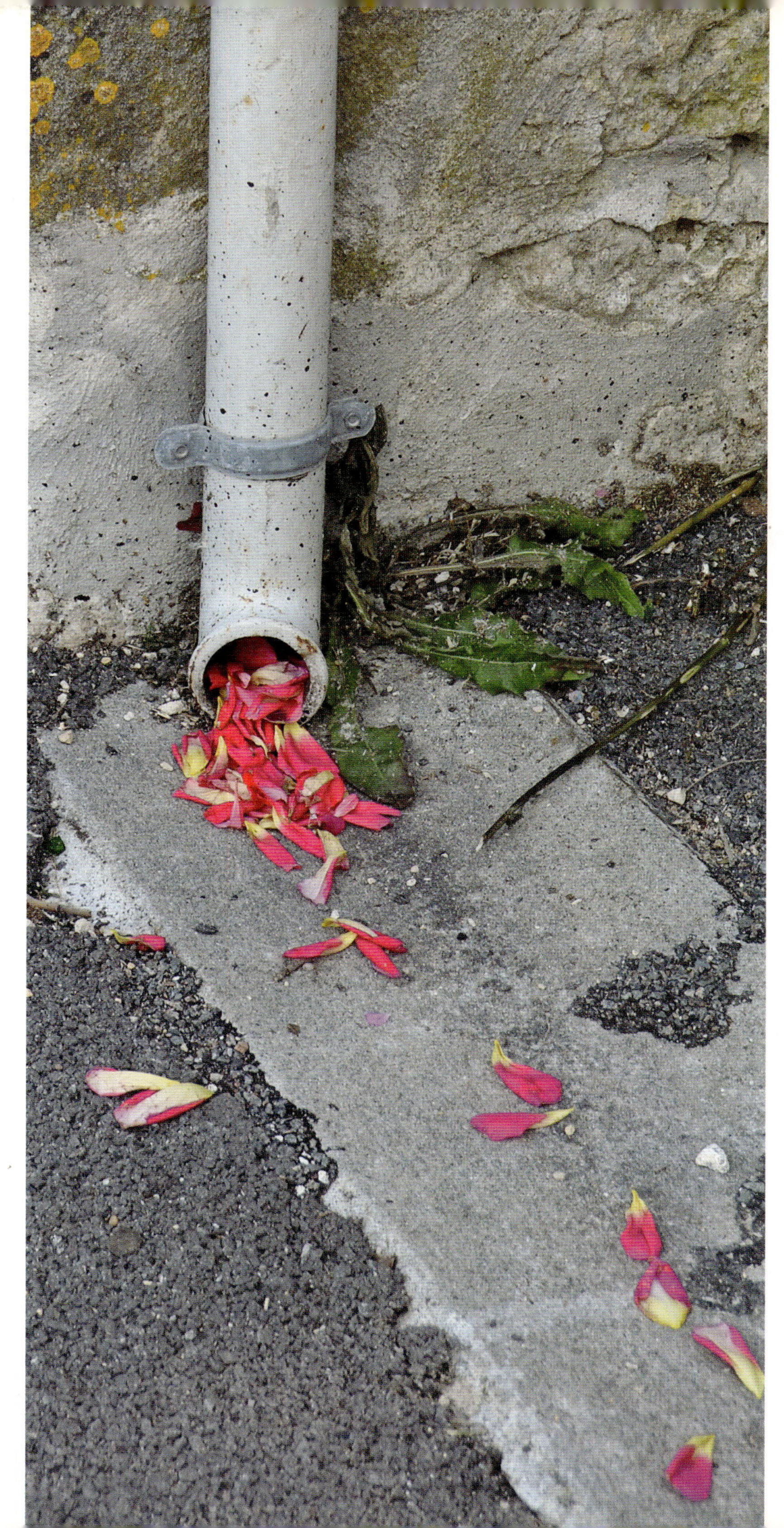

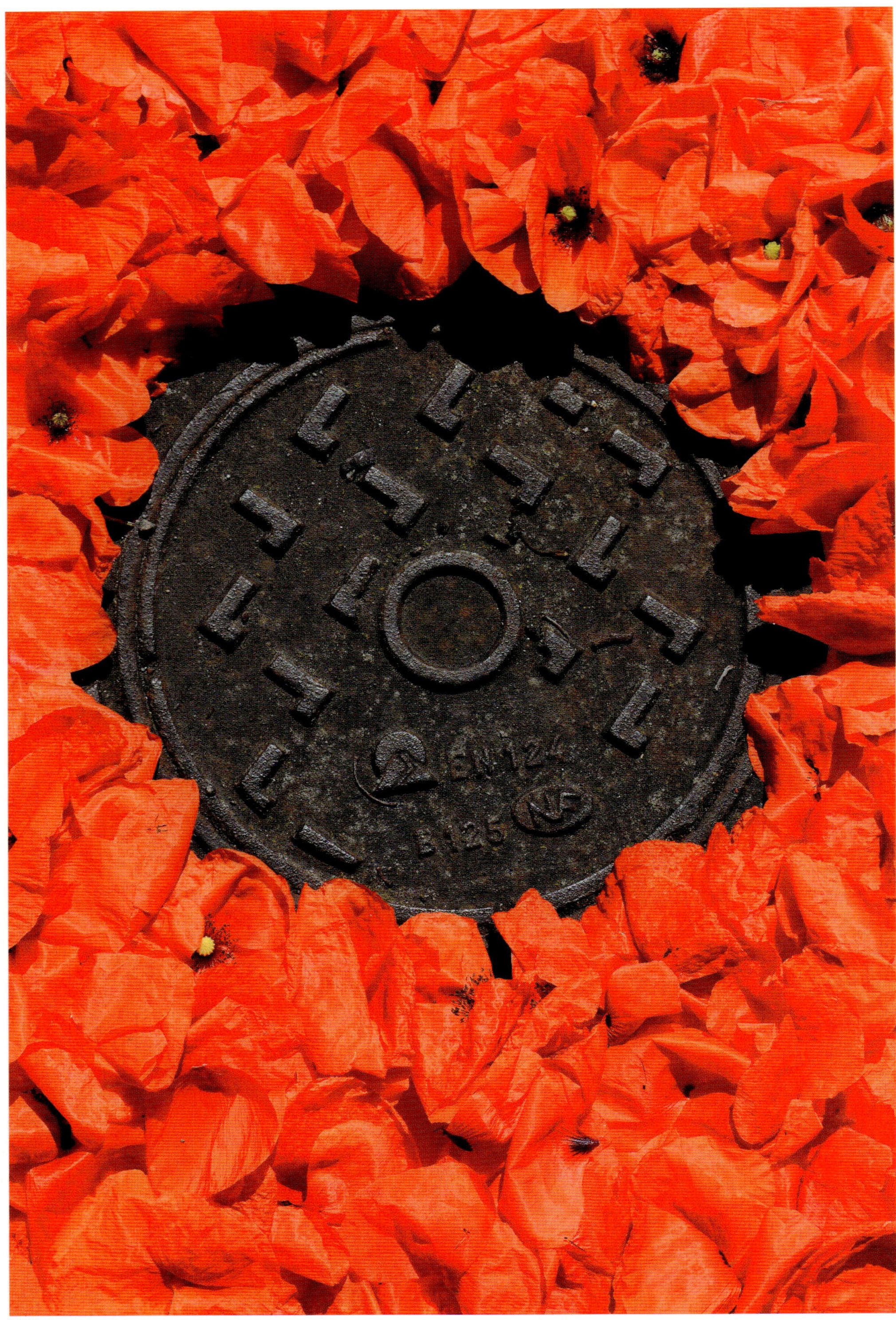

Poppies also bloom in town!

Both the town poppy and the country poppy are extremely fragile, and not a little effort is required to use them on a windy day.

But if you're crafty and patient, you can achieve some beautiful results!

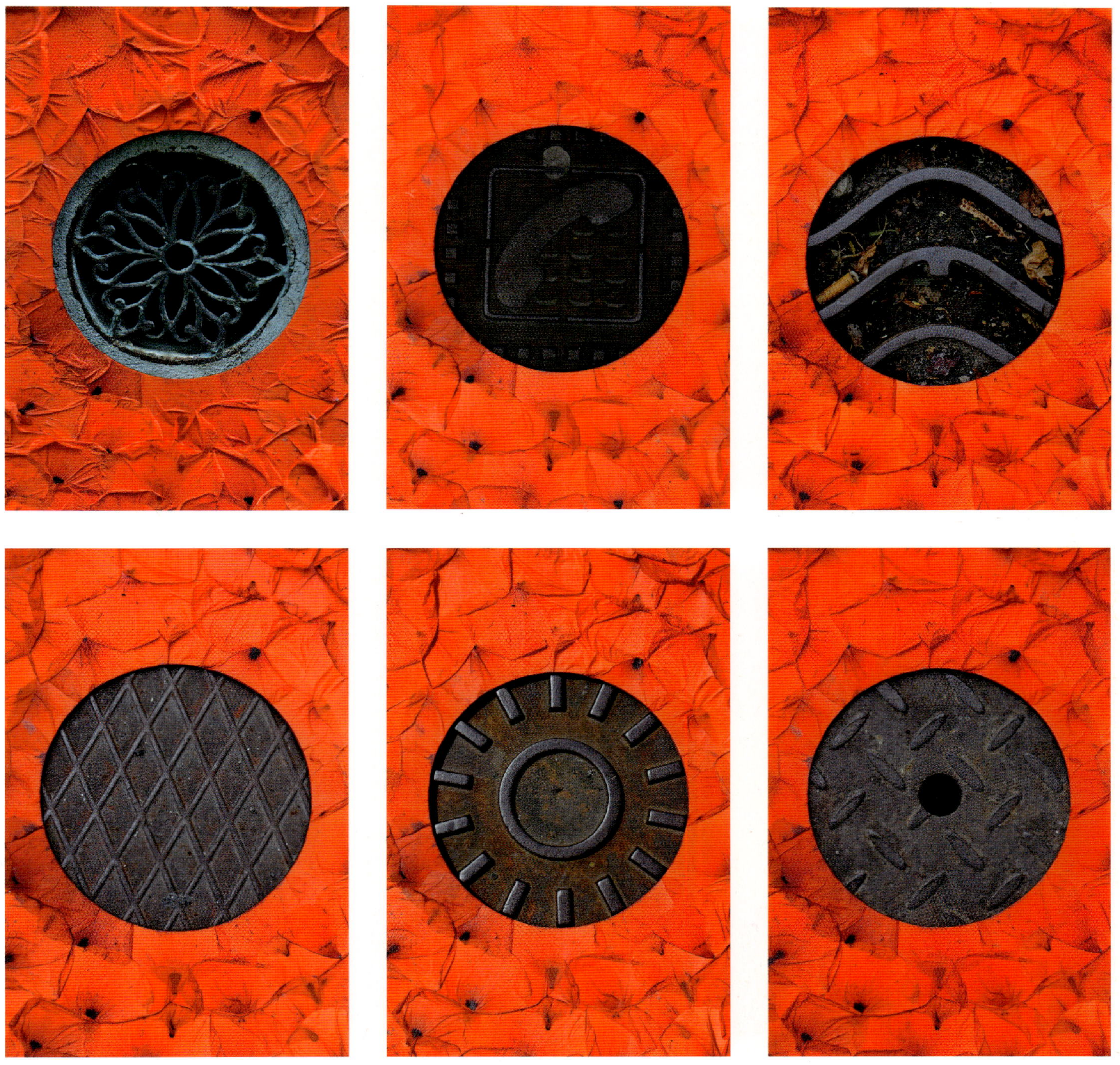

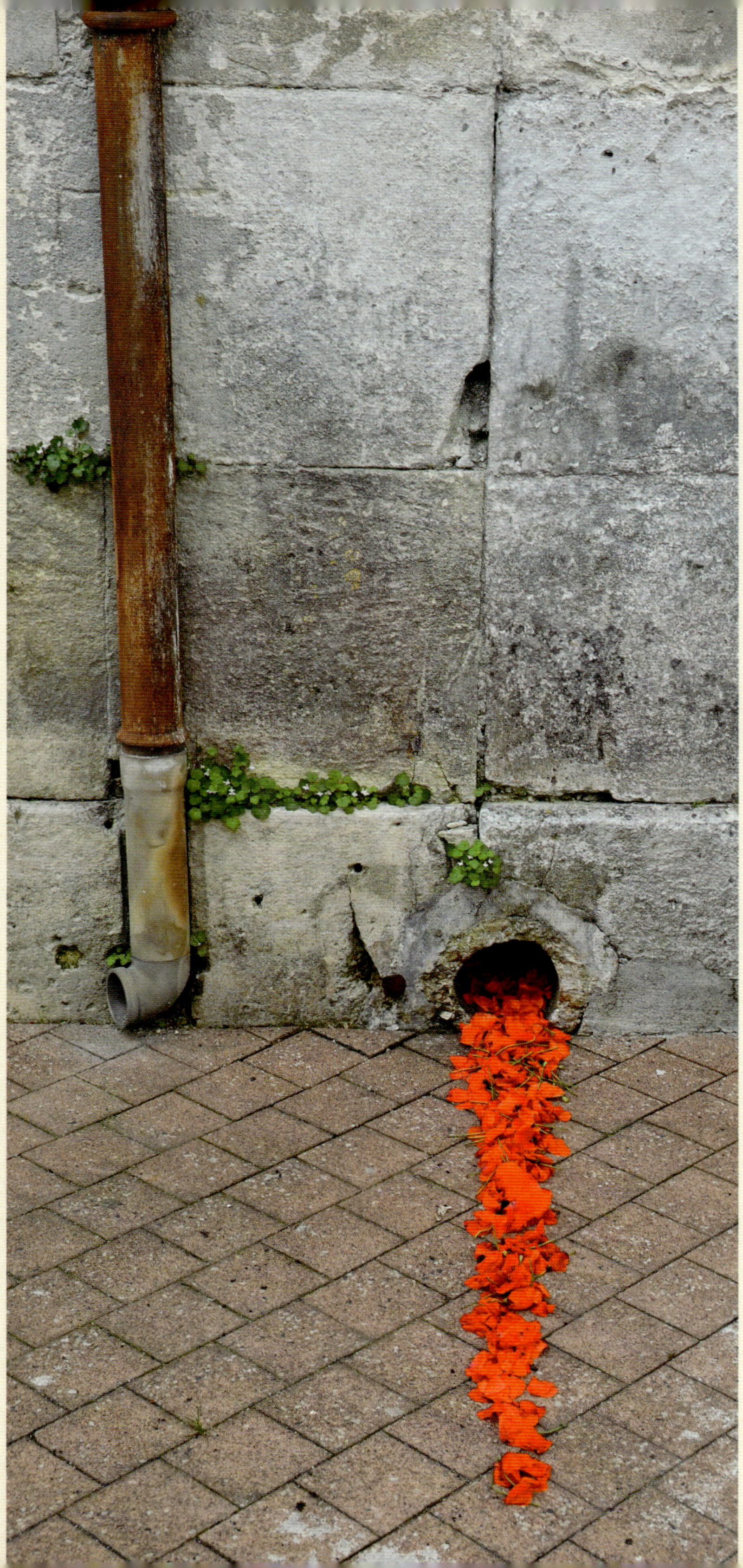

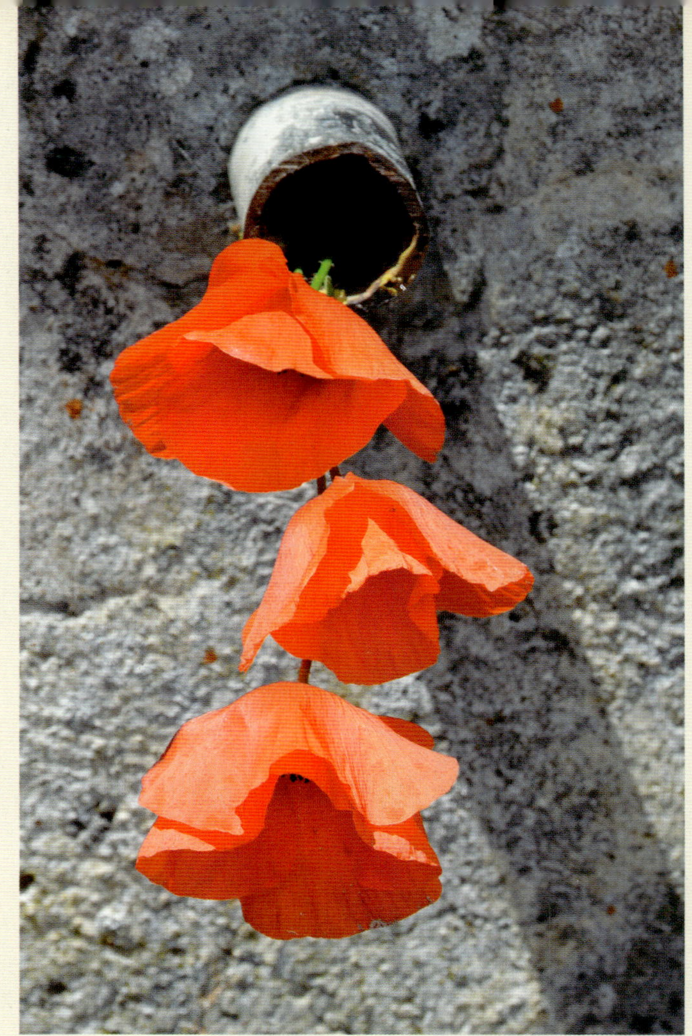

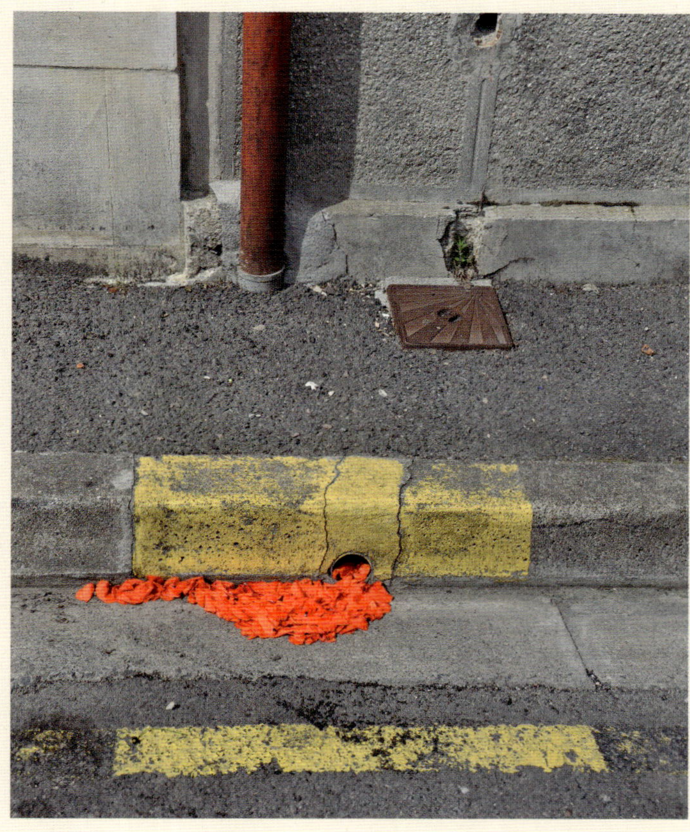

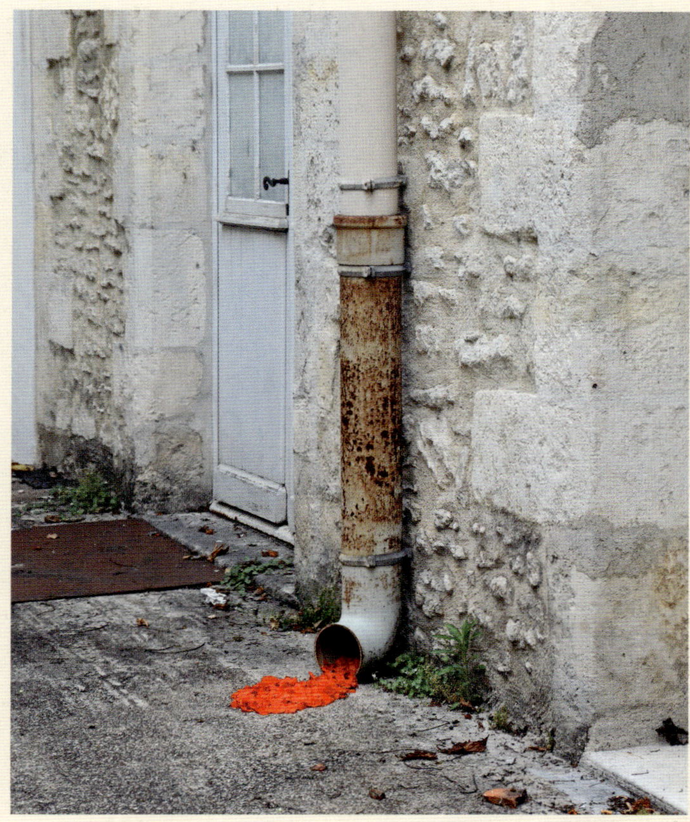

Poppies rush and tumble, through drains, out of pipes and along gutters, overflowing in a scarlet blaze. Where will they end up?

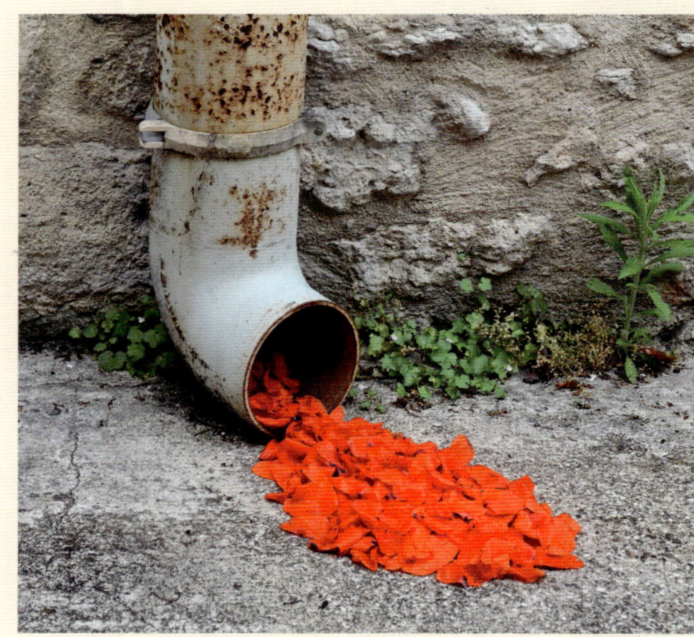

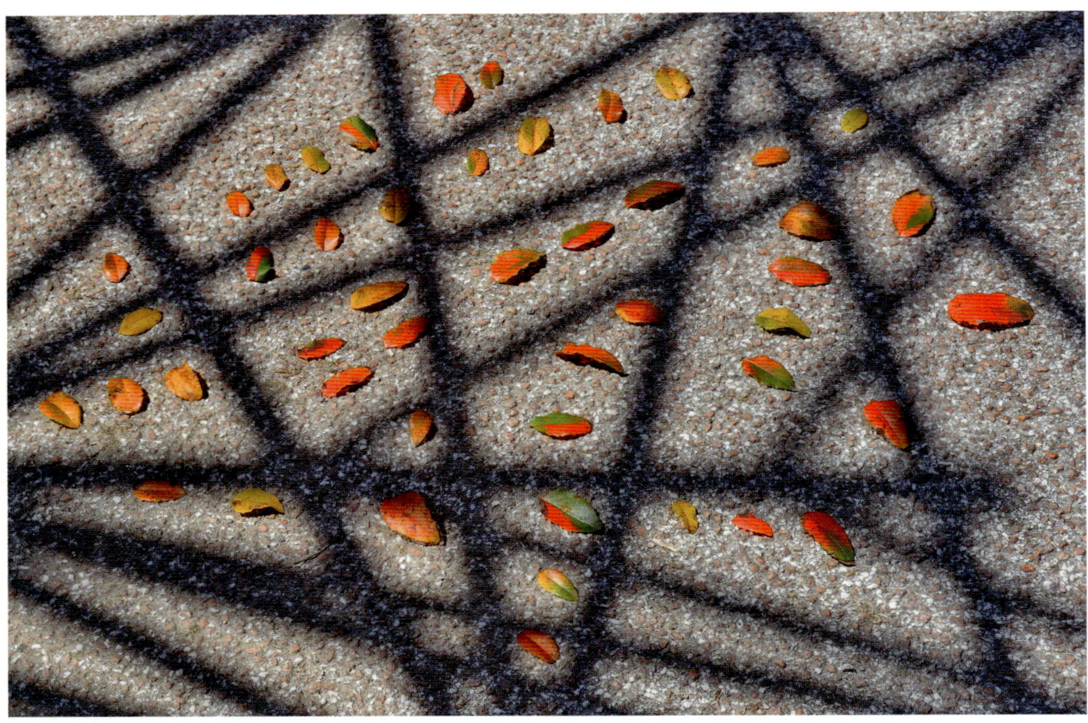

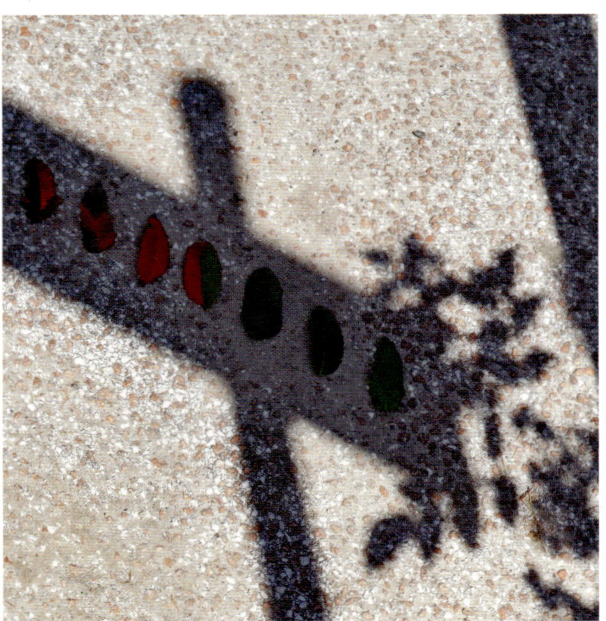

Everyone knows you can't catch a shadow, but why not use their ephemeral, shifting nature to create some truly special pieces?

If there's a shape you'd really like to make, but don't have the freehand composition skills to do so, an obliging shadow can serve as a stencil. But you'd better work quickly before it moves too far!

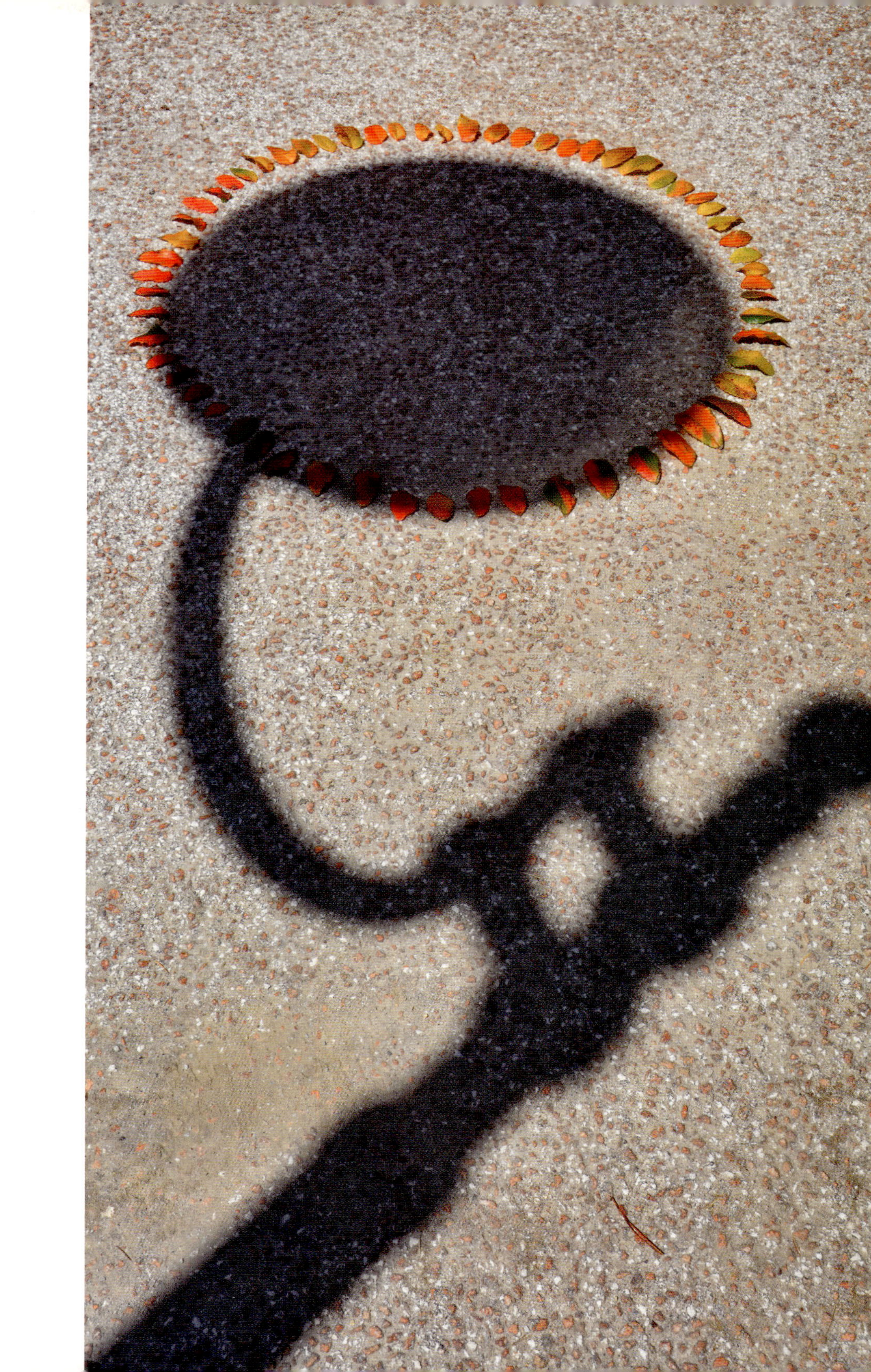

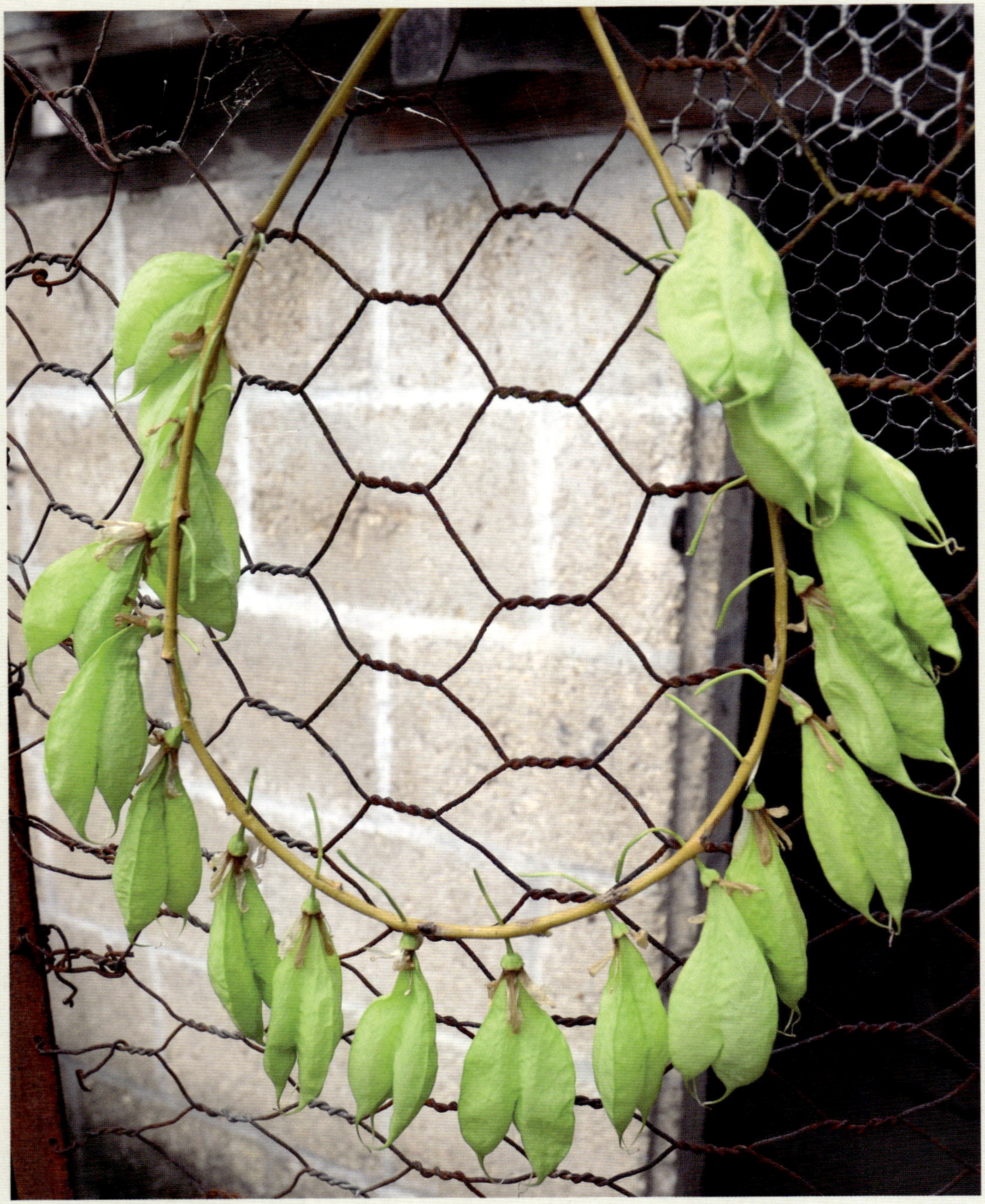

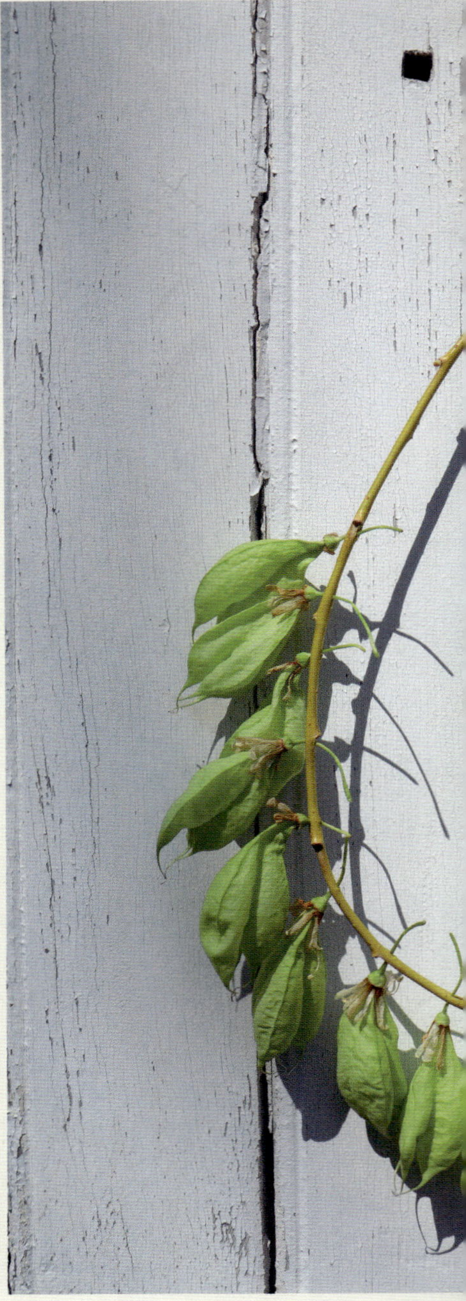

Attach leaves to this flexible willow twig by making a series of small notches about 1 cm long down the middle of the twig, taking care not to split it entirely. Then stick each stalk in one of the little notches.

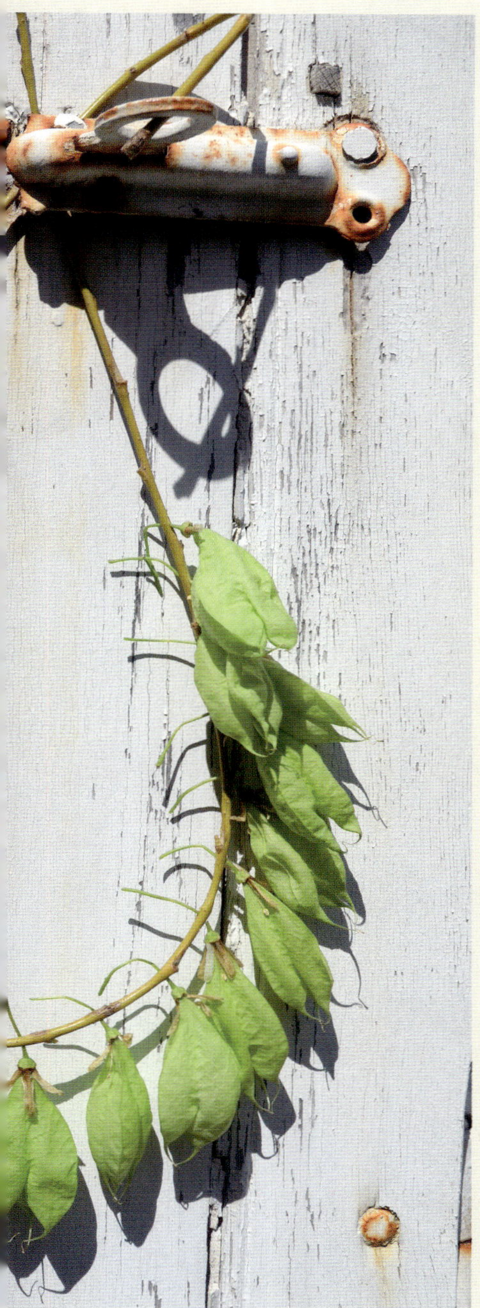

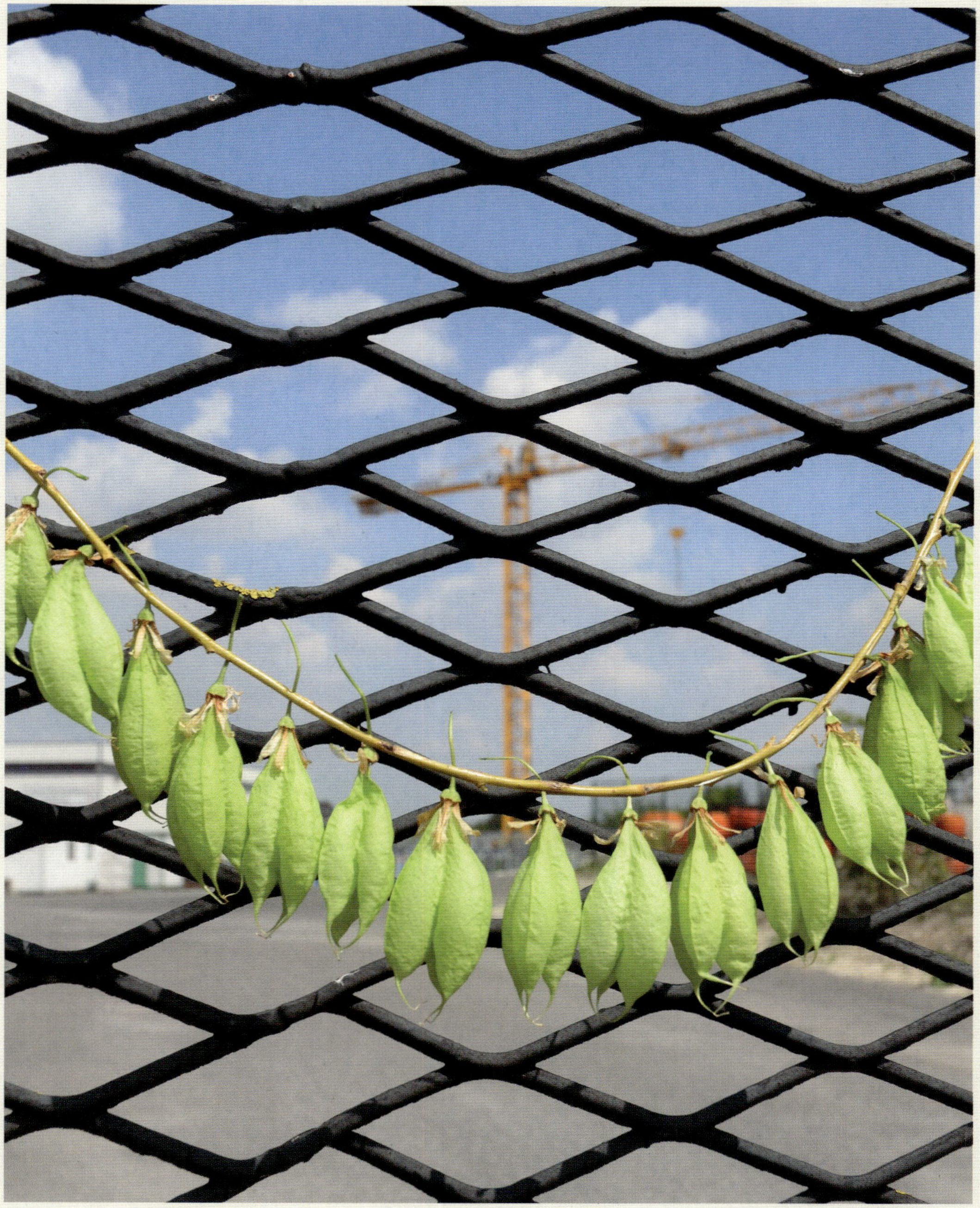

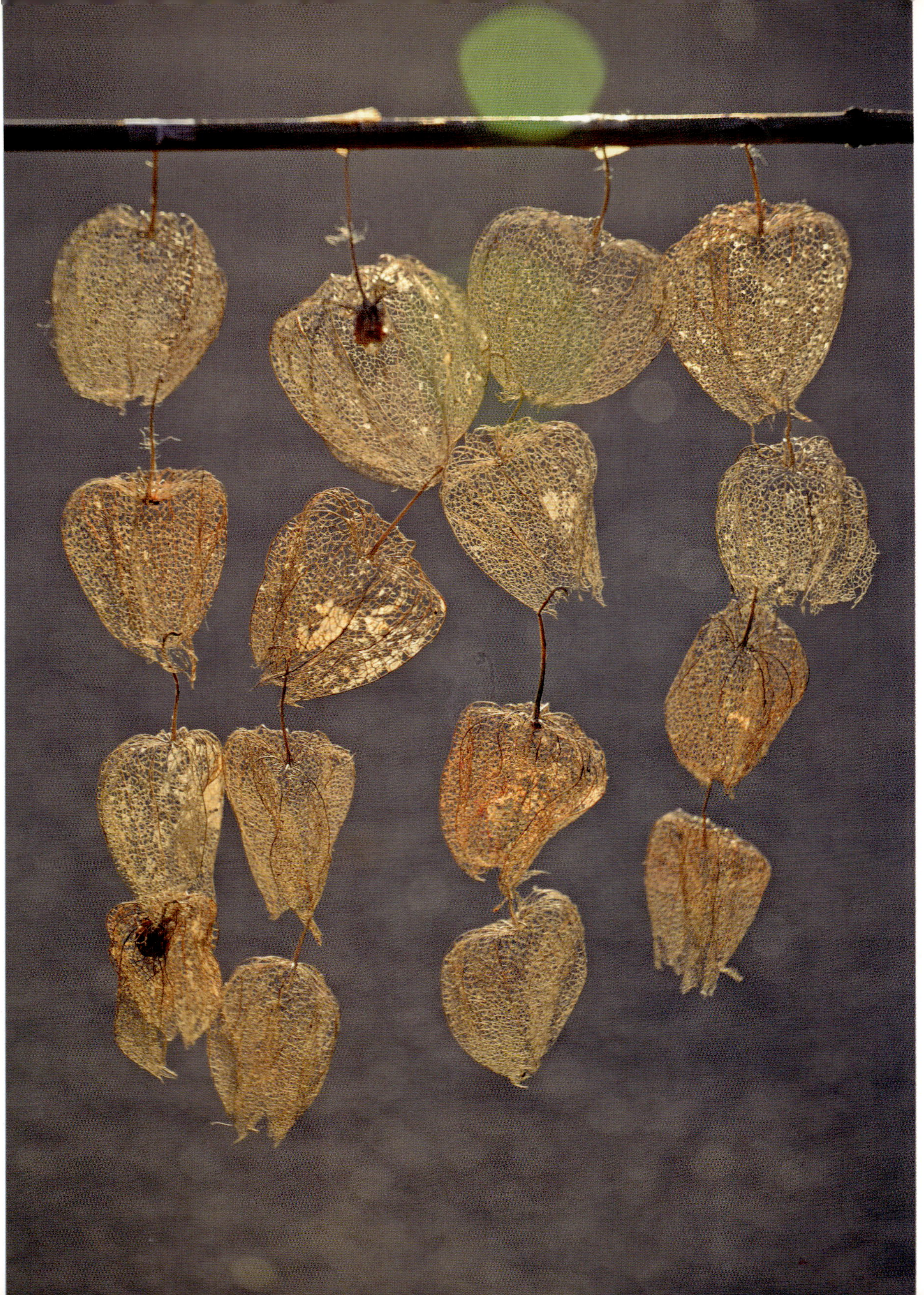

Gossamer thin physallis leaves glow translucent against the soft light of a summer evening.

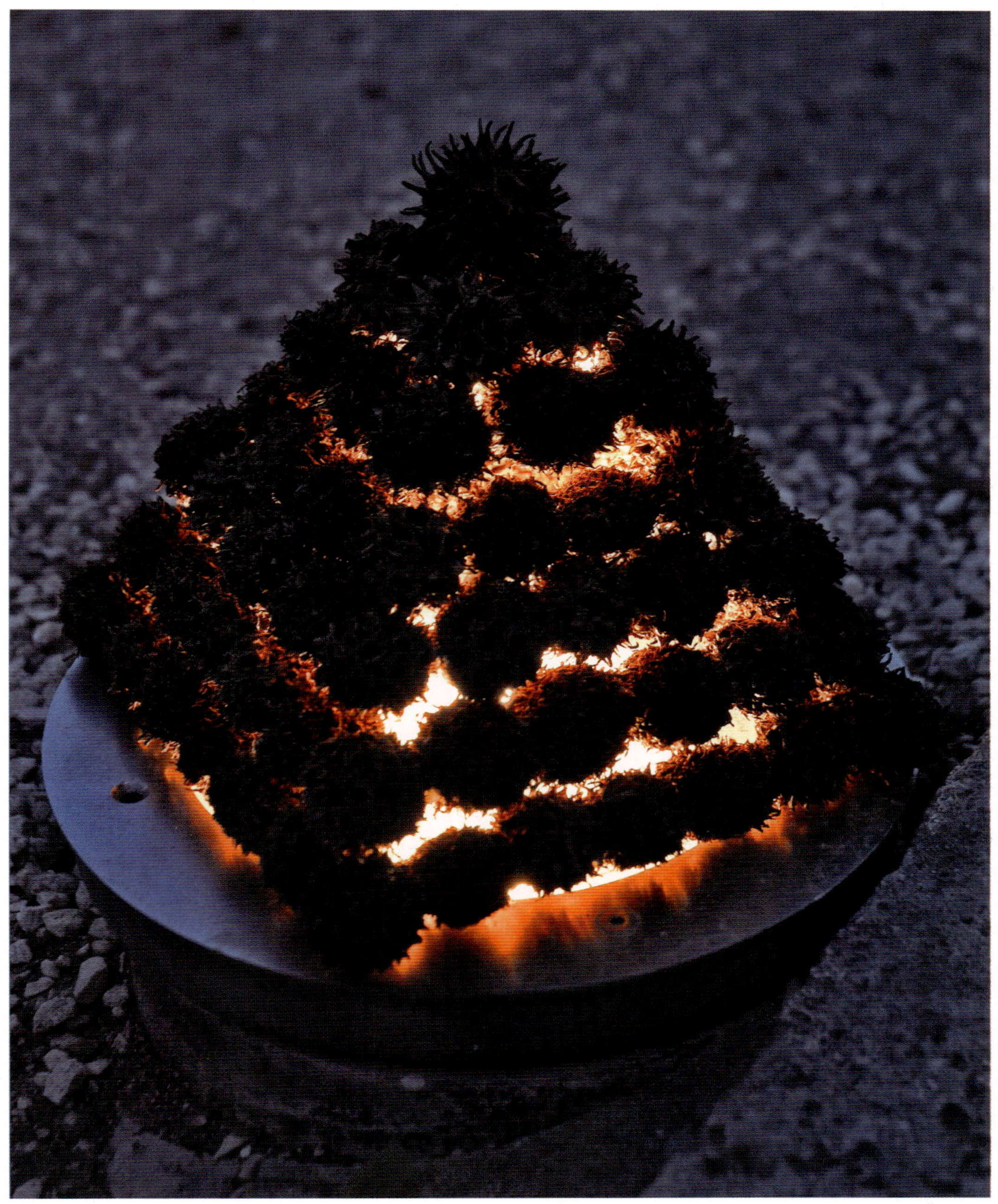

I used fruit of the Australian pine (*Casuarina equisetifolia*) to make this pyramid above a lamp, but you could use thistle heads or spiky horse chestnut balls to achieve a similar effect.

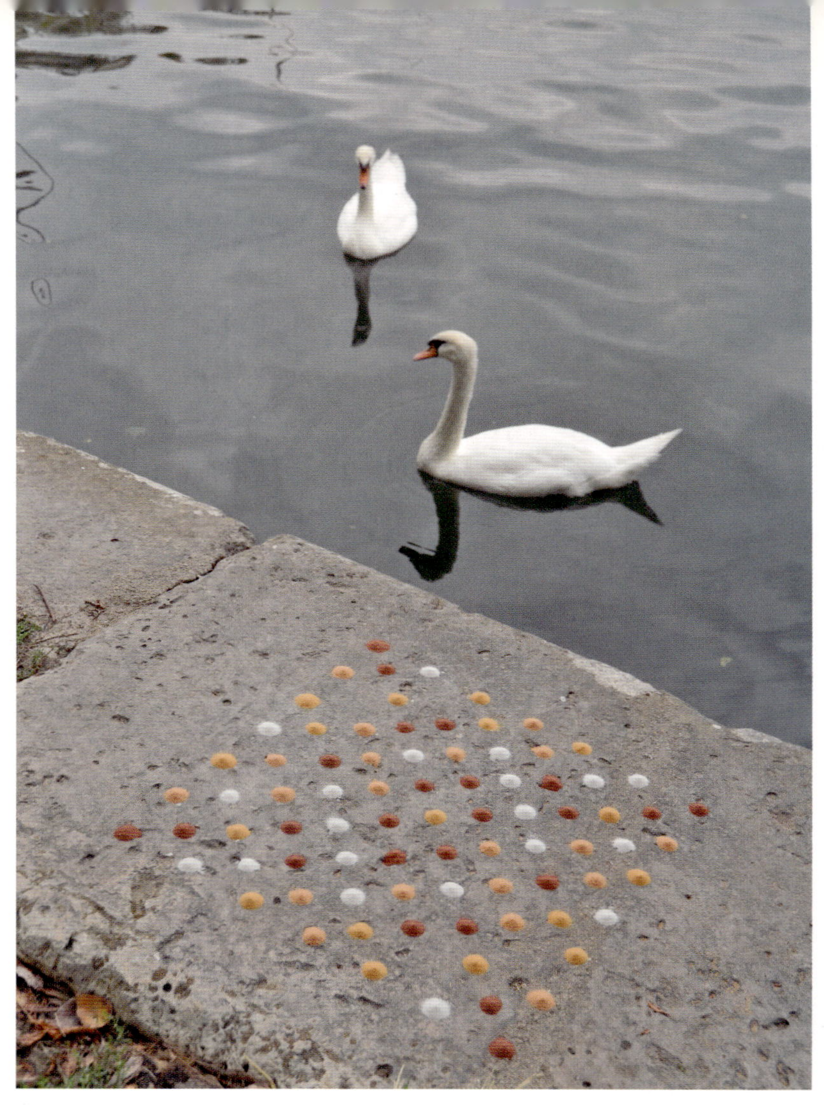

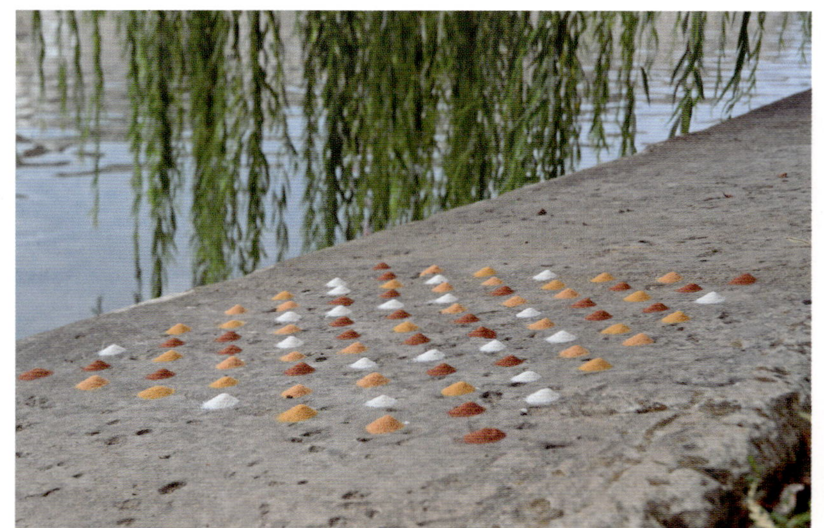

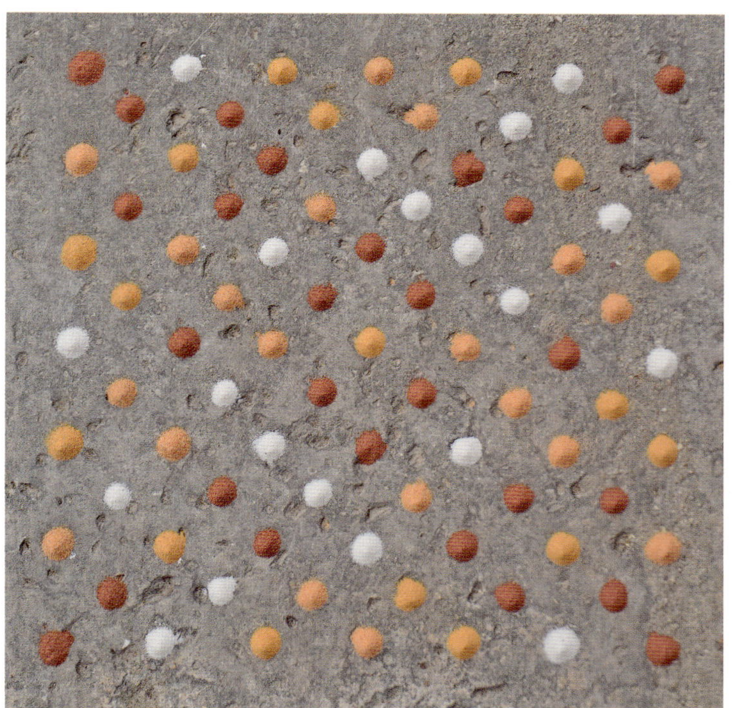

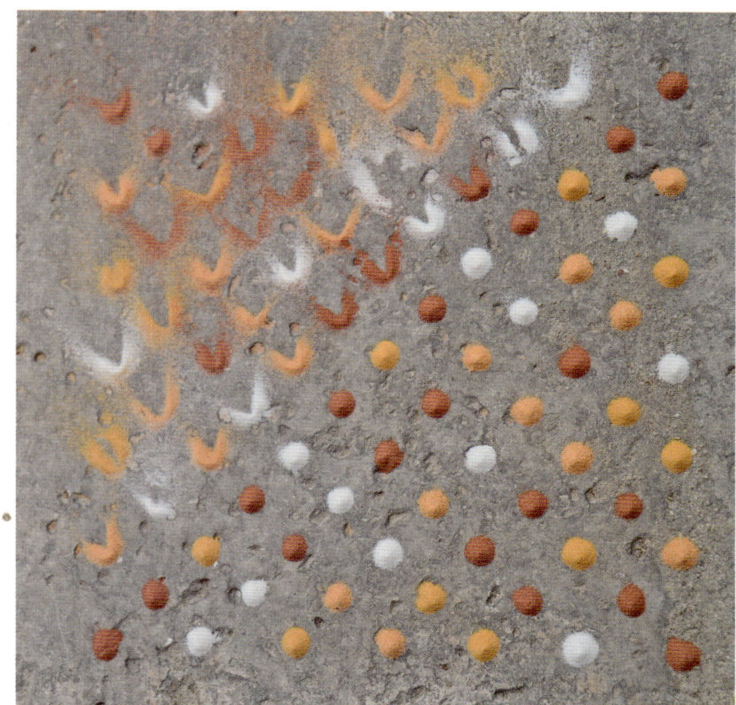

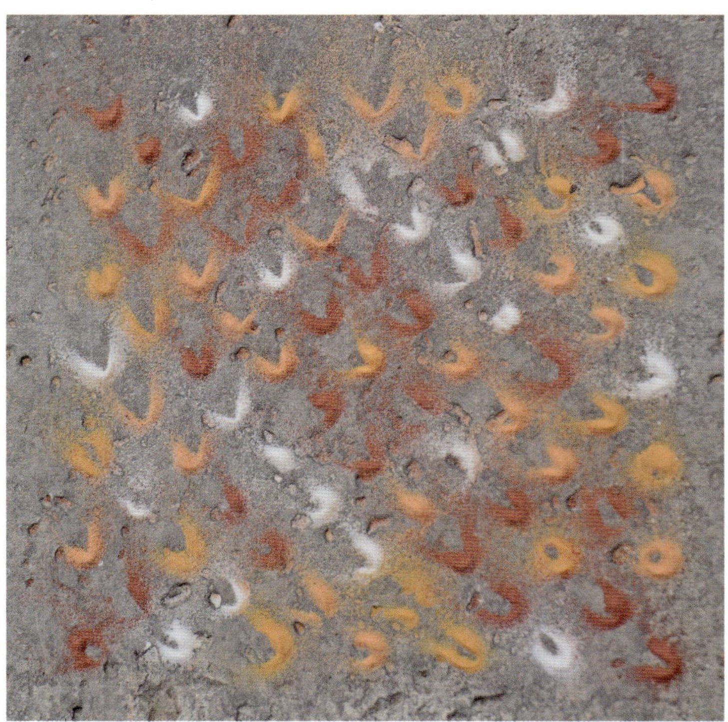

Kolams or *rangolis* are graphic patterns made by women in India, using chalk or rice powder poured from the palm of their hand or through their fingertips. These ephemeral installations are made in front of houses or dwellings each morning to bring prosperity and welcome guests, and are handed down from mother to daughter.

I used very fine sand and ochre, poured from a small bottle with a spout.

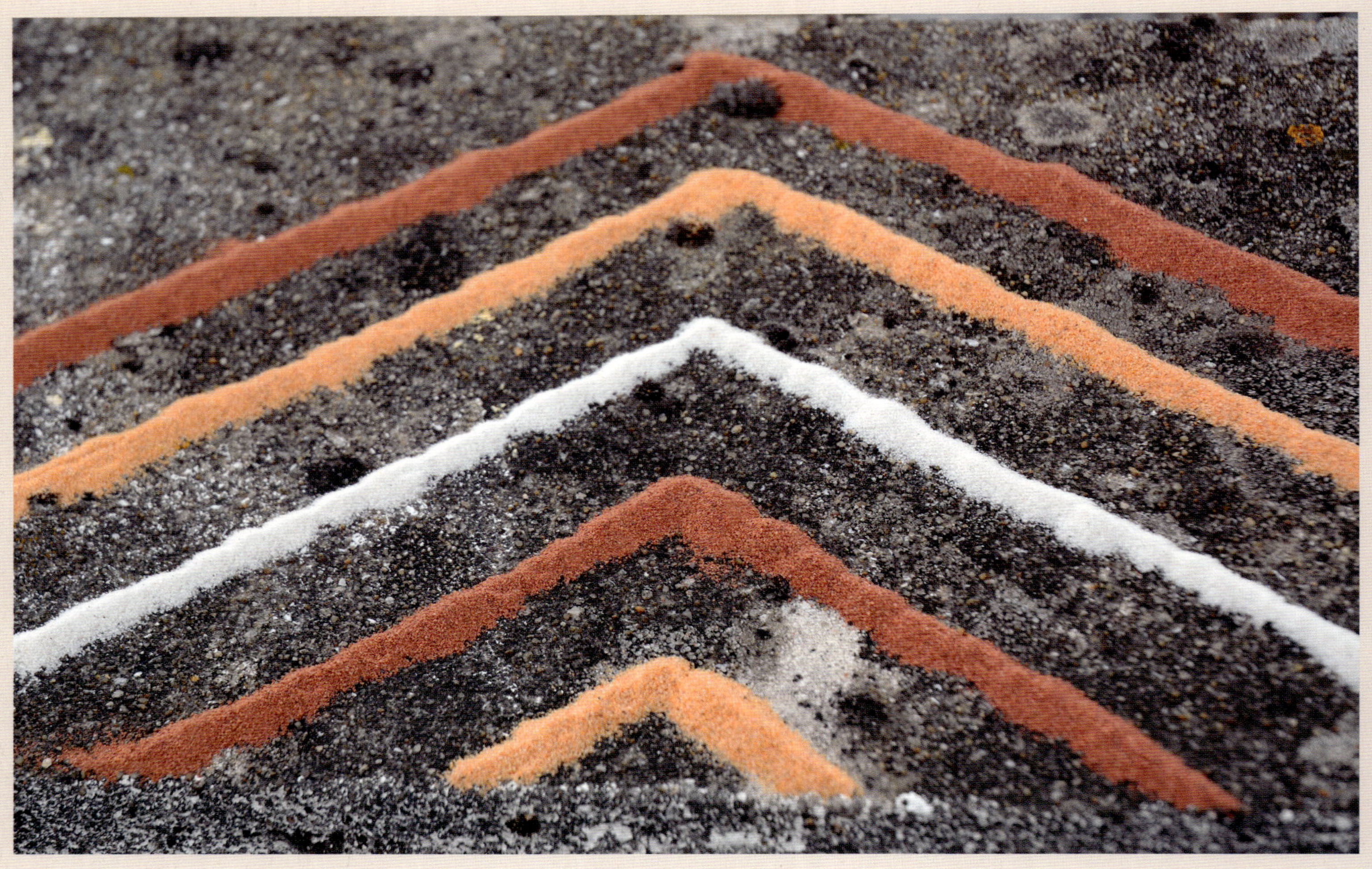

Use a rough surface to achieve an interesting contrast of textures.

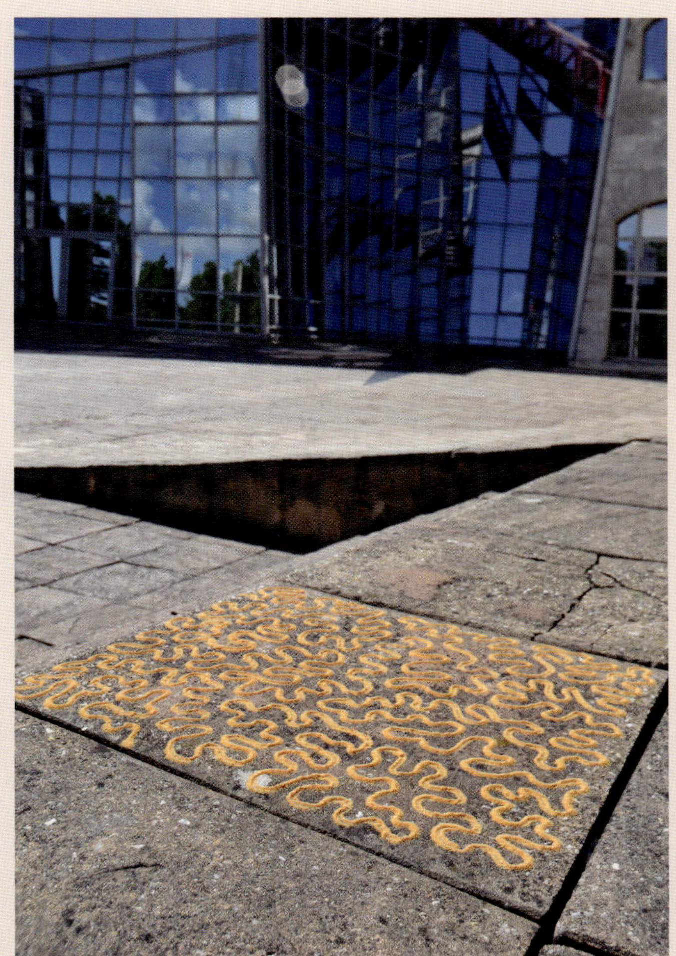

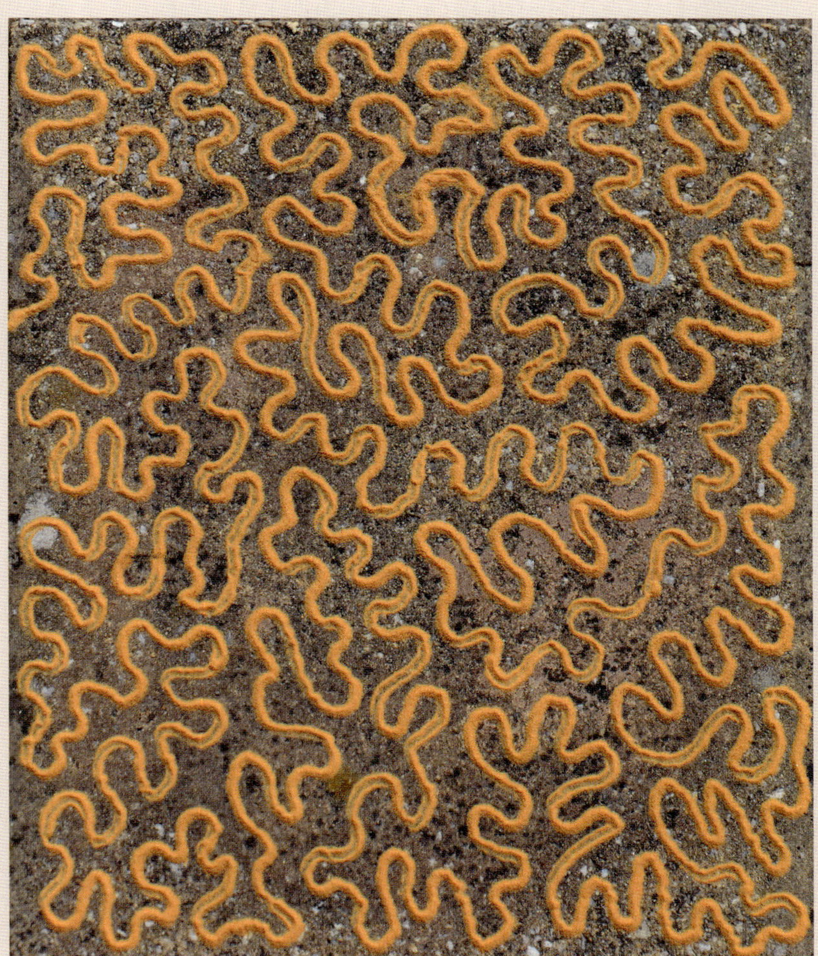

India folklore dictates that all lines should be joined to prevent evil spirits entering a pattern, and thus the home, and girls take great pride in making complex patterns in a single long movement of their hand or without standing up.

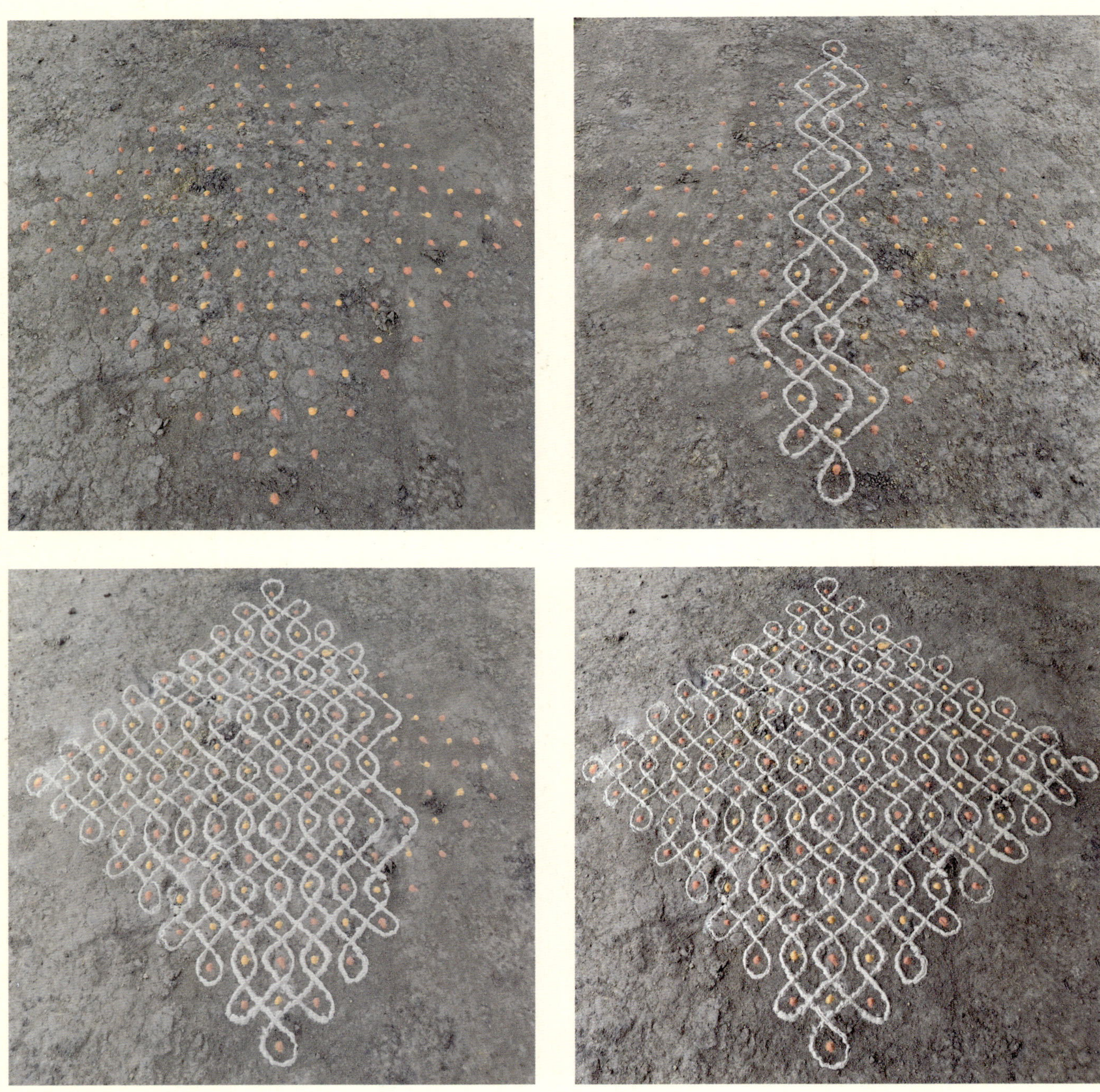

Use seeds, small fruits and even different types of earth to form patterns and shapes. Once you start, the possibilities are endless.

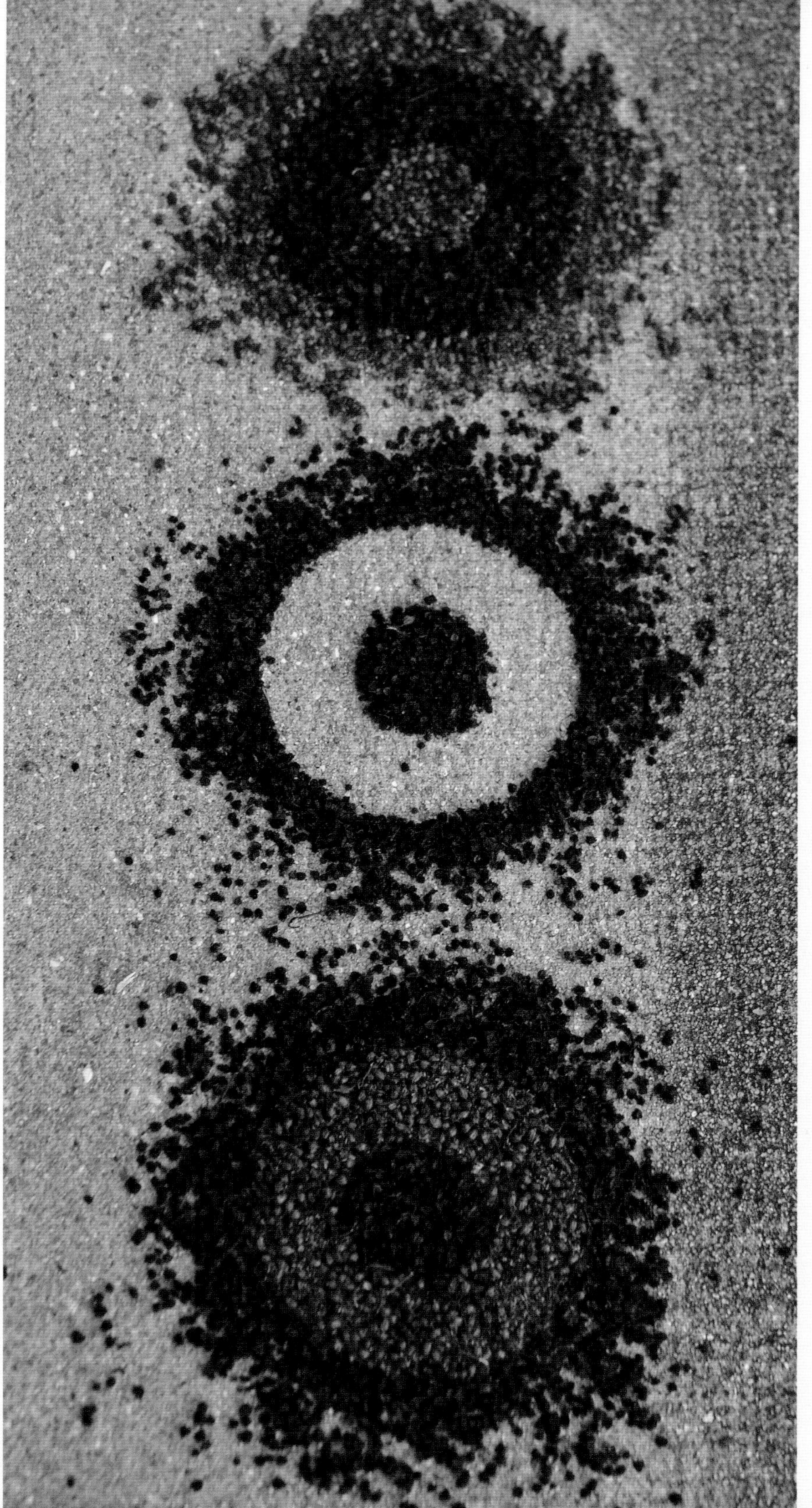

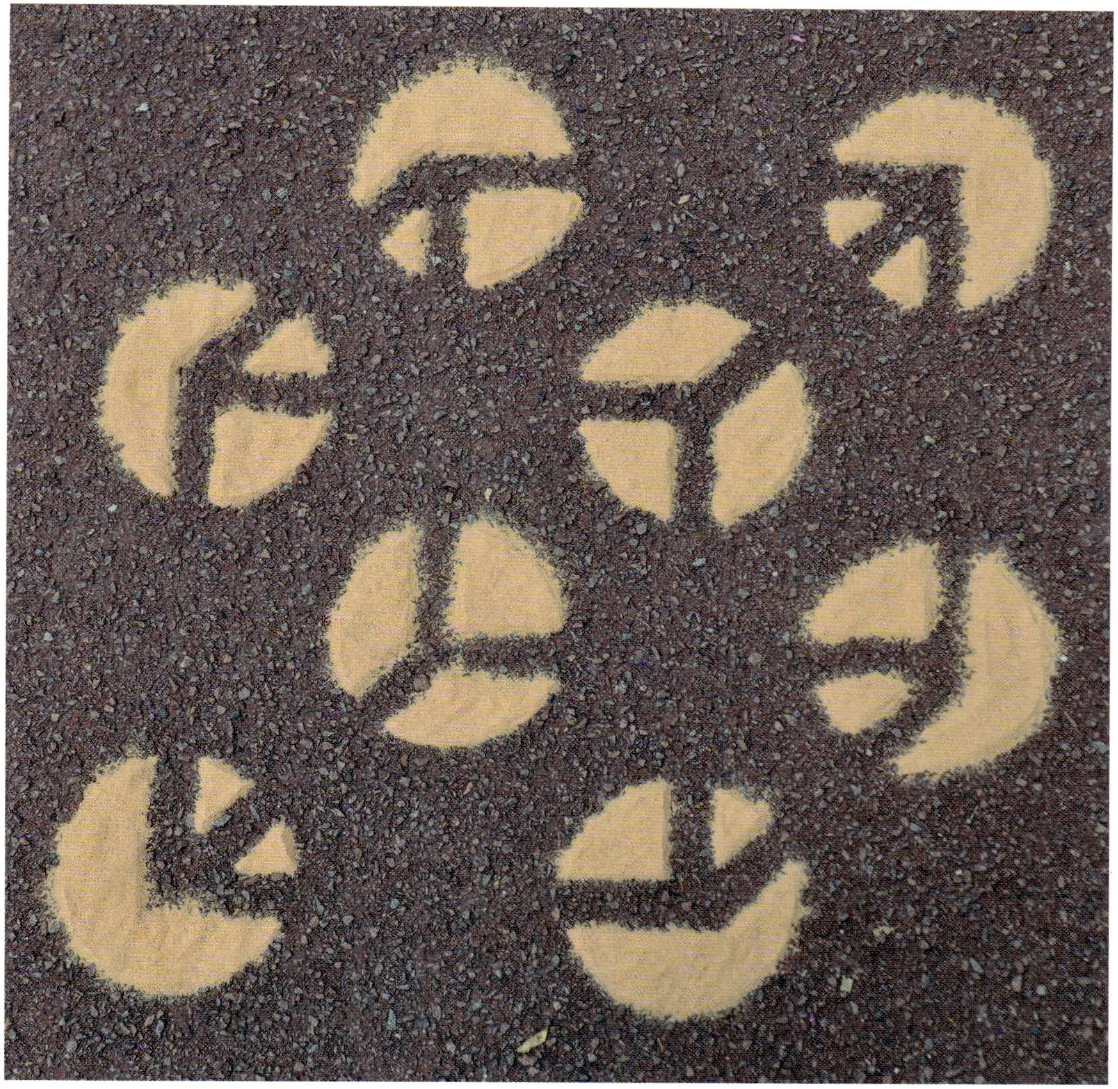

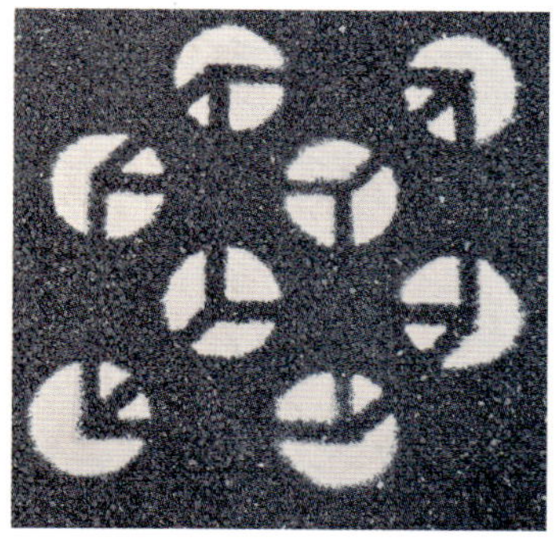

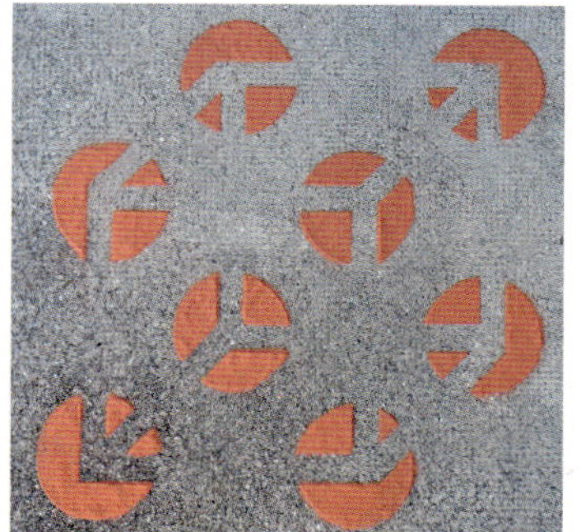

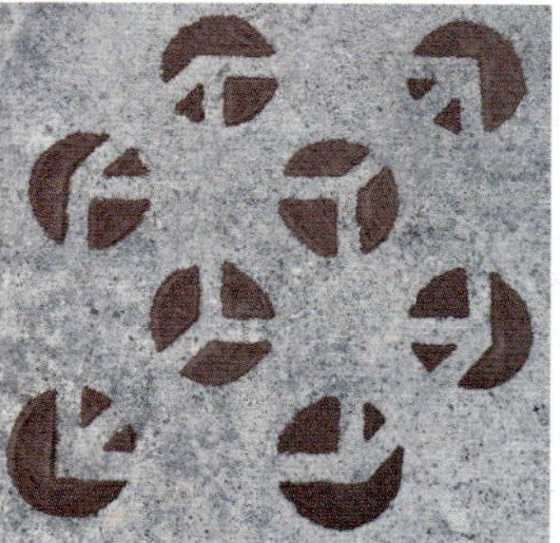

To create this shape, called a Necker cube, and to easily reproduce it several times, I made a stencil. After drawing the shape on a piece of cardboard, I cut out the eight little circles with a craft knife. But a cardboard stencil is quite fragile, so it's better to use a more robust, yet flexible material if you want to reproduce a shape many times. Make sure that the stencil is pressed firmly against the surface on which you are working in order to ensure a sharp image.

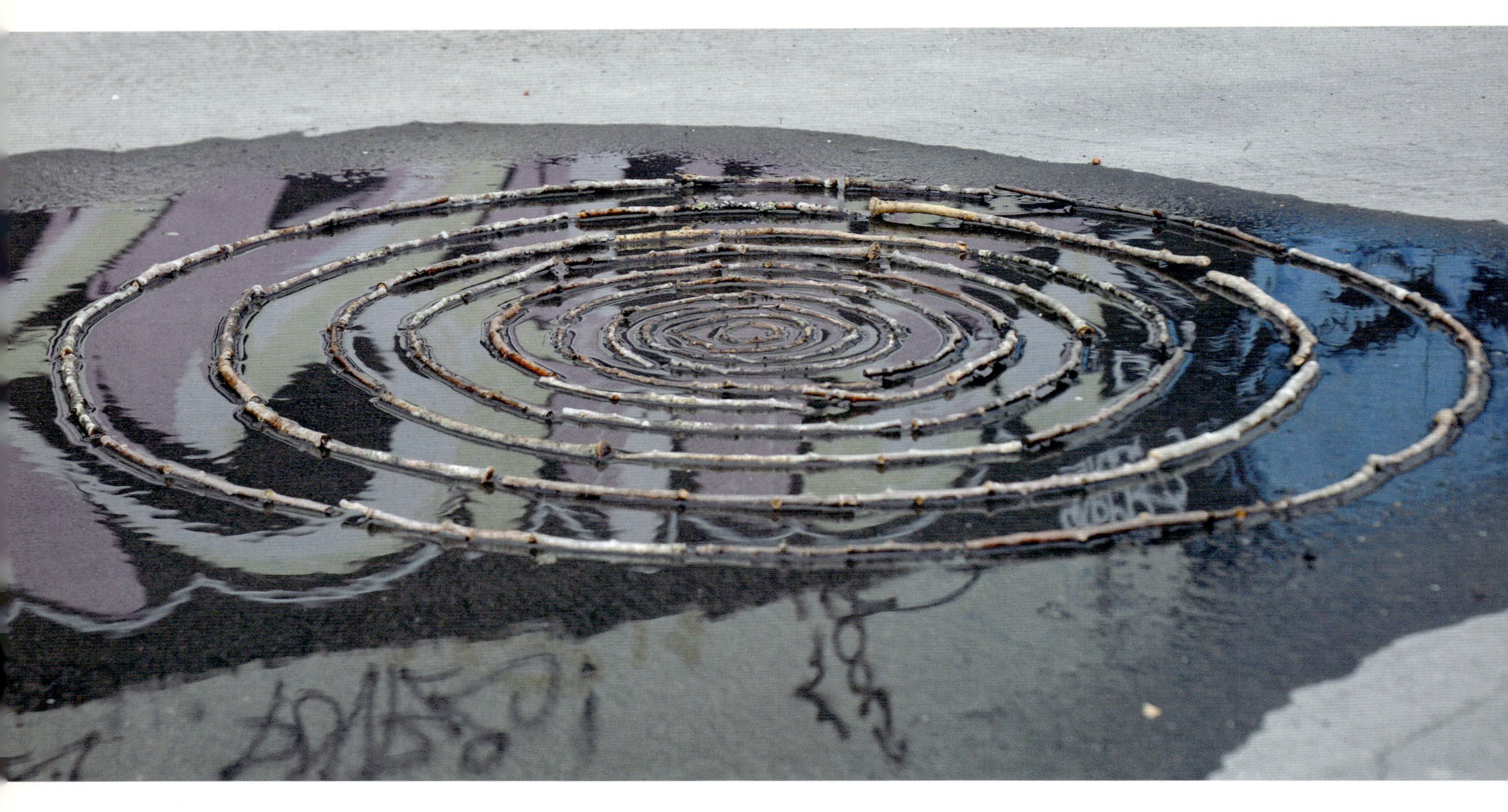

One of the oldest artforms on the planet counterpoints one of the newest, or is it the other way round?

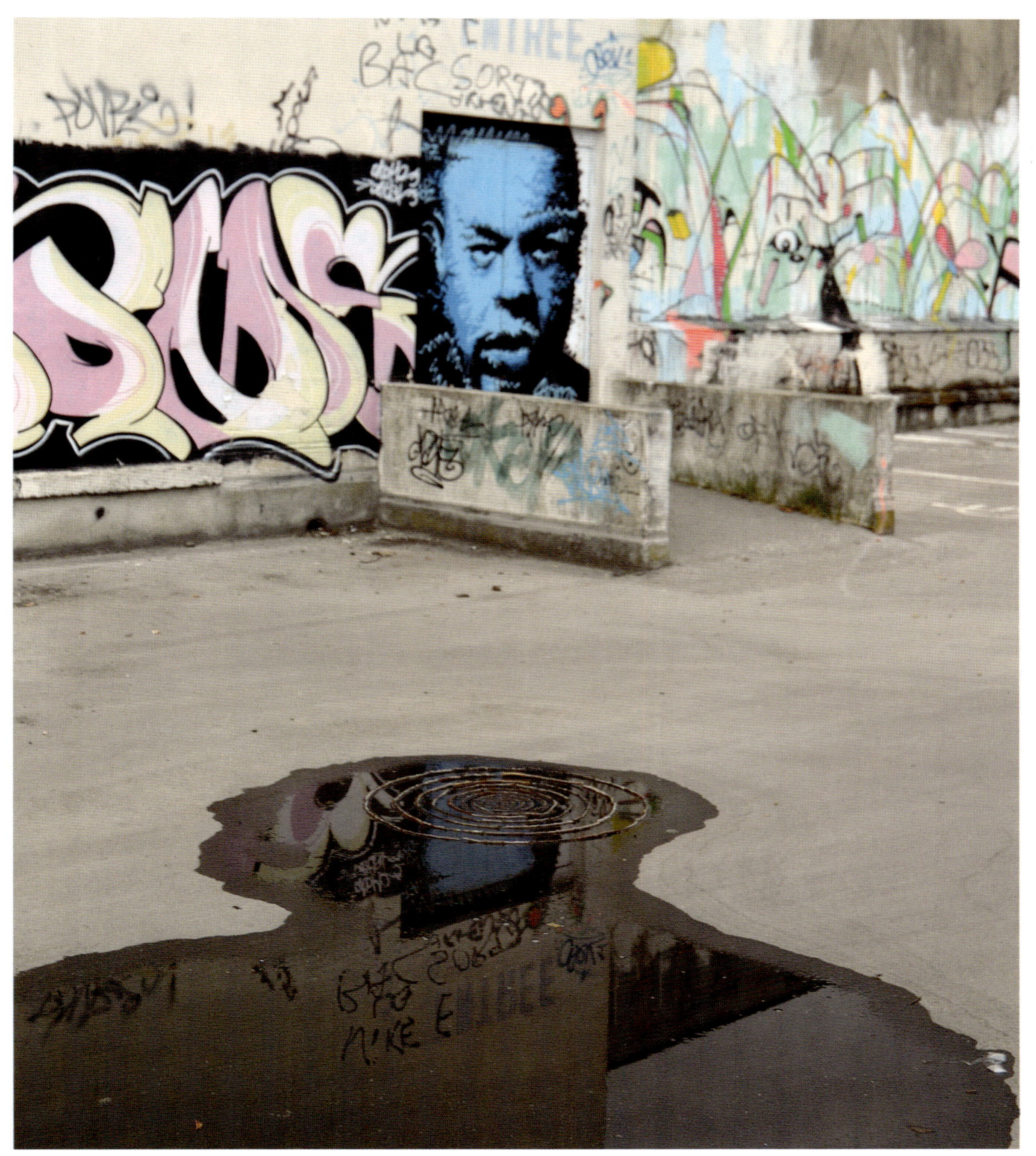

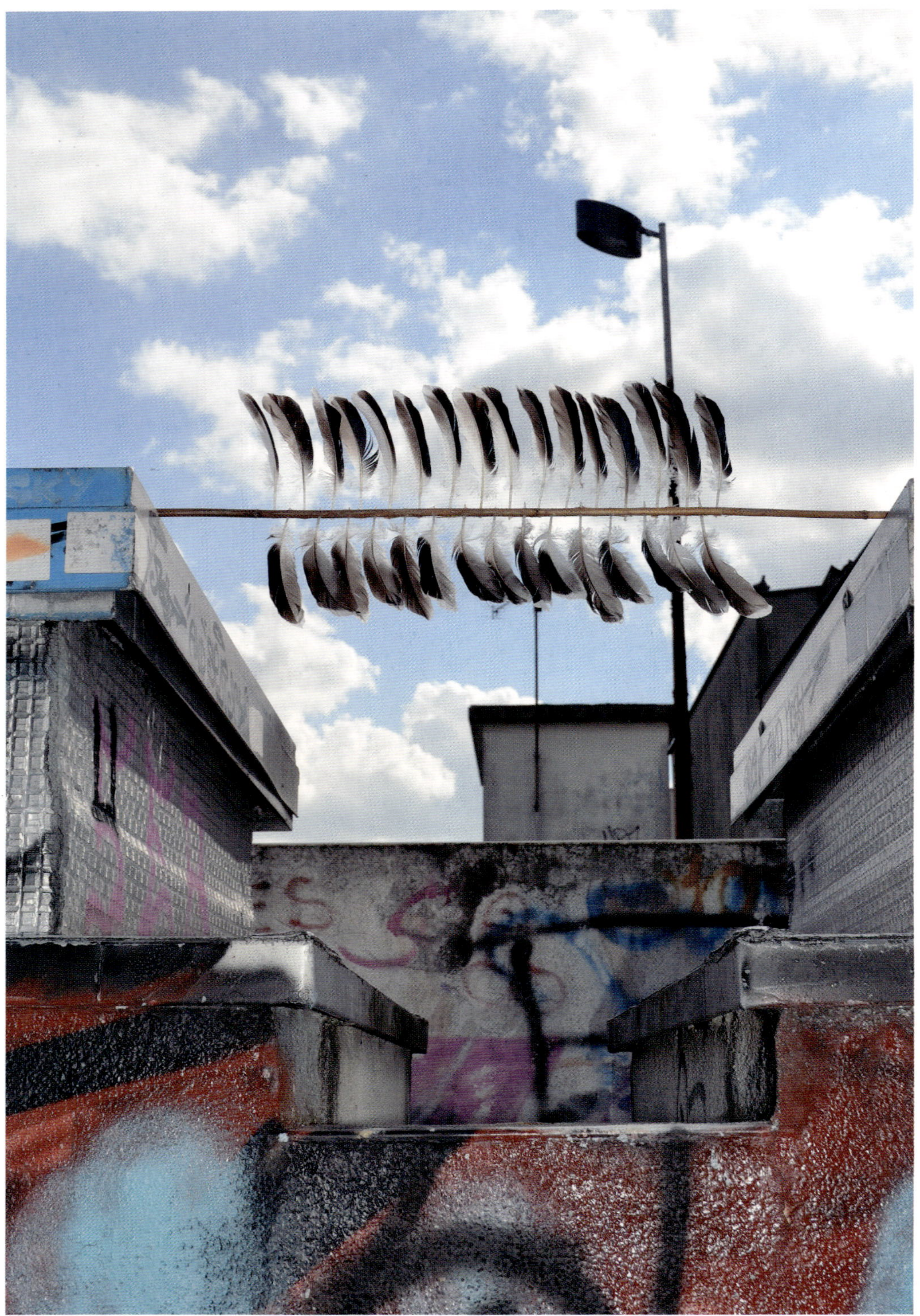

Feathers are wondeful to use, not only because of their texture and lovely hues, but also because they tend to be somewhat hardier than petals and leaves. Installations involving feathers may not last a whole season, but there's a good chance they'll still be fluttering in the breeze when you return next week.

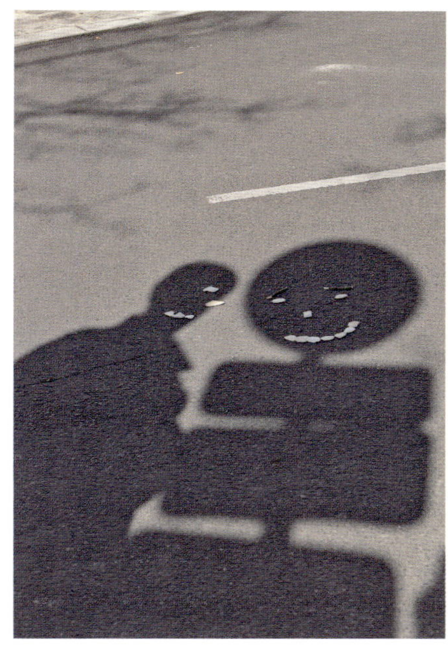

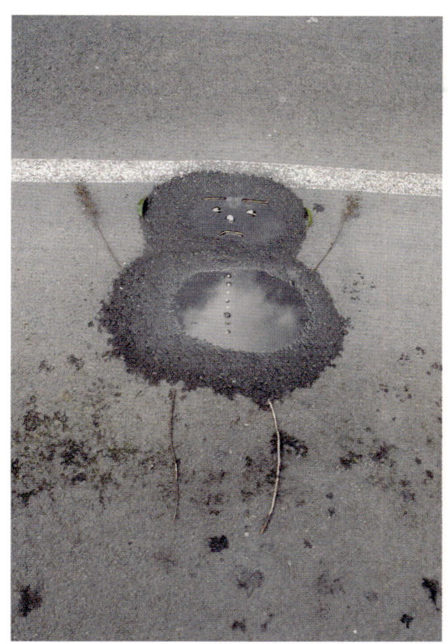

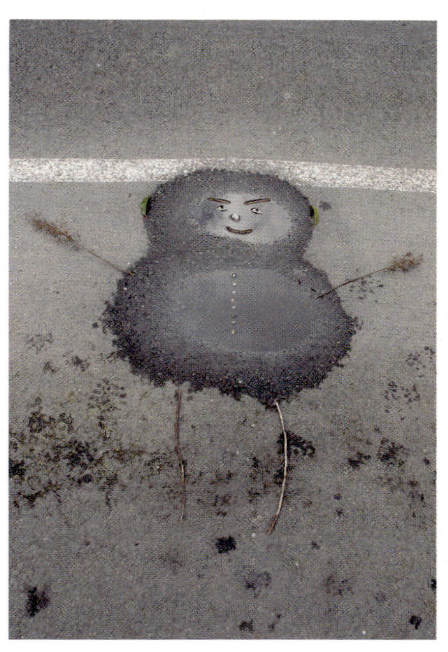

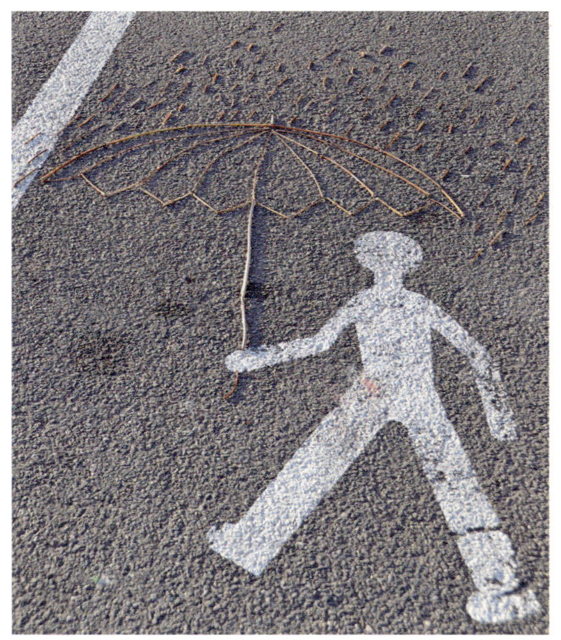

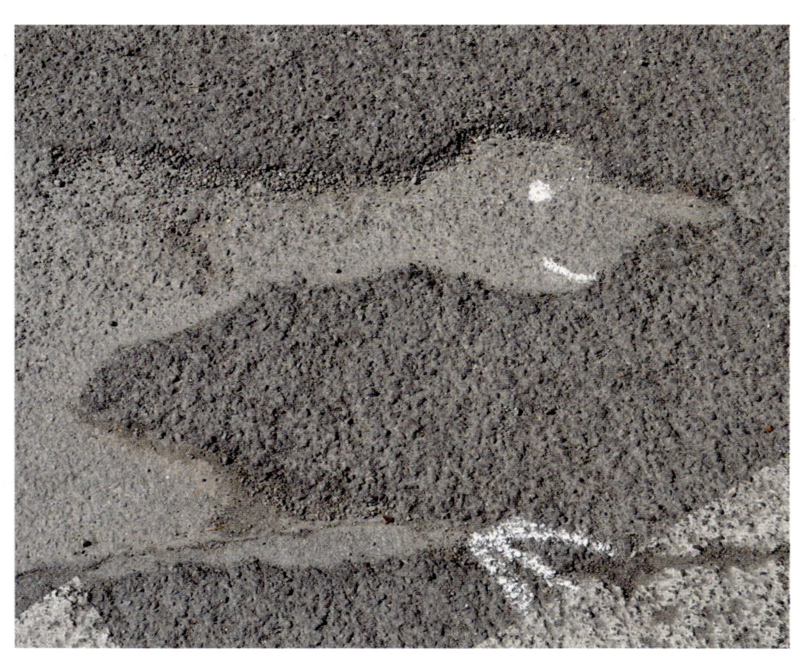

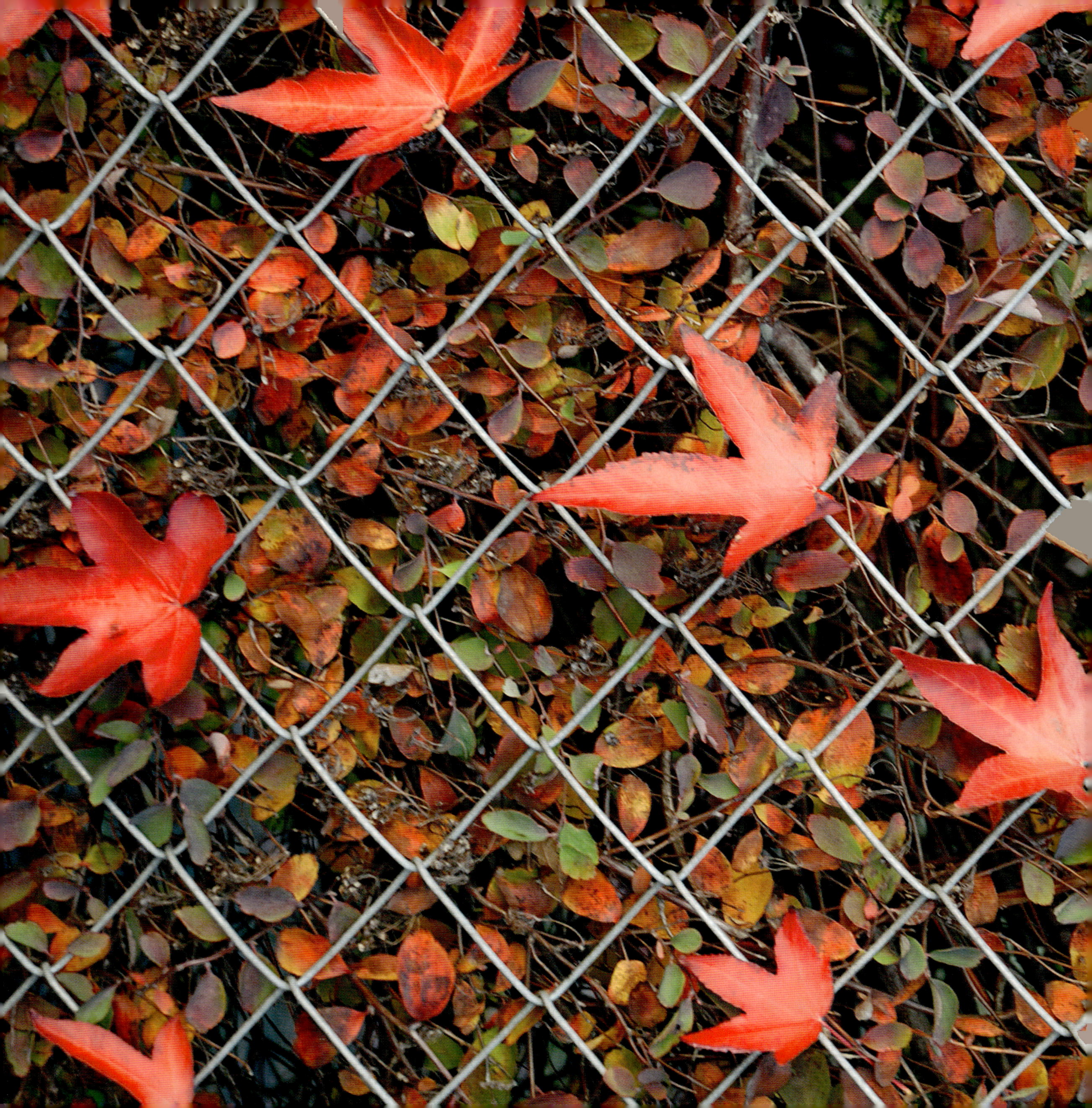

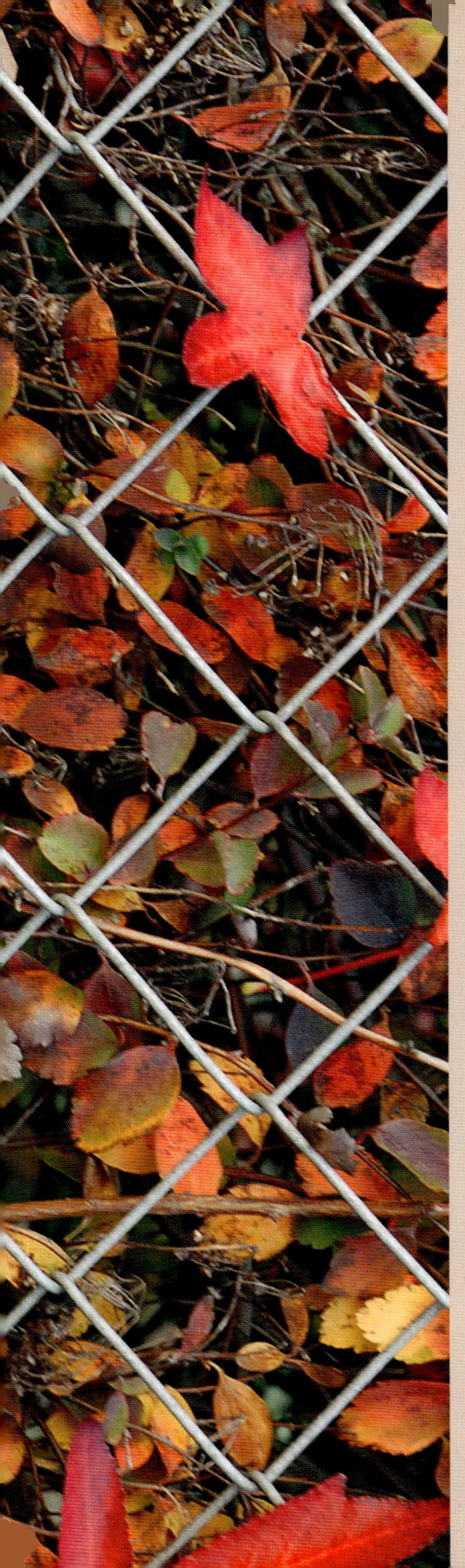

AUTUMN

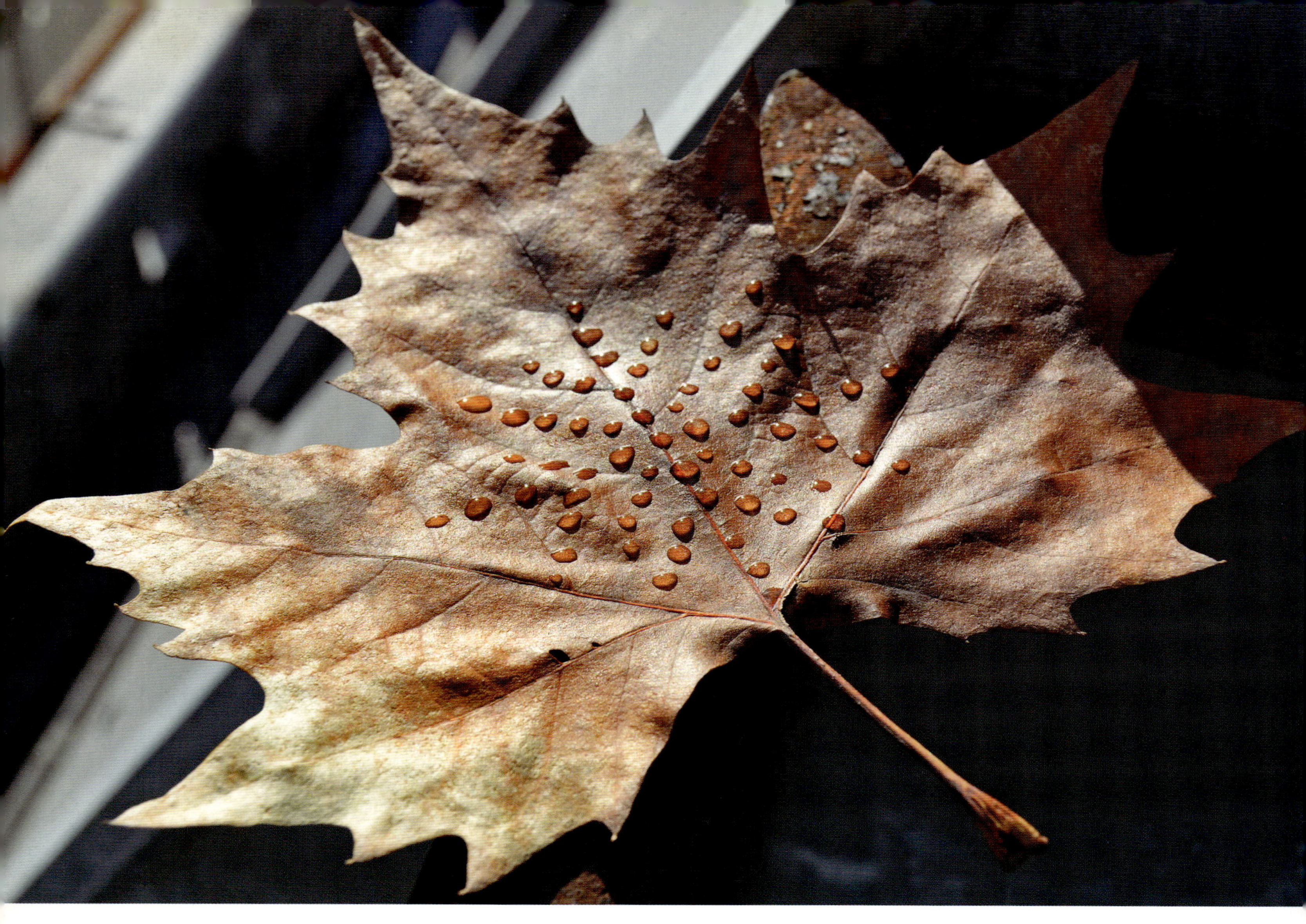

Water droplets sit harmoniously on a plane leaf.

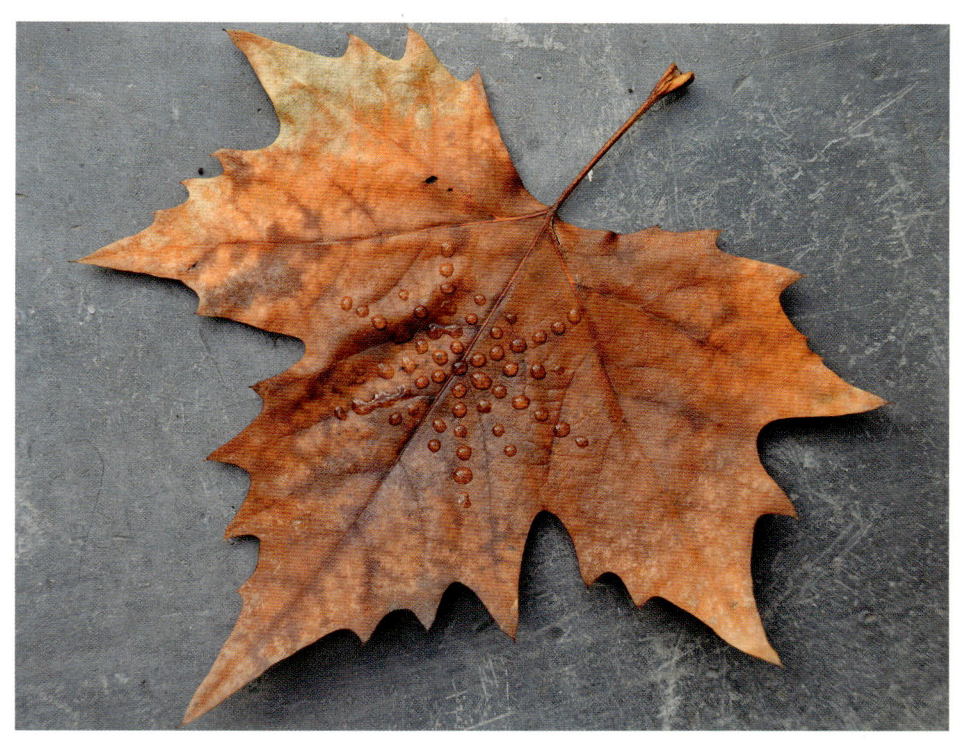

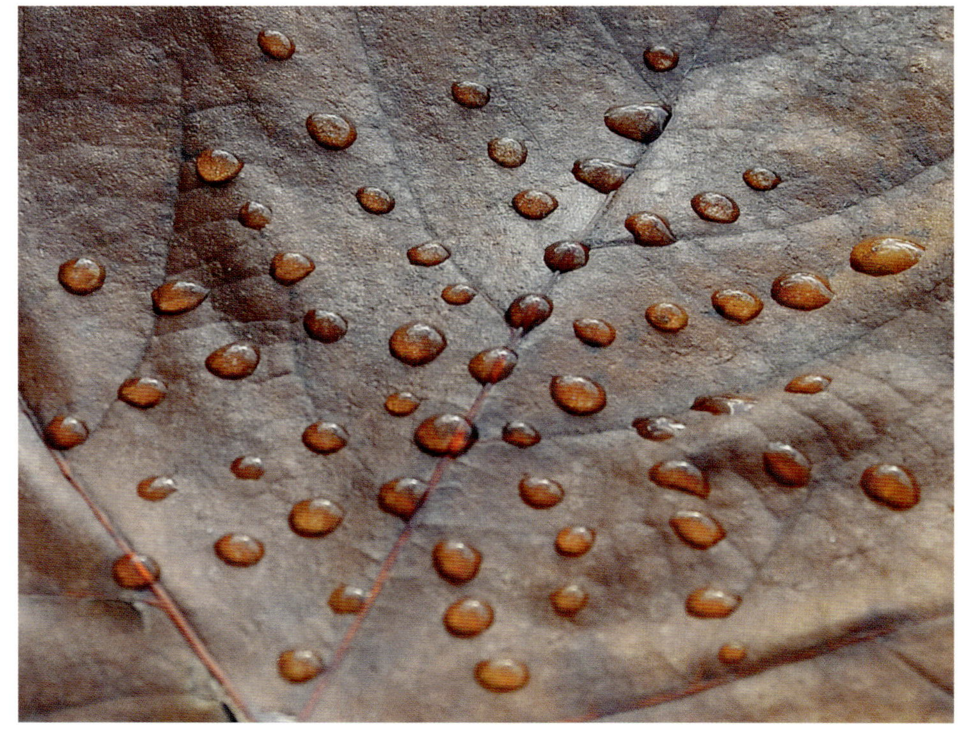

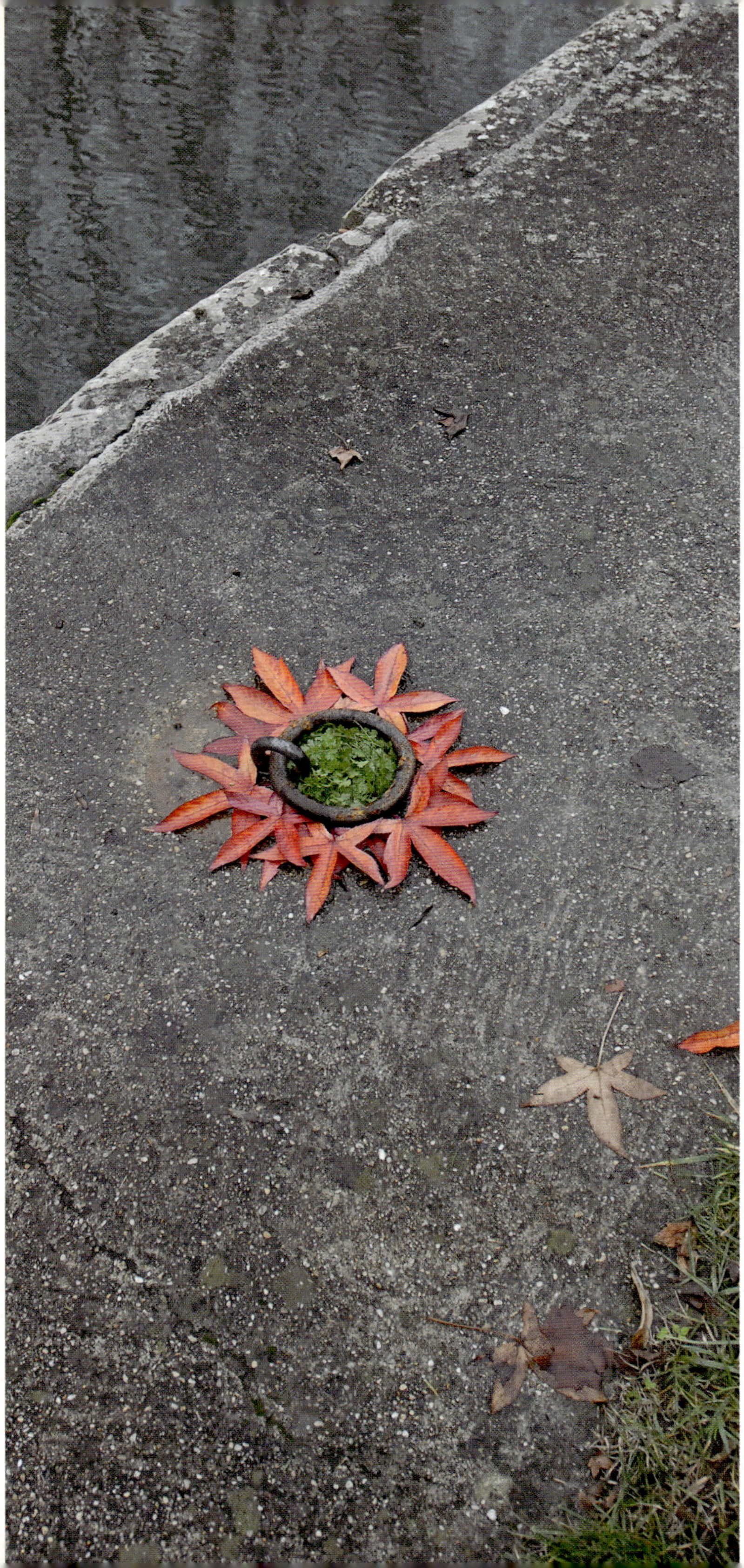

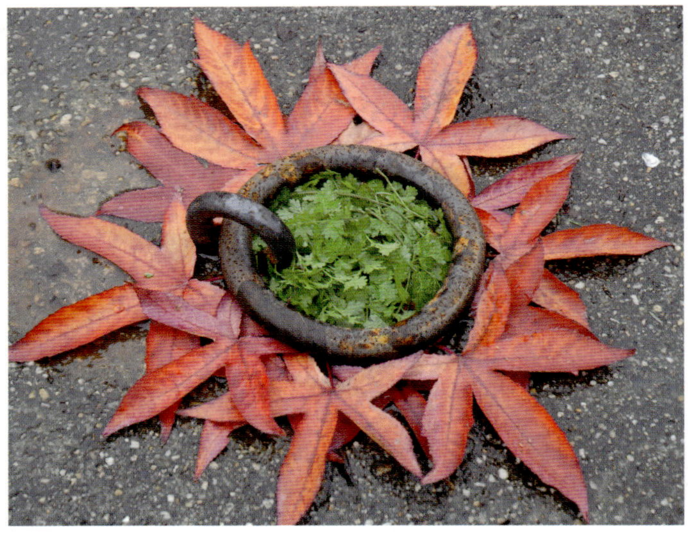

Maple leaves surround a metal ring with a centre of parsley leaves.

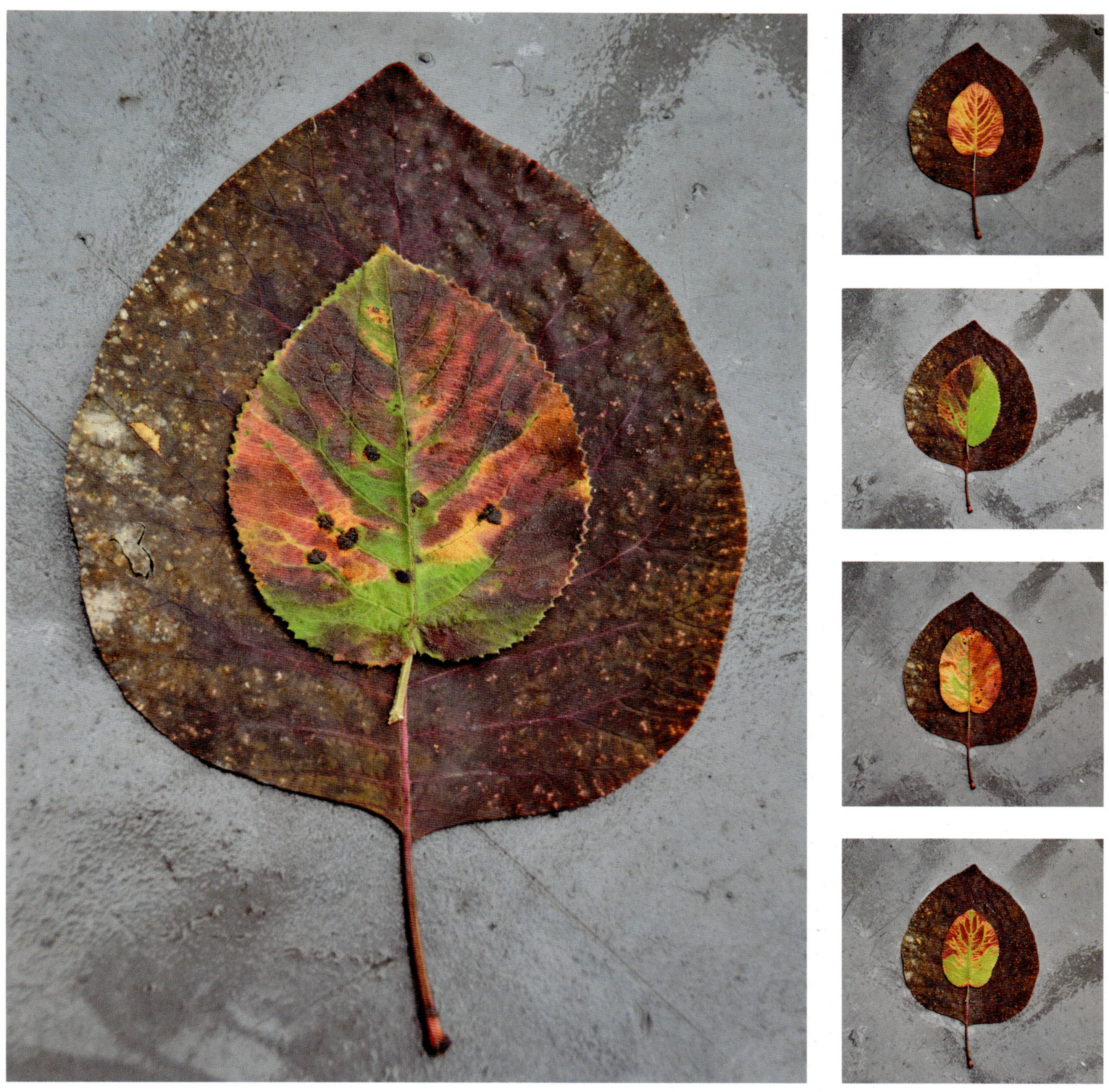

Autumn sees leaves turn an astonishing range of colours: yellow, green, brown, orange, red, green, yellow, brown, red...

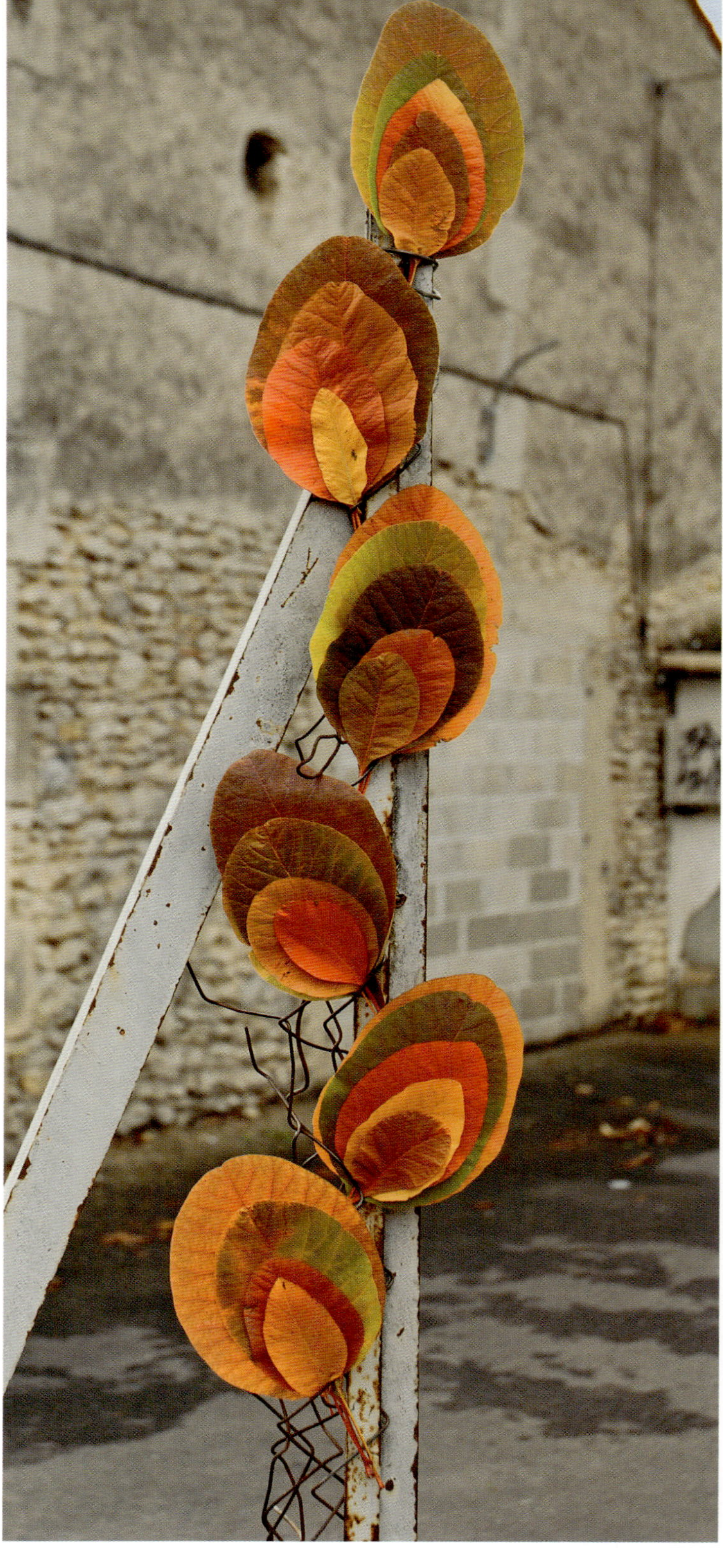

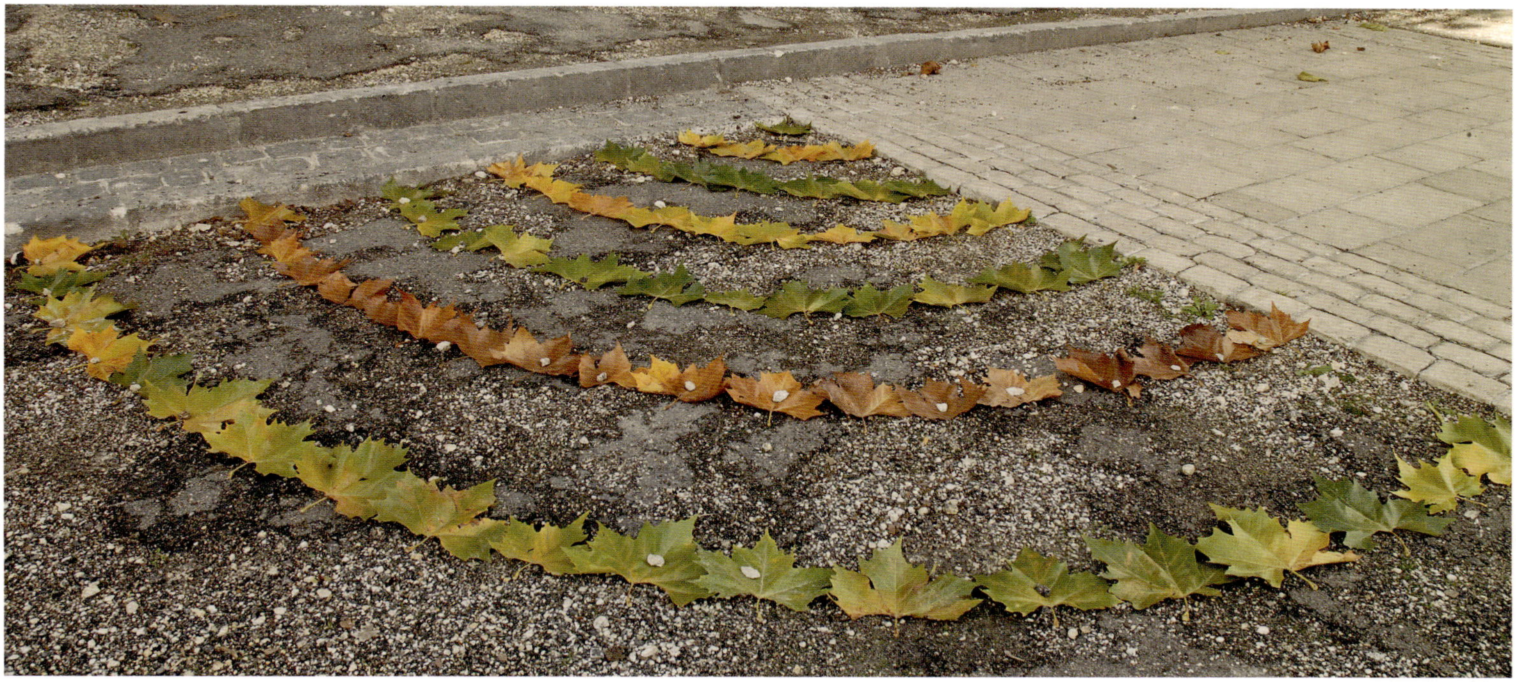

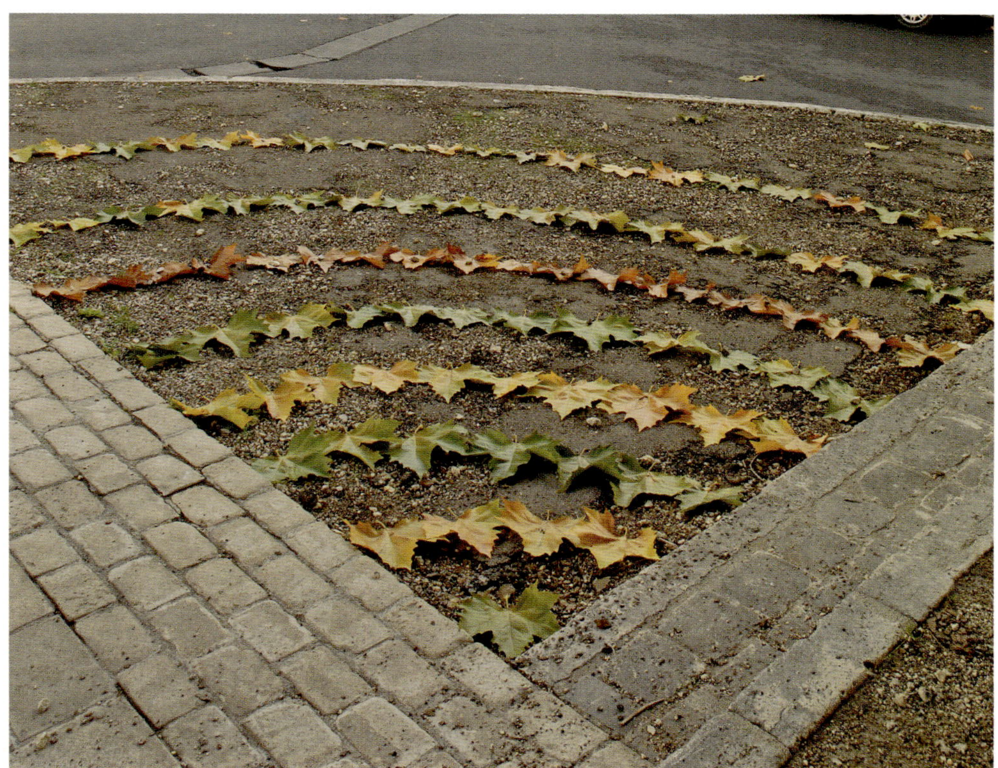

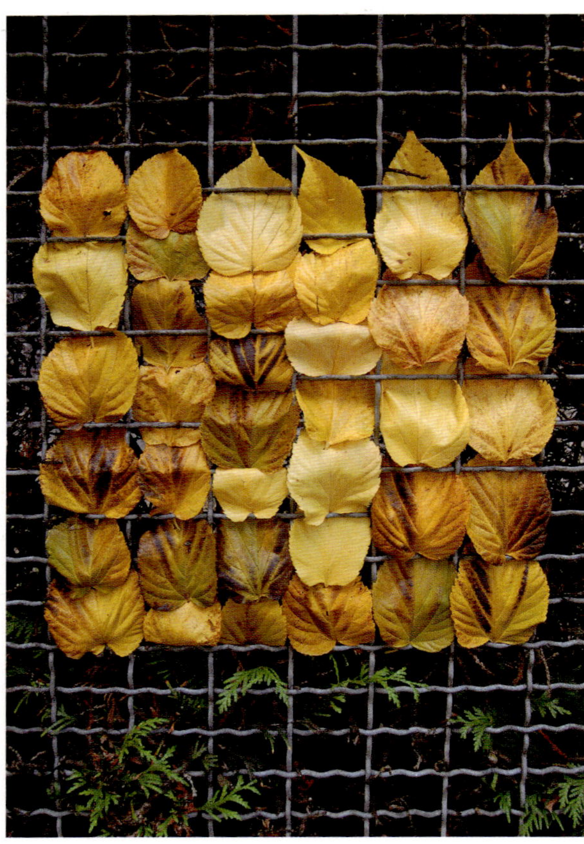

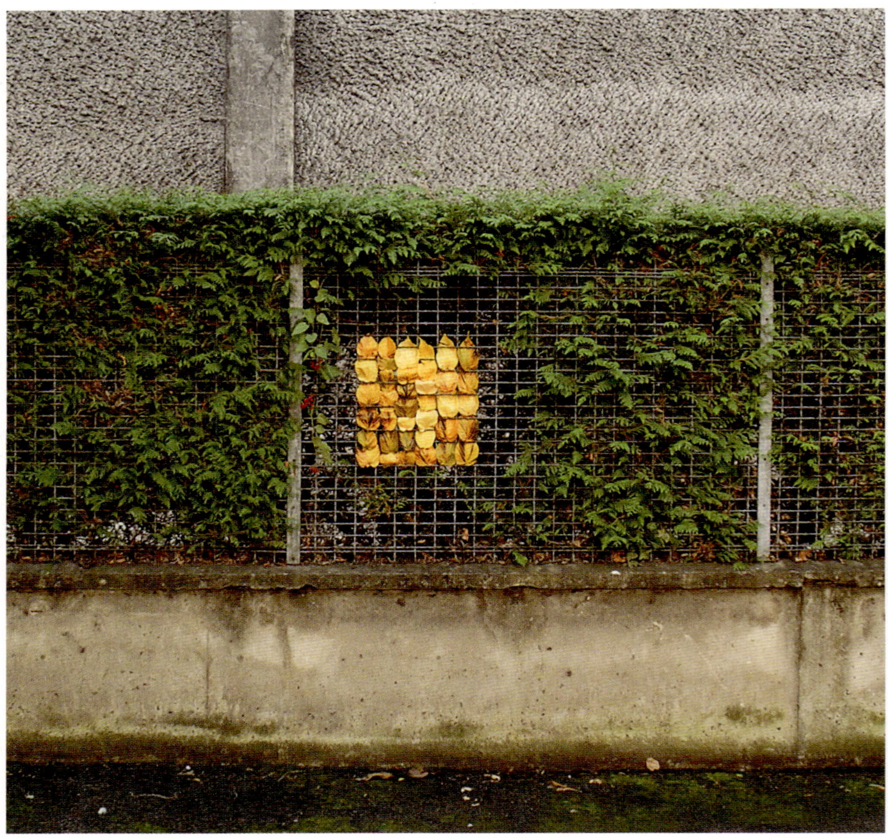

A golden square of linden leaves brings a bold bright splash to this imprisoned hedge.

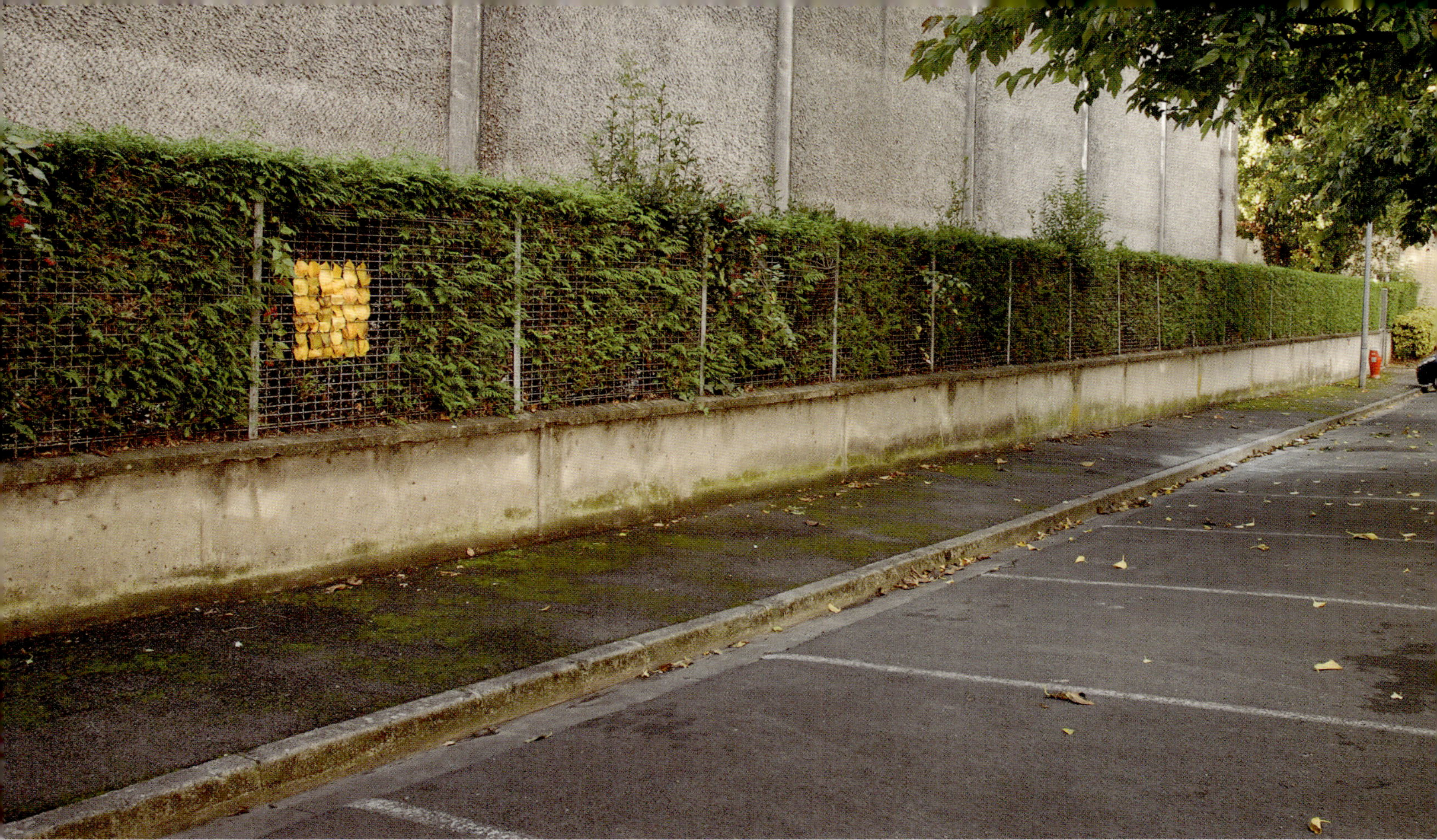

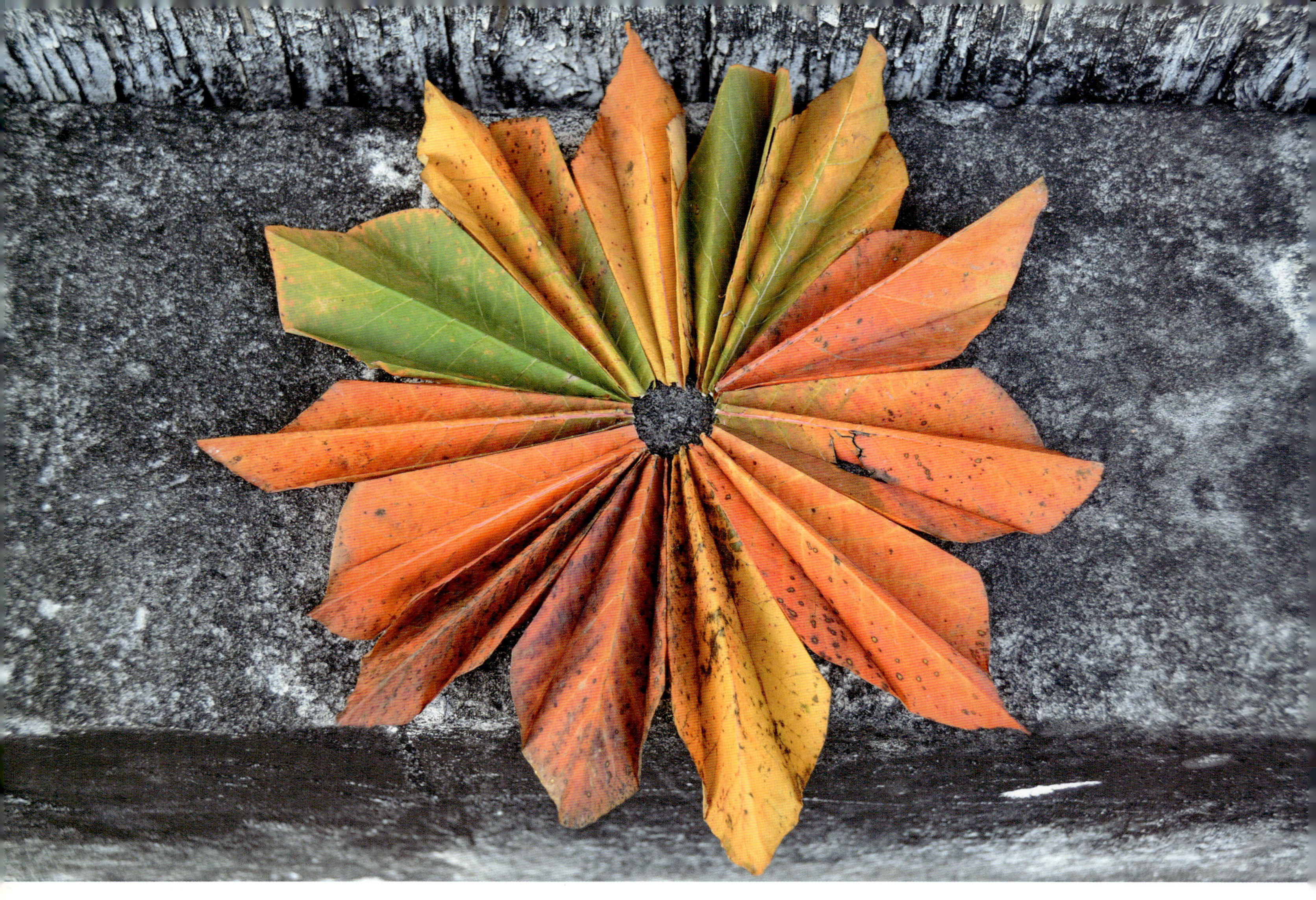

Folded smoke tree leaves fixed together with a natural glue of water, flour and sugar.

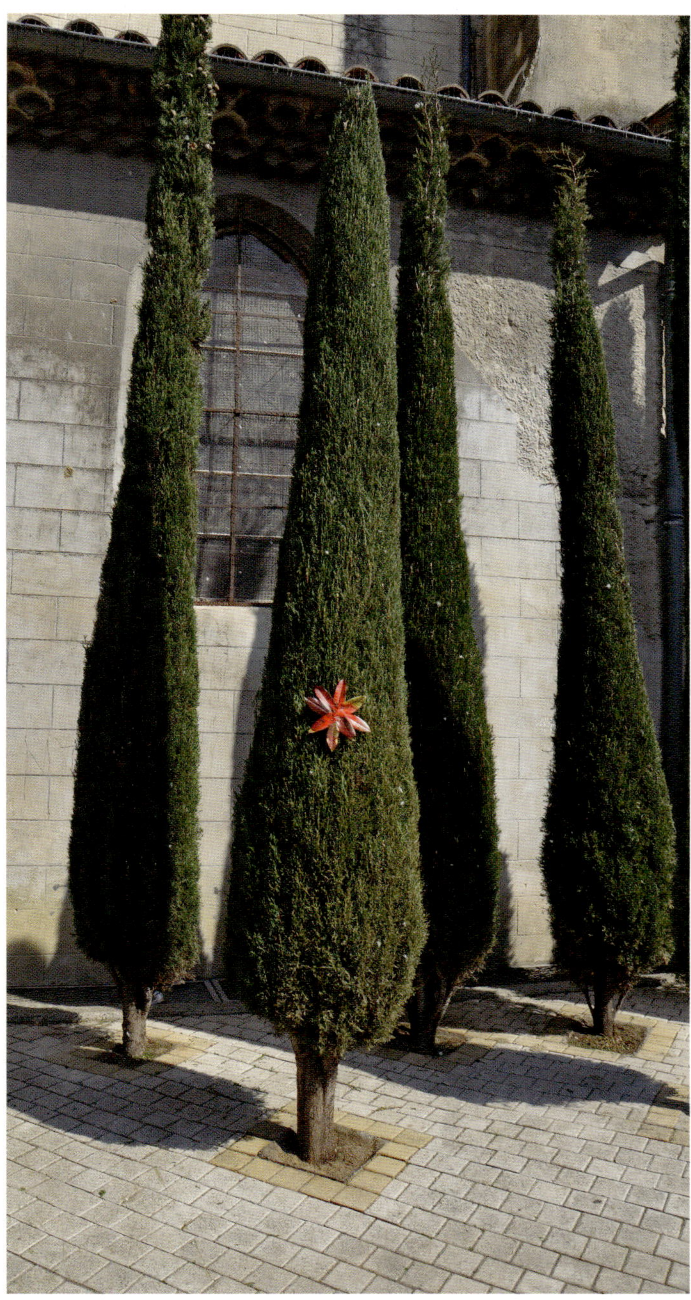

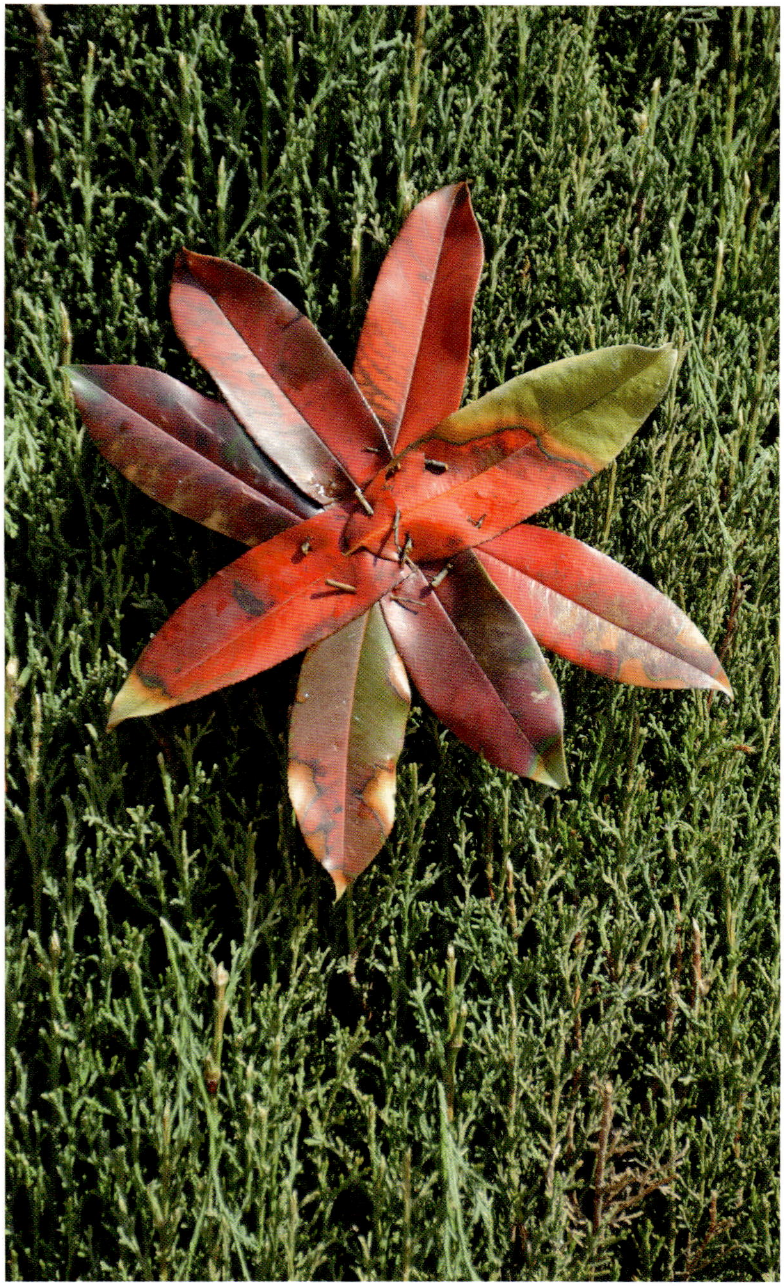

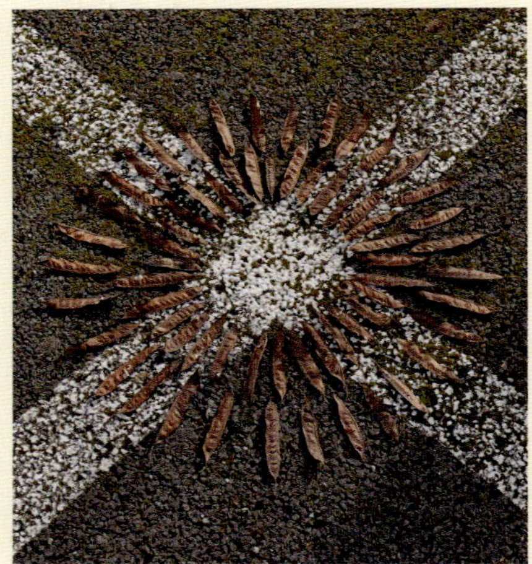

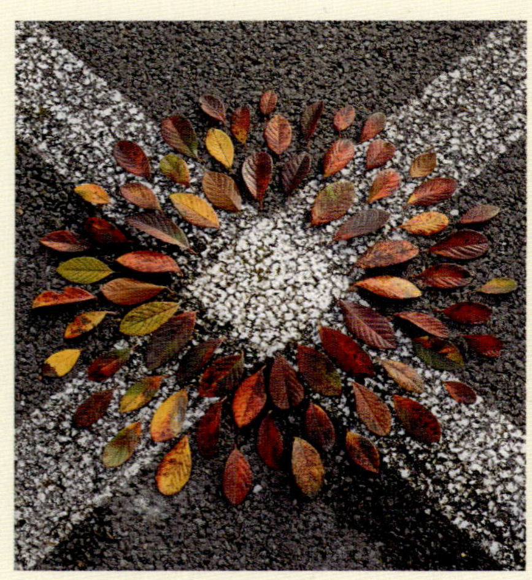

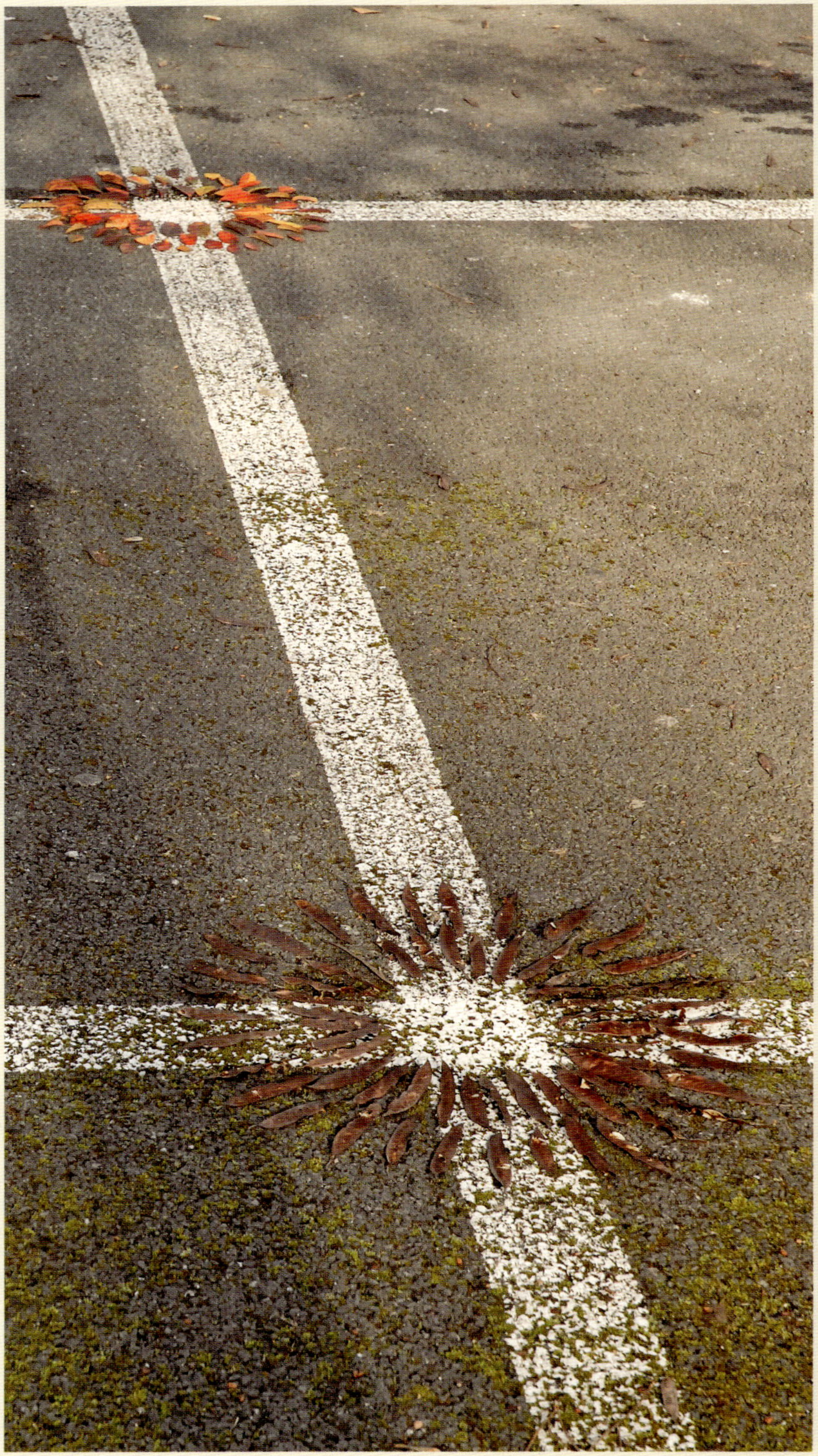

Installations made with black locust pods and cotoneaster leaves.

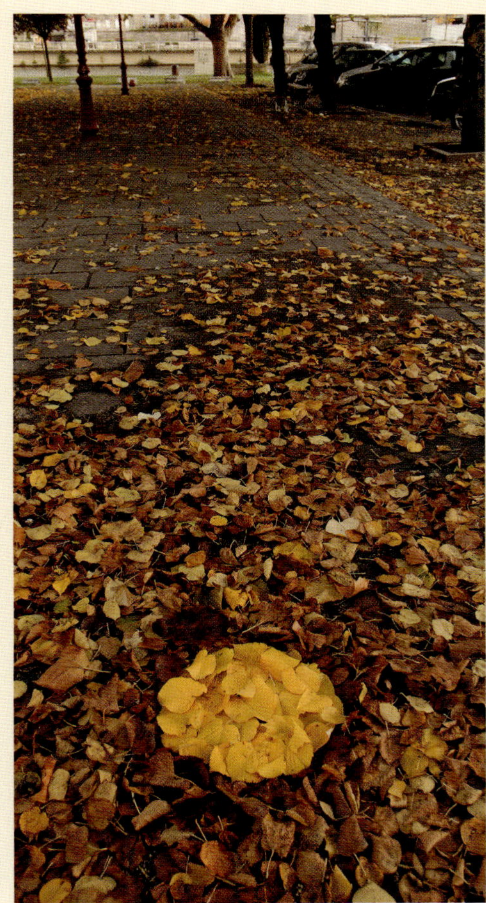

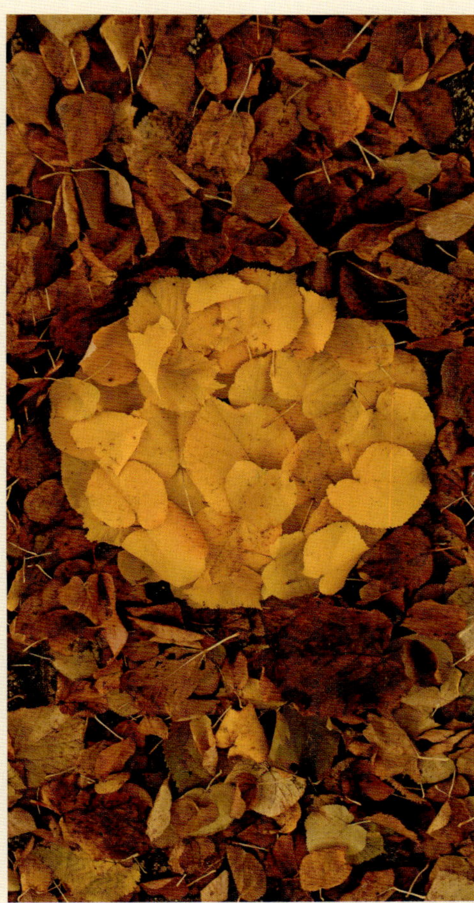

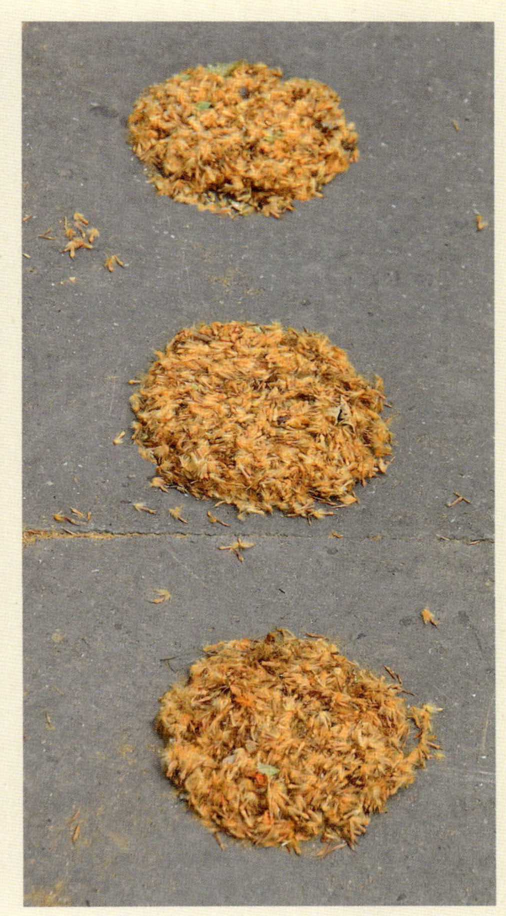

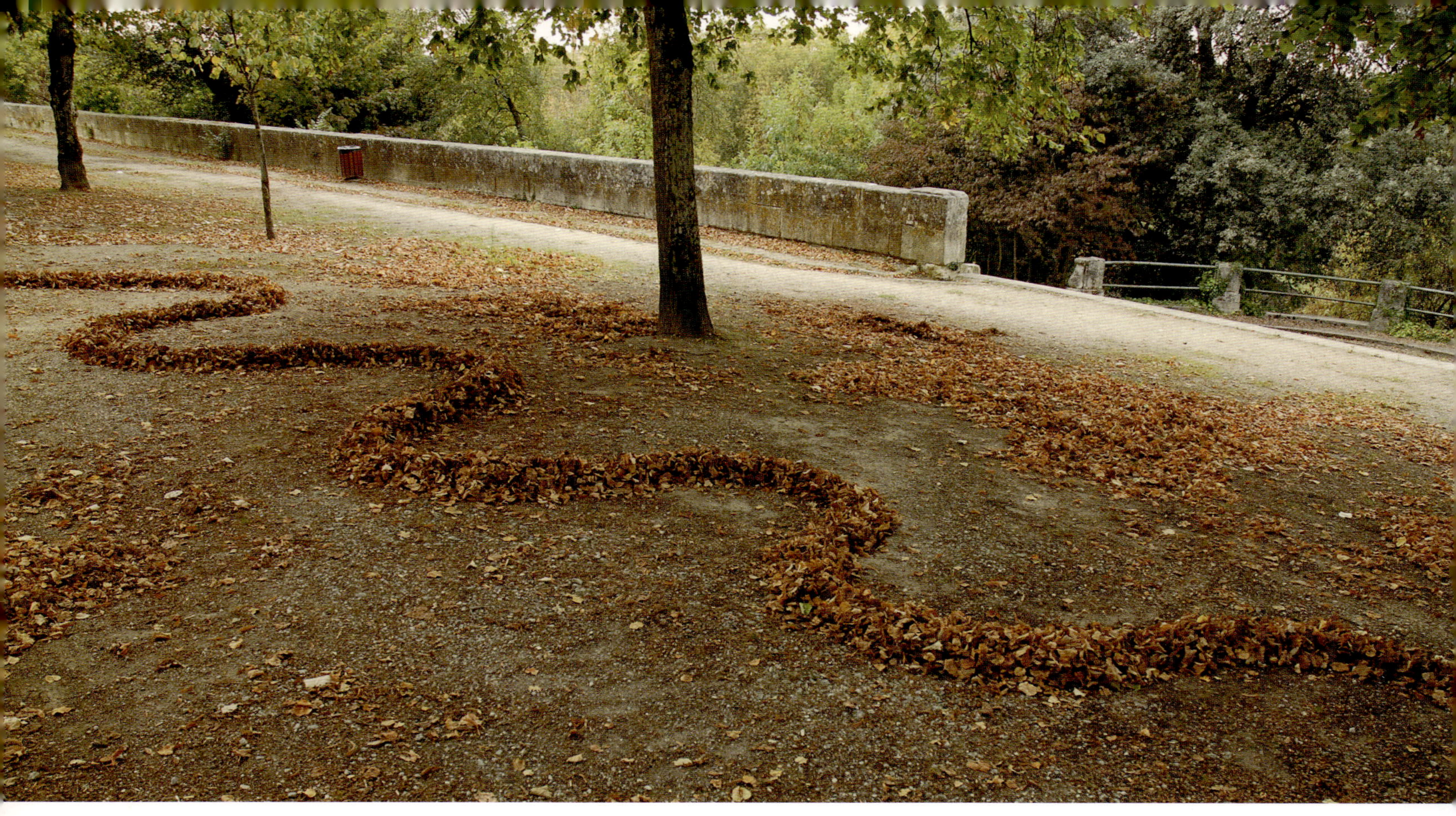

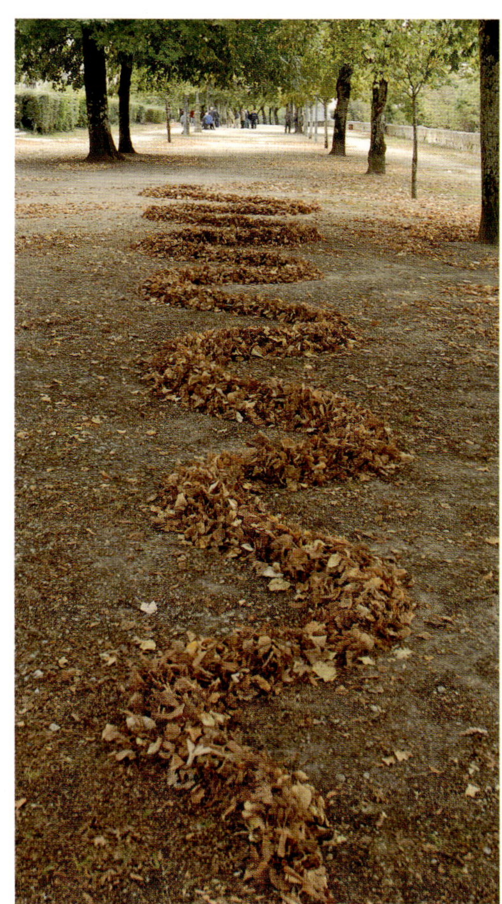

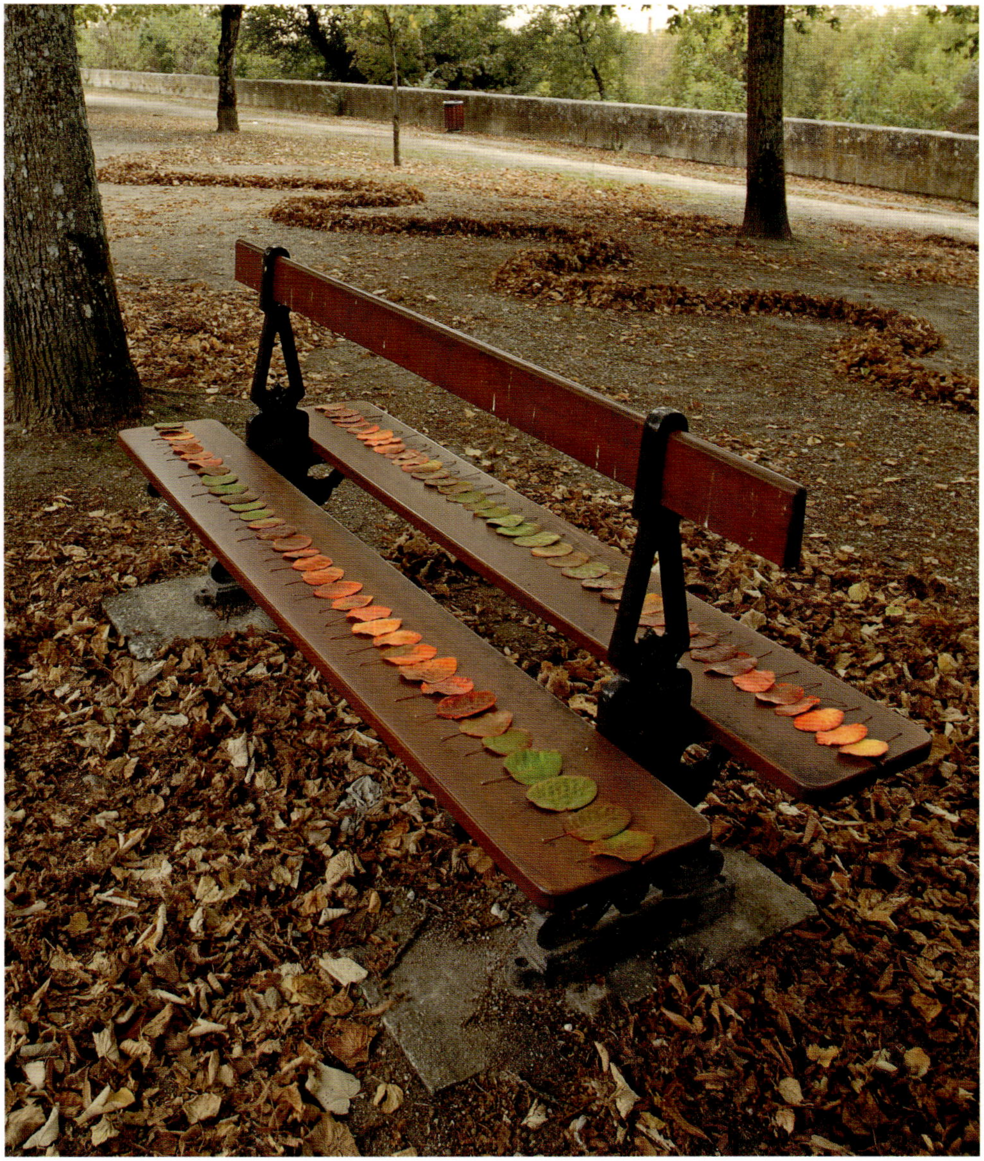

Smoke tree leaves take a break after putting on a show.

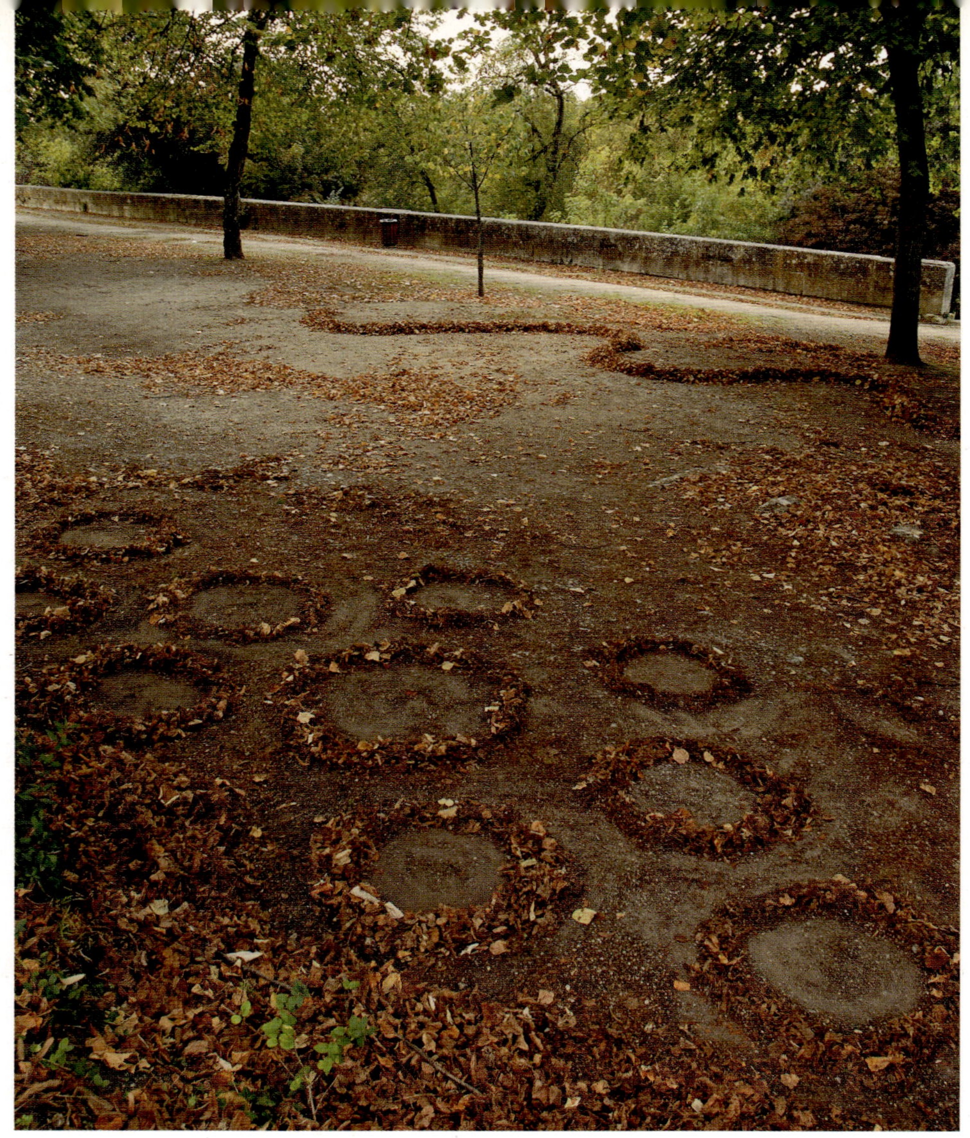

Circles of fallen linden leaves.

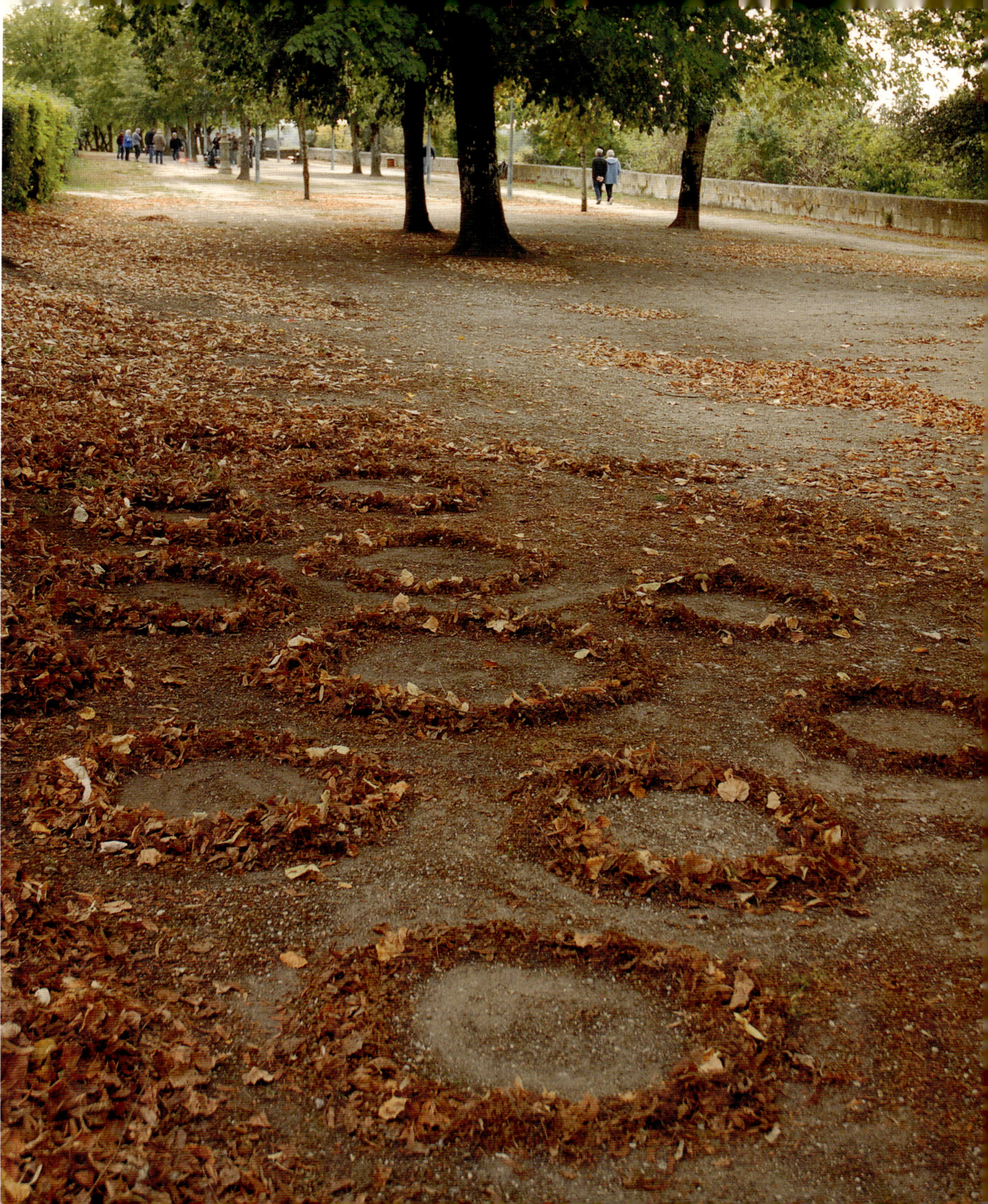

You can spend a while creating a lovely piece, such as this square of chestnuts, only to return later to see it disturbed or even vanished!

The ephemeral nature of land art is part of its attraction, but do take photographs to preserve something of your work.

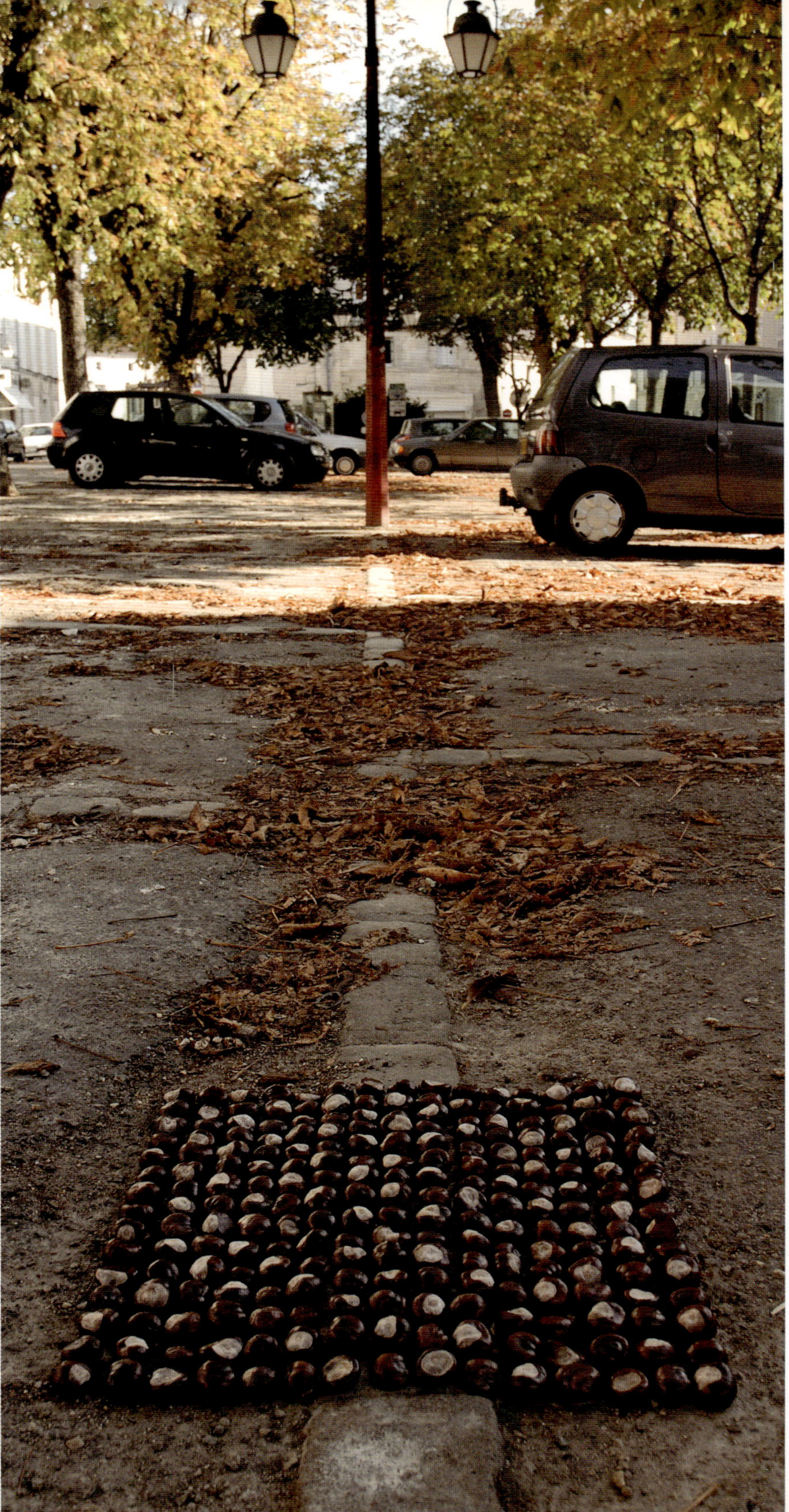

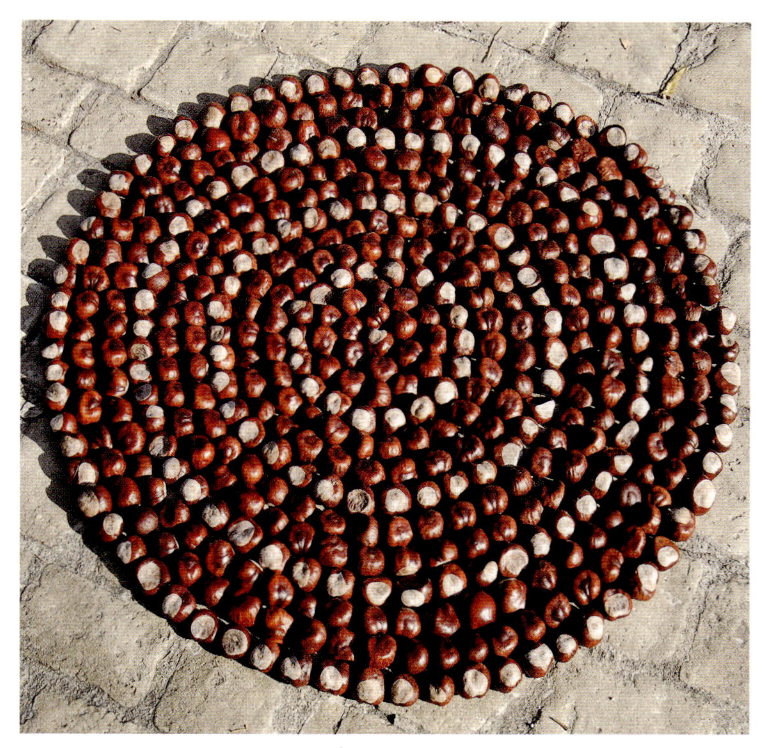

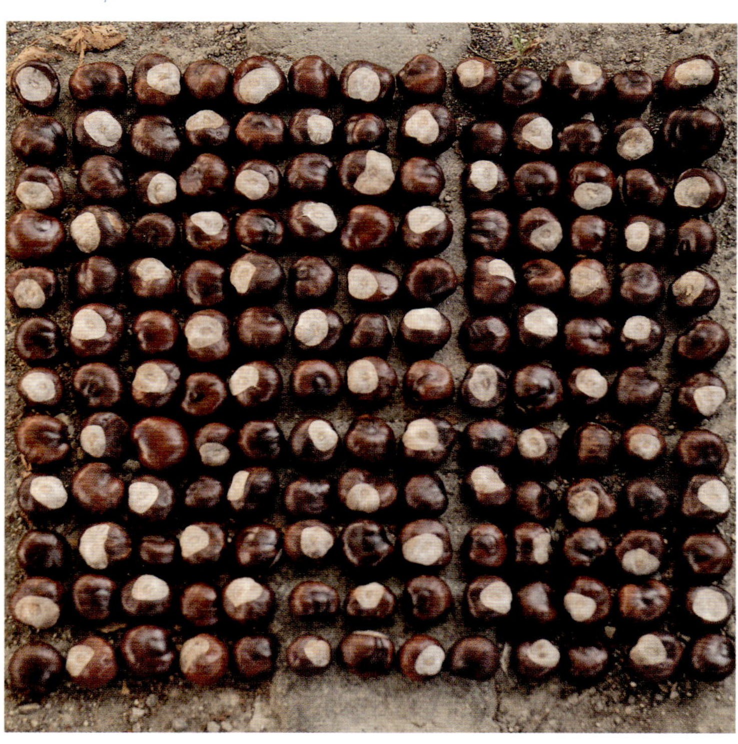

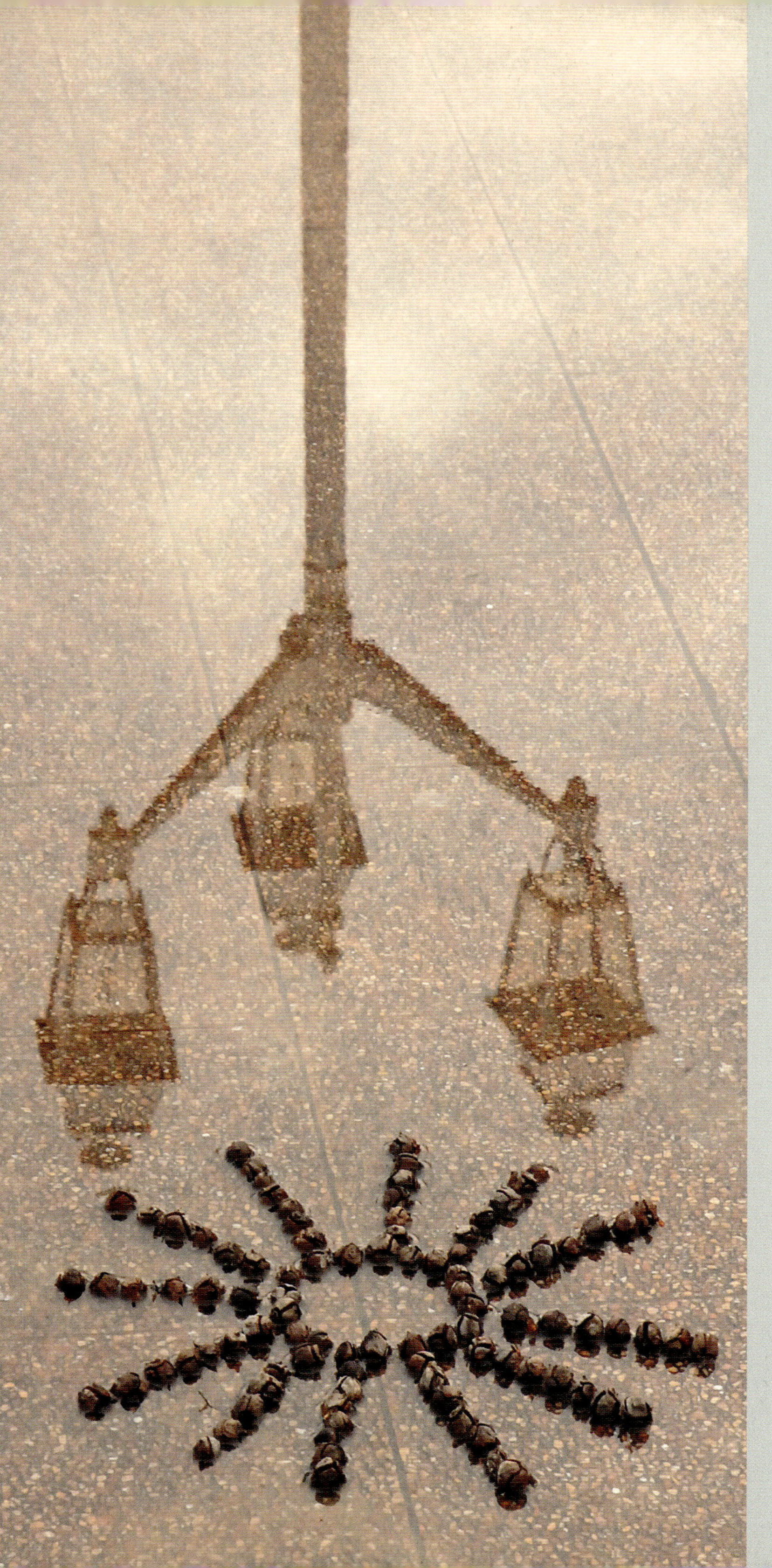

Sun after the rain.

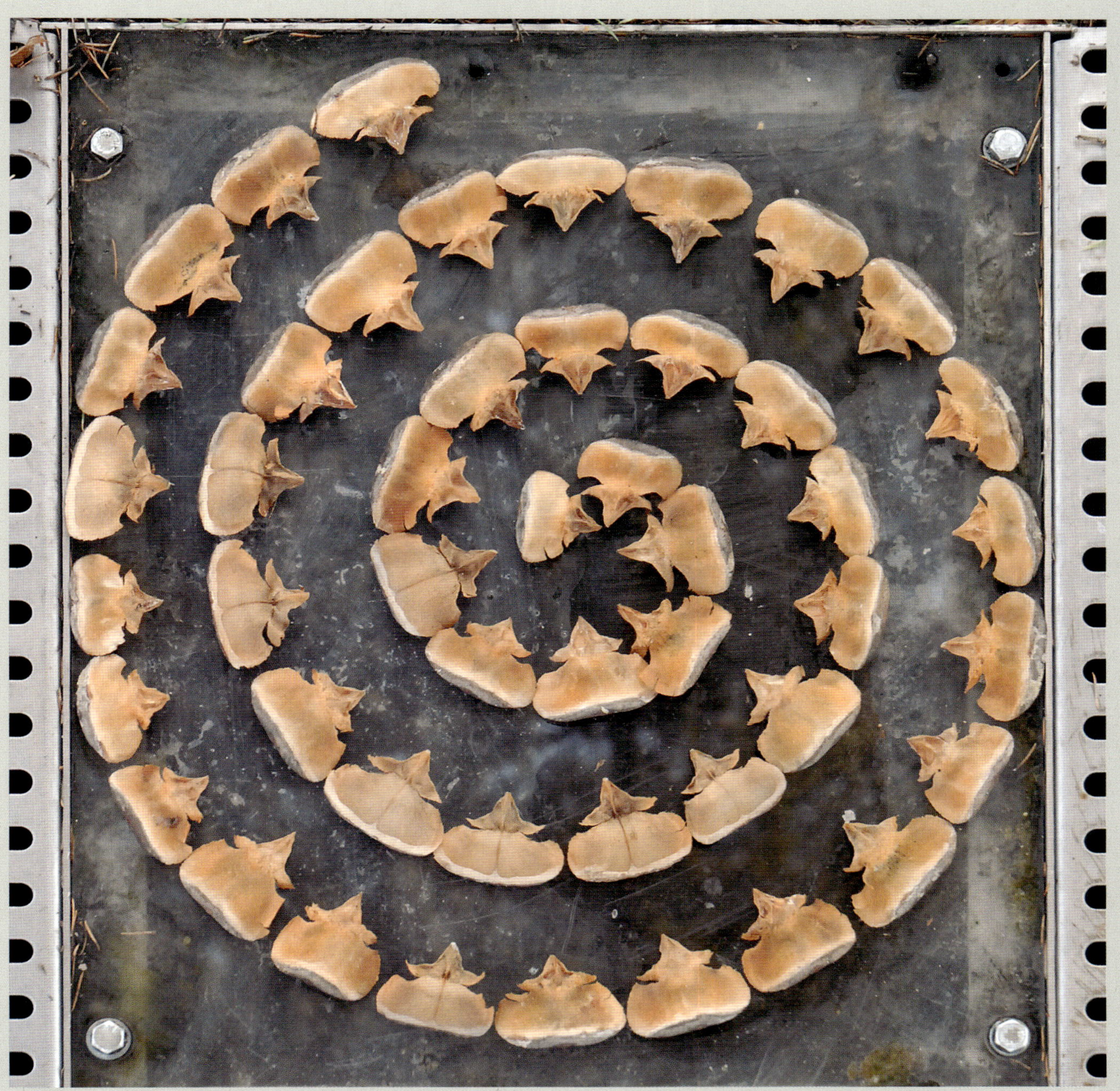

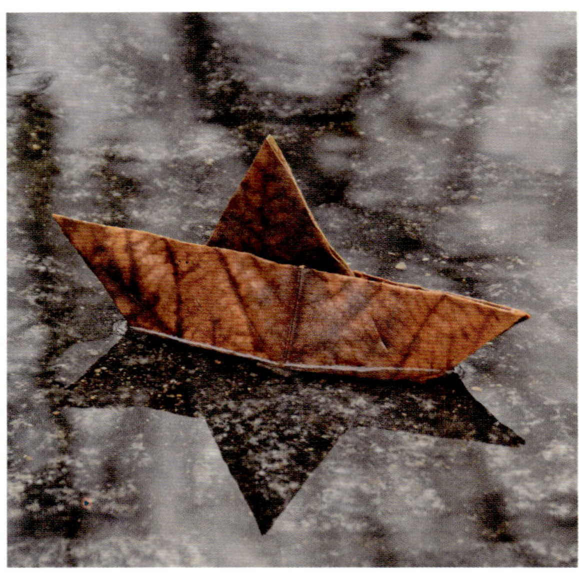

This little boat was made from two large horse-chestnut leaves. I chose leaves that had just fallen from the tree and were not yet entirely dry, otherwise they would have been too fragile and might have torn easily. I folded the leaves just like you would make a paper boat, and used sloe thorns to hold them in place.

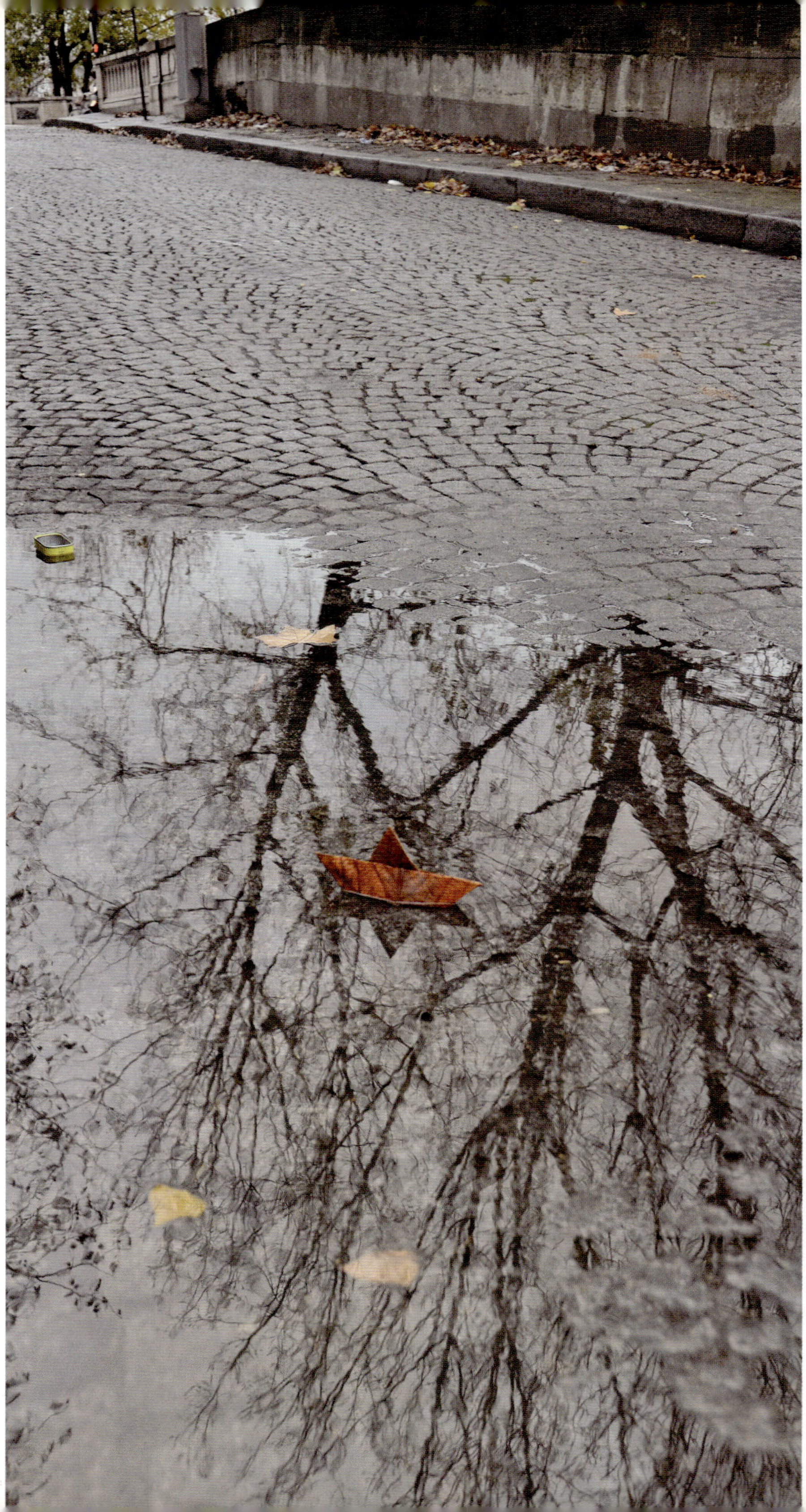

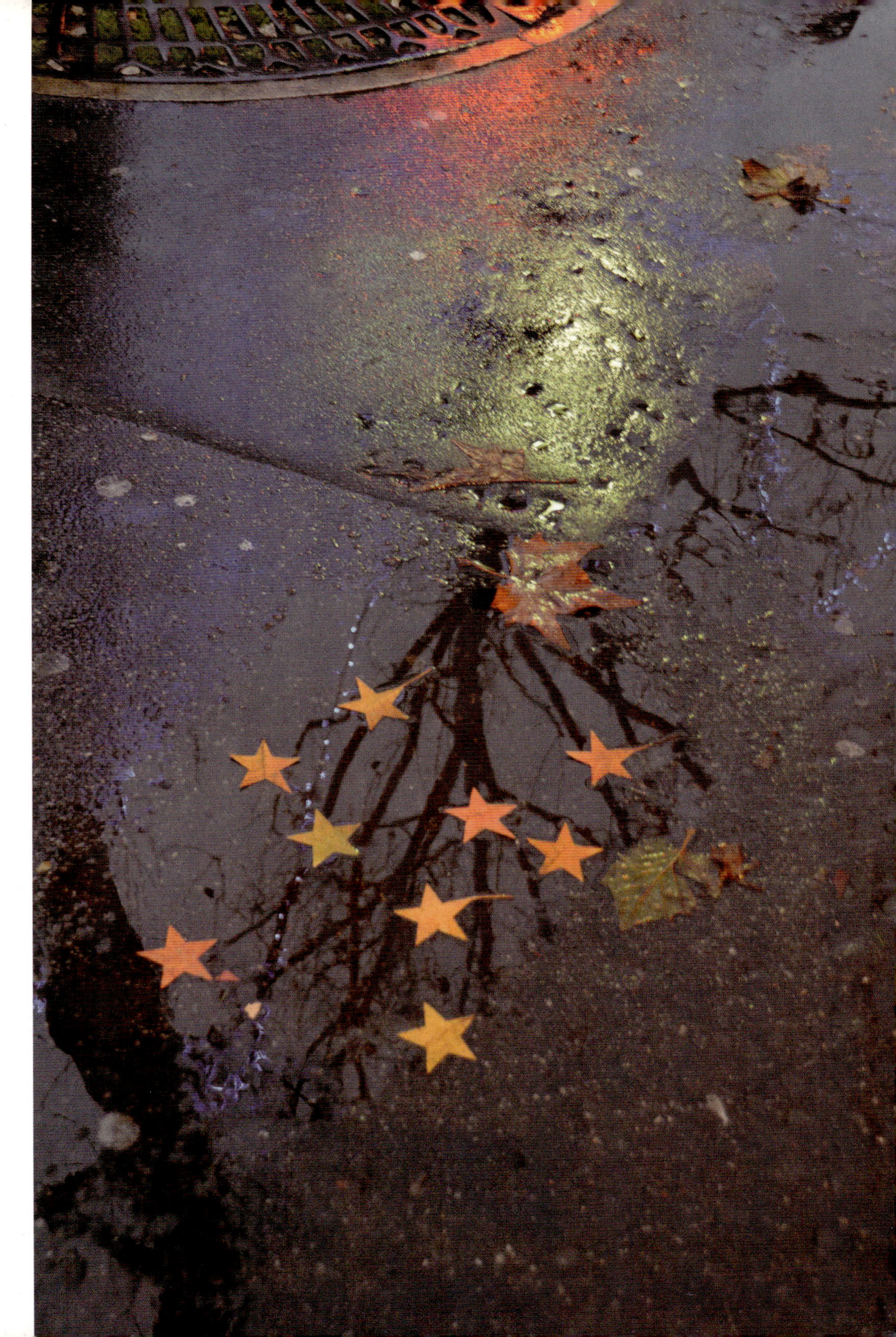

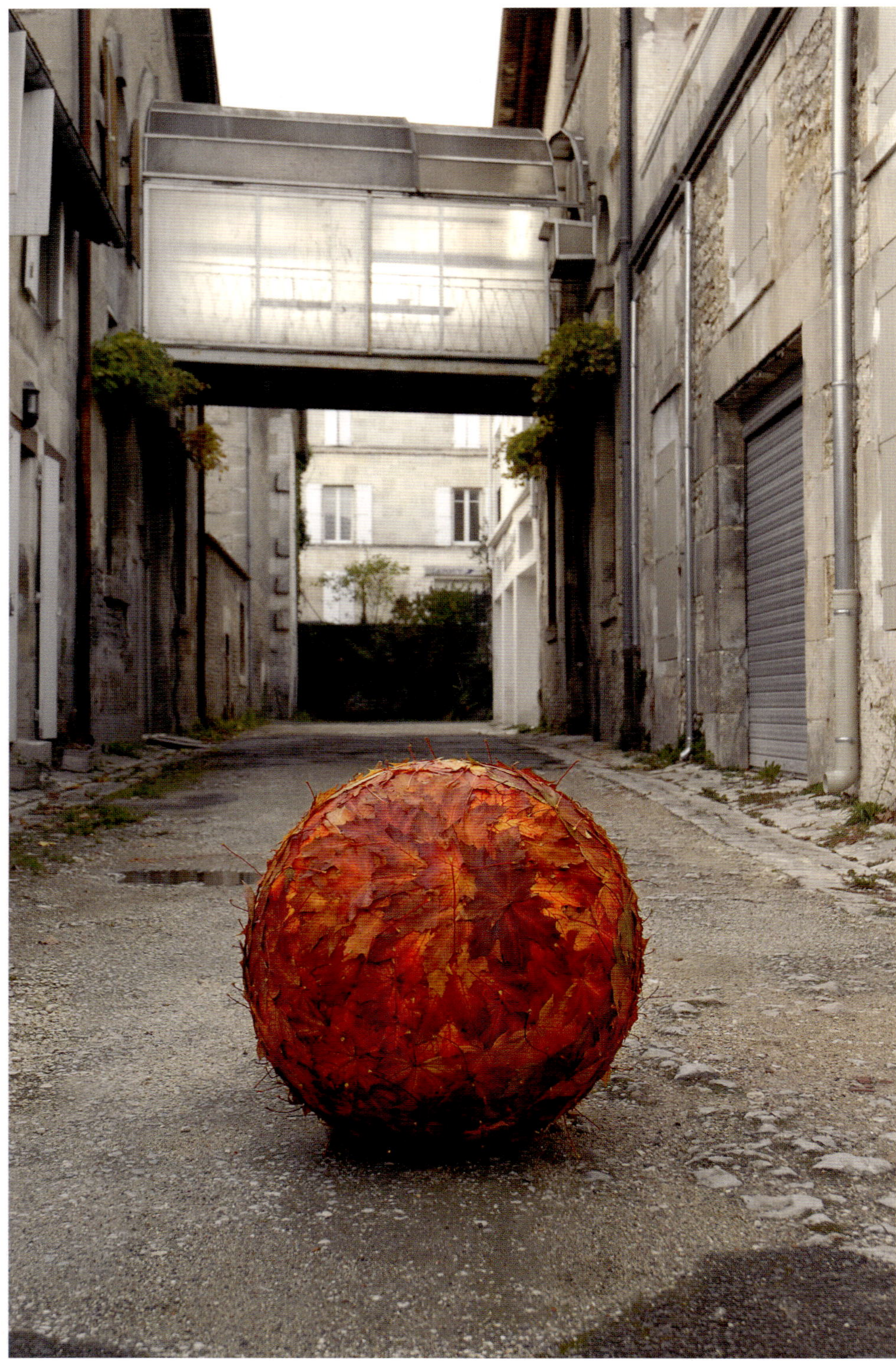

The longest and most difficult part of this installation is collecting the leaves and above all making the sphere to which they are affixed. You can use a foam ball or one made from fencing.

Many of the installations in this book were created on-site using natural elements gleaned from the surrounding area. Others that could be moved were created beforehand then taken to interesting sites and placed there, even used several times in different locations to create a series.

It's great fun and very creative to wander the town with your piece tucked under your arm looking for the right spot, the best light or an interesting juxtaposition of elements and background.

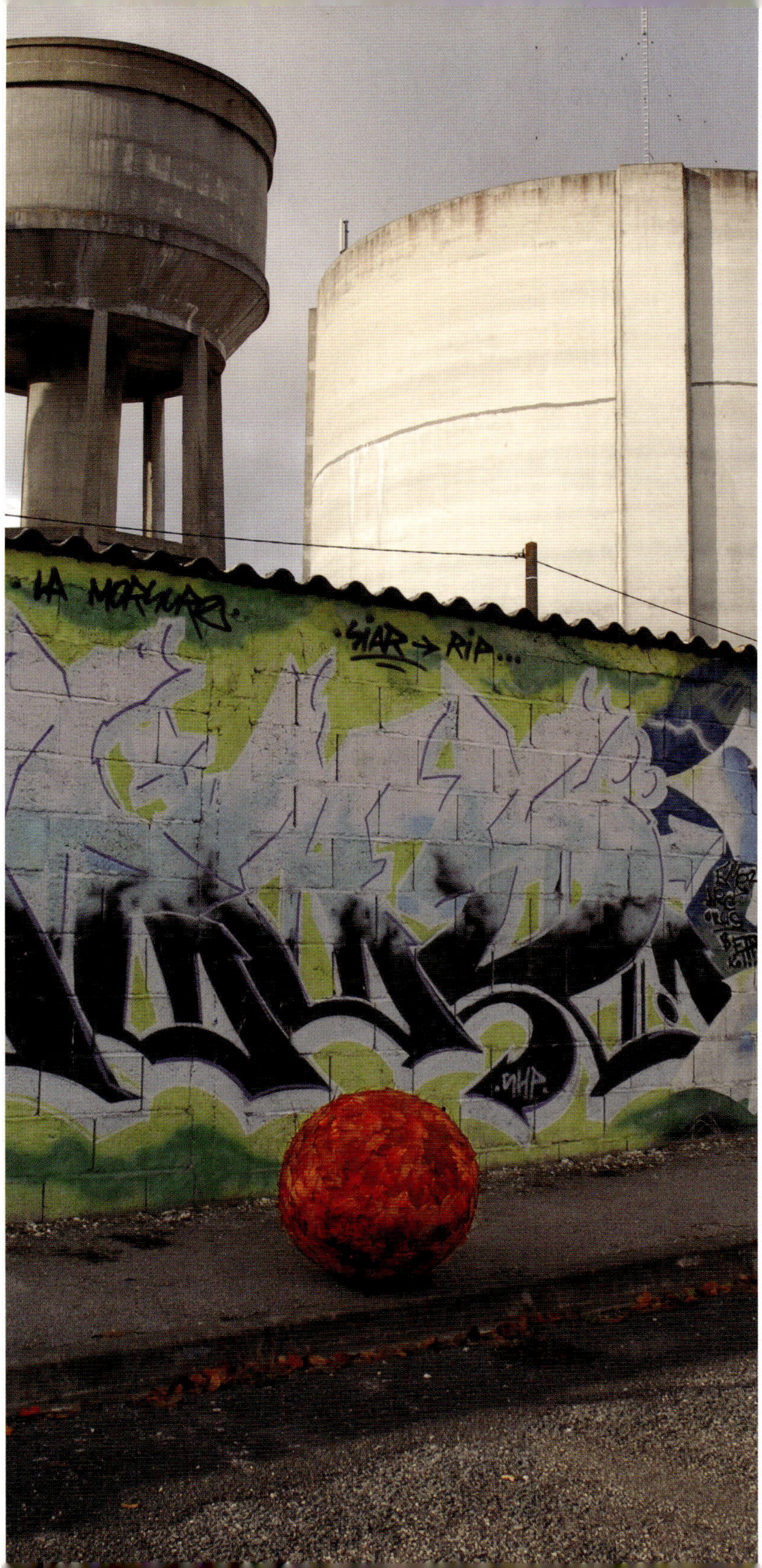

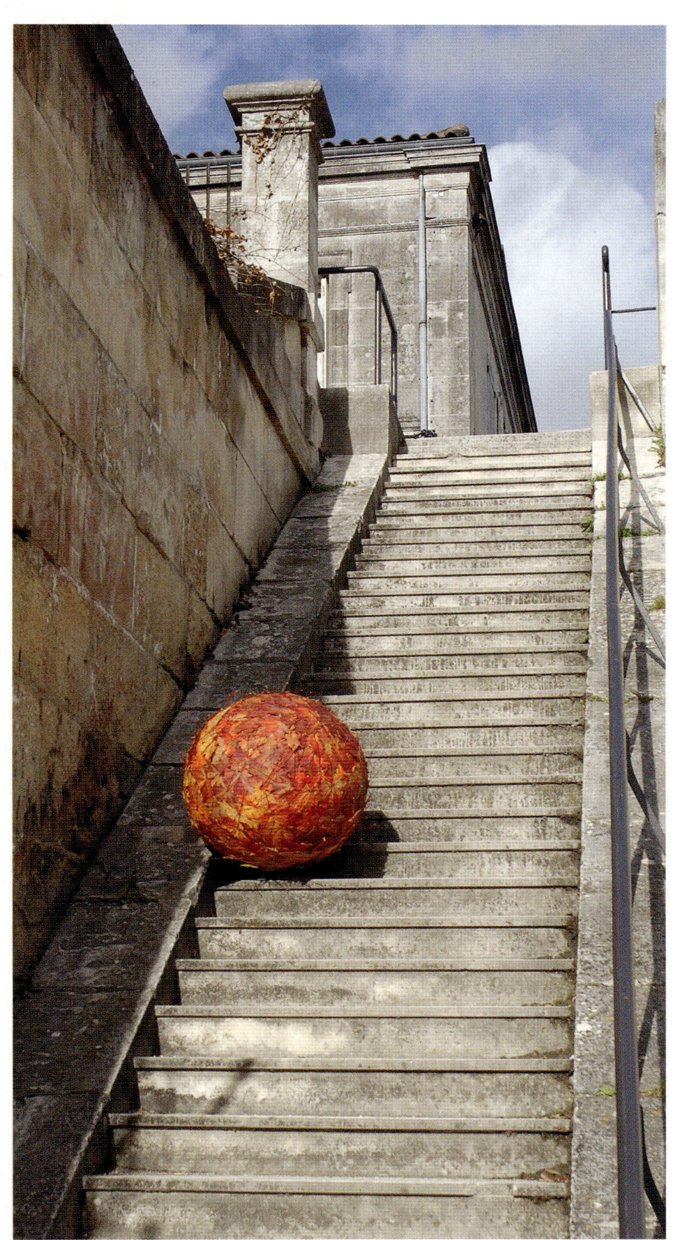

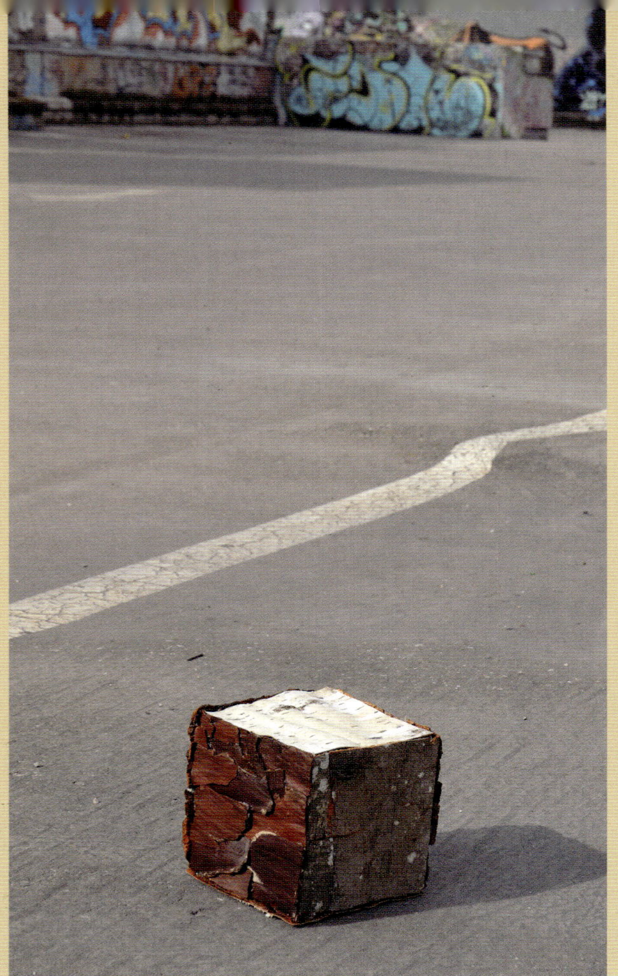

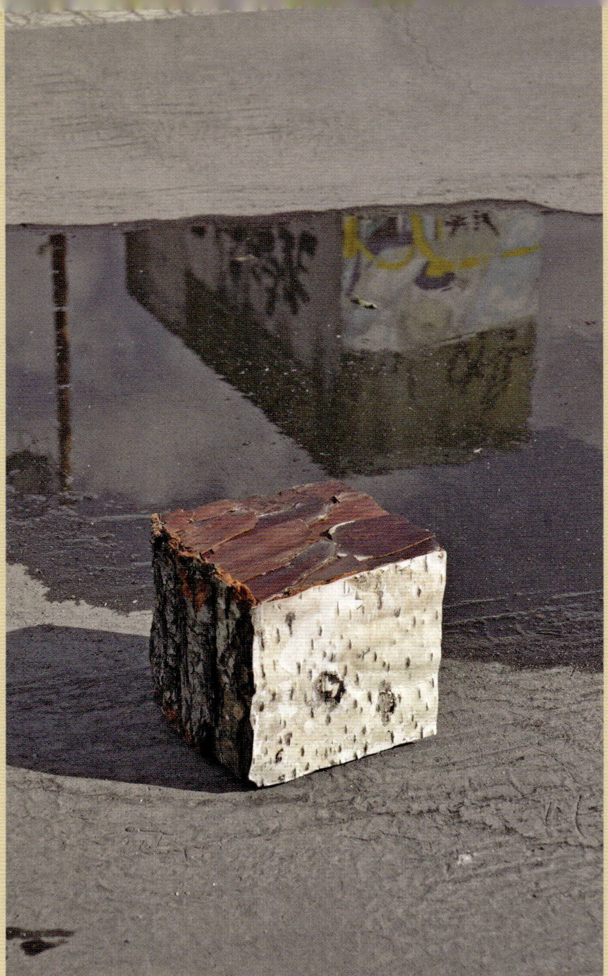

Box made from birch and pine bark.

I used dried sunflower stems from my garden to make the cube. They are both rigid yet flexible, and are fixed together with sloe thorns. I then made holes in the sunflower stems to hold the feathers.

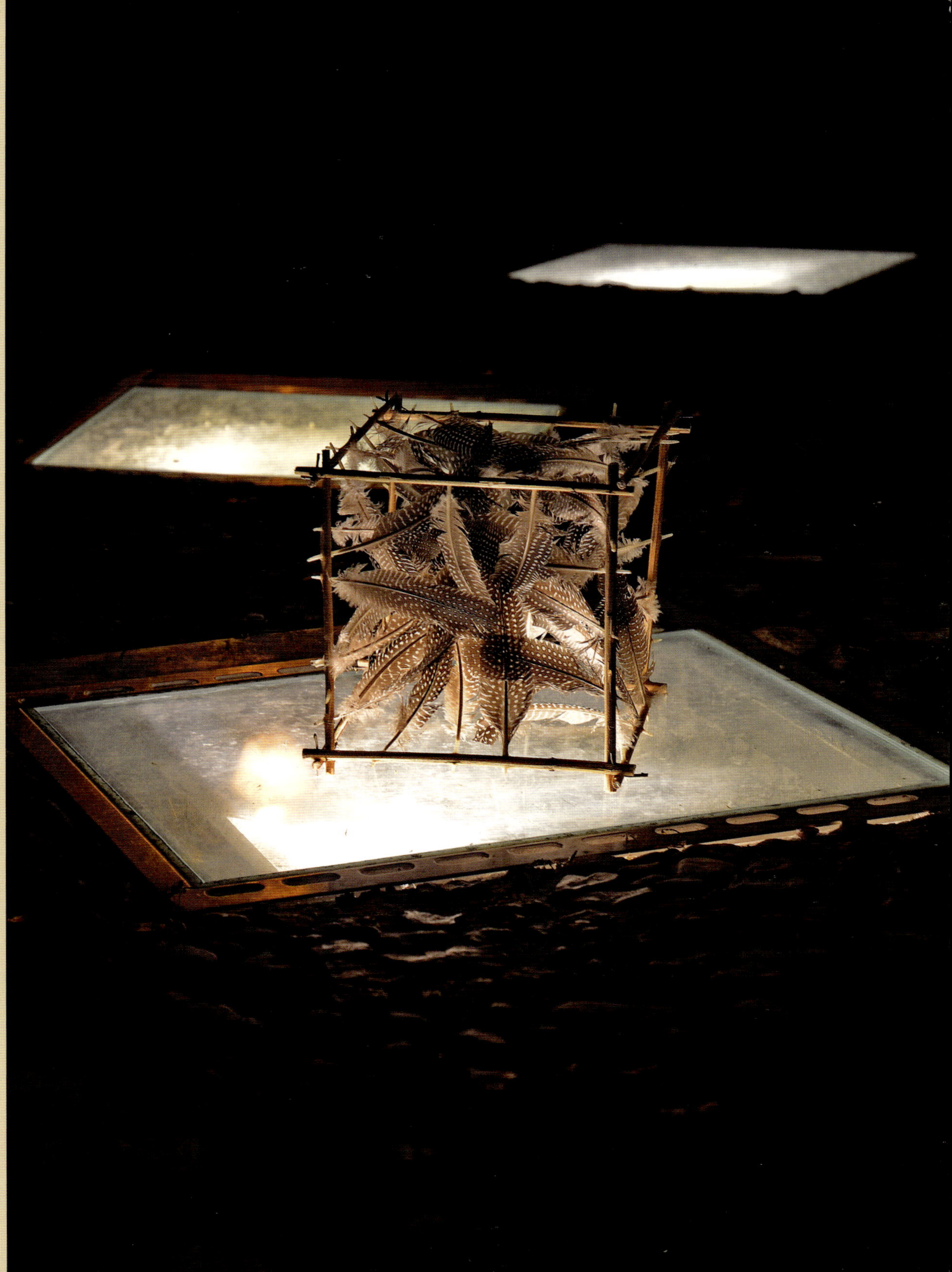

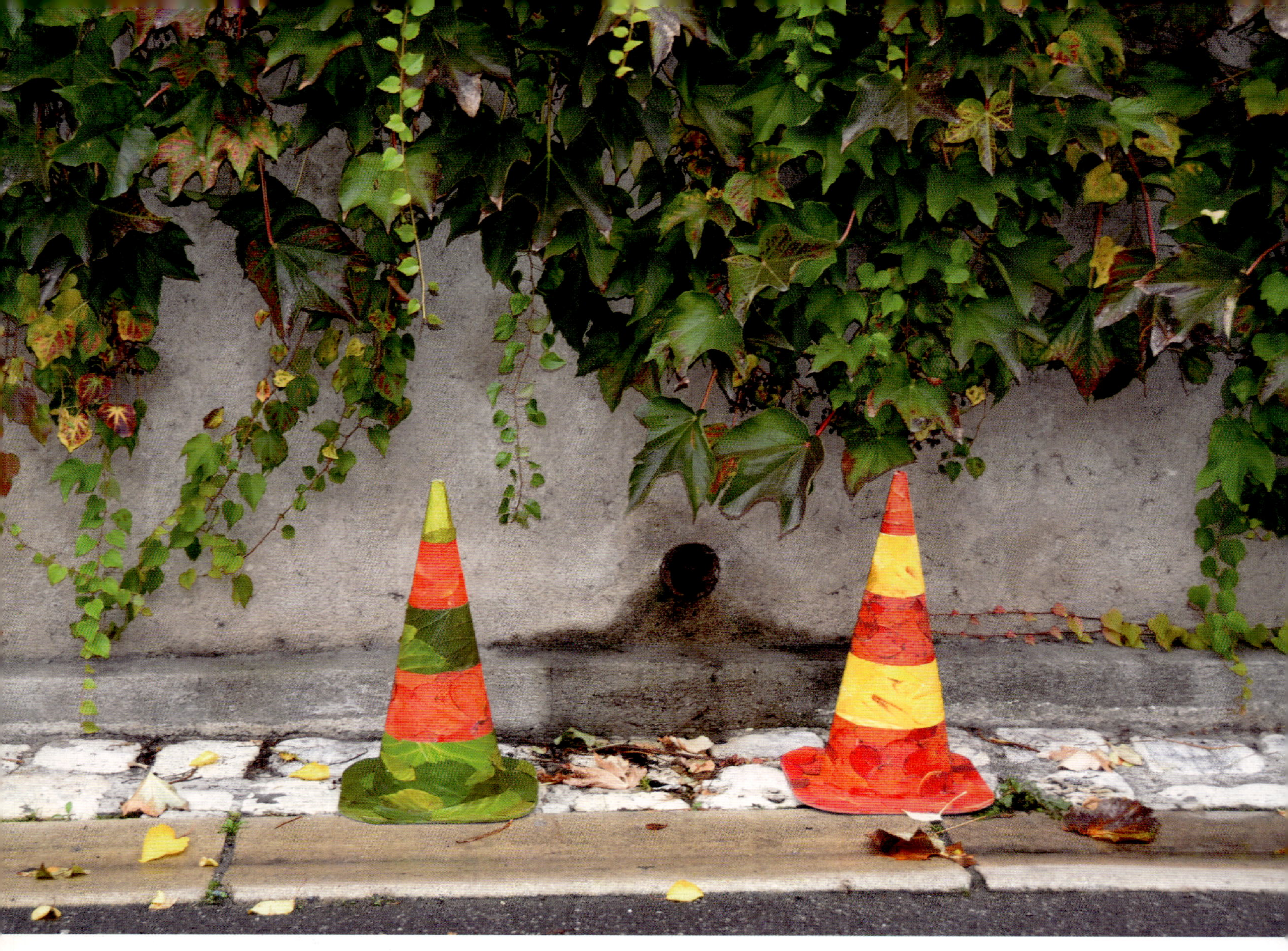

I try to use natural elements as much as possible, but in this case I made the traffic cones from cardboard, before mixing up a glue of water, flour and sugar to stick on the leaves.

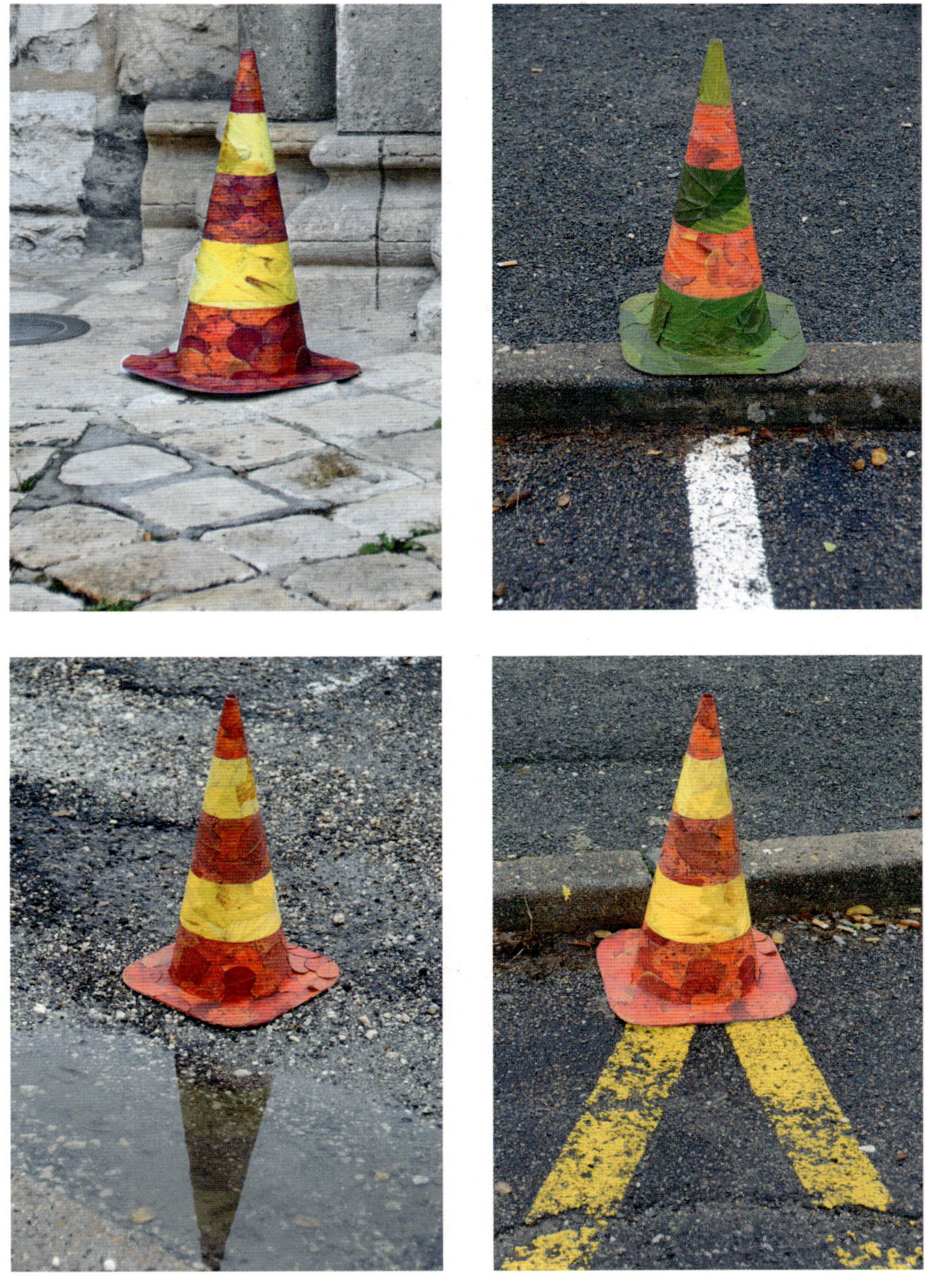

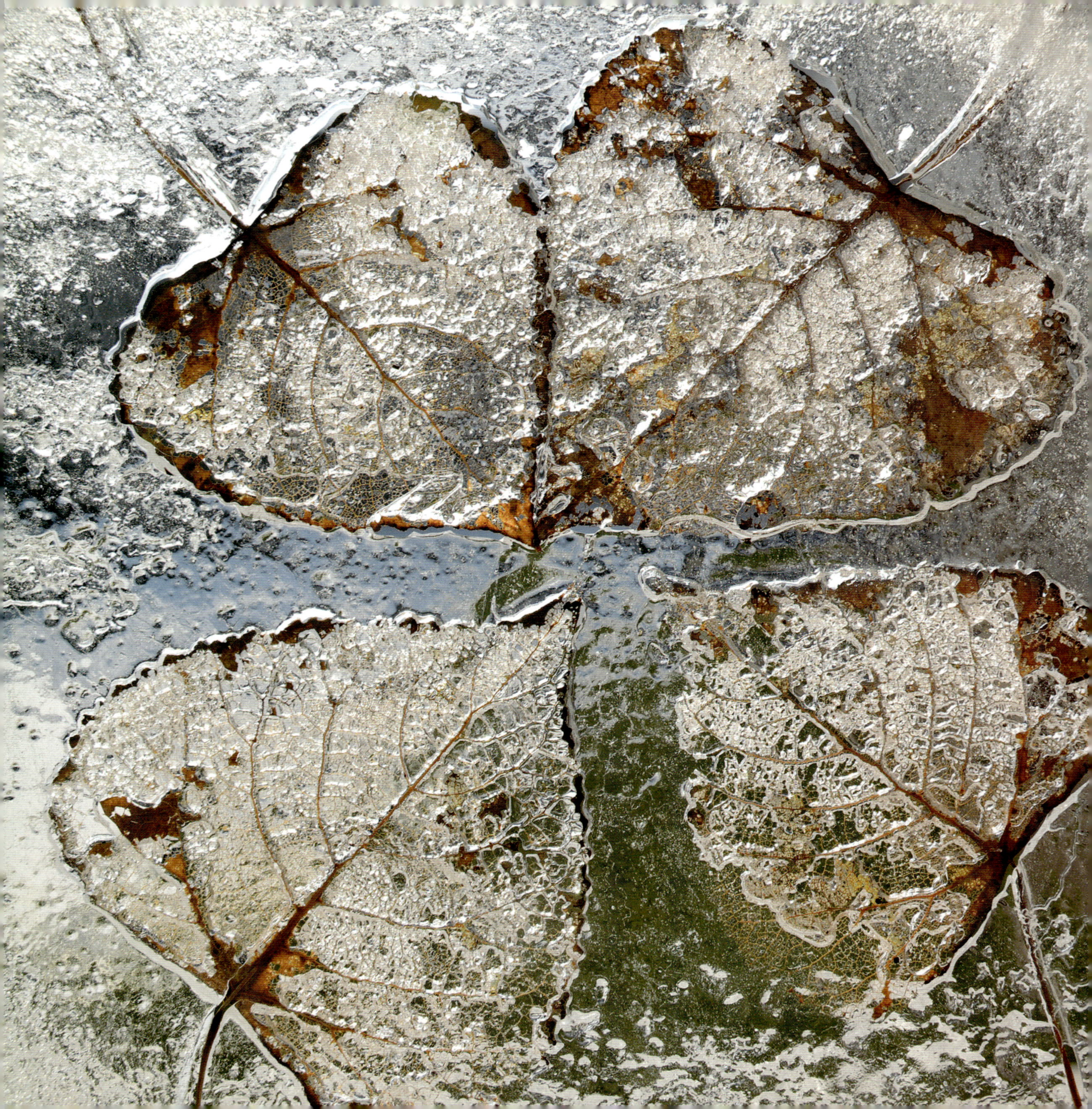

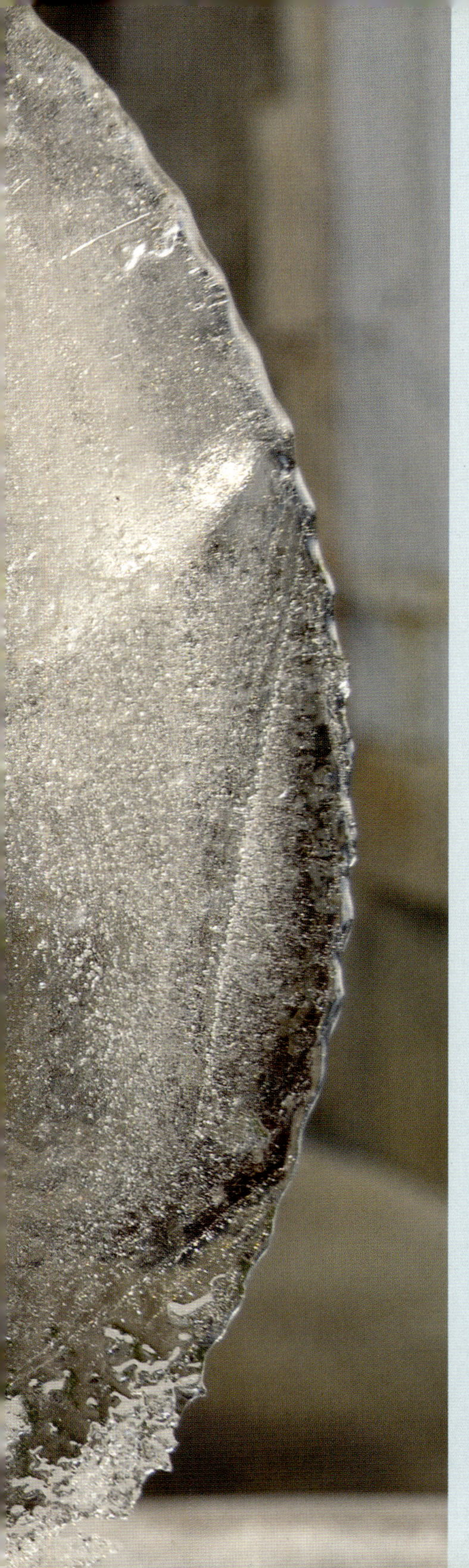

WINTER

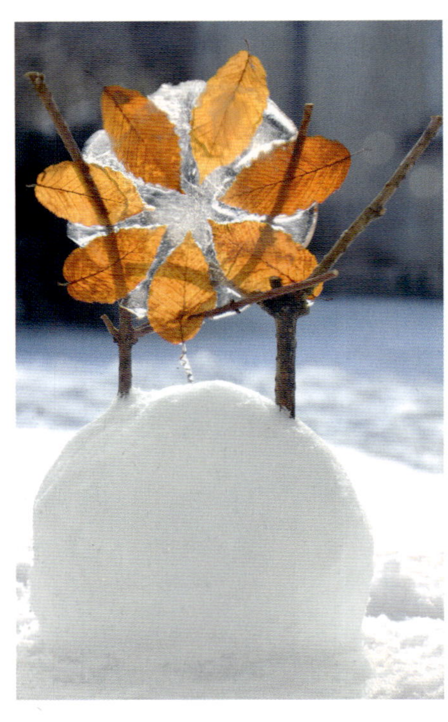

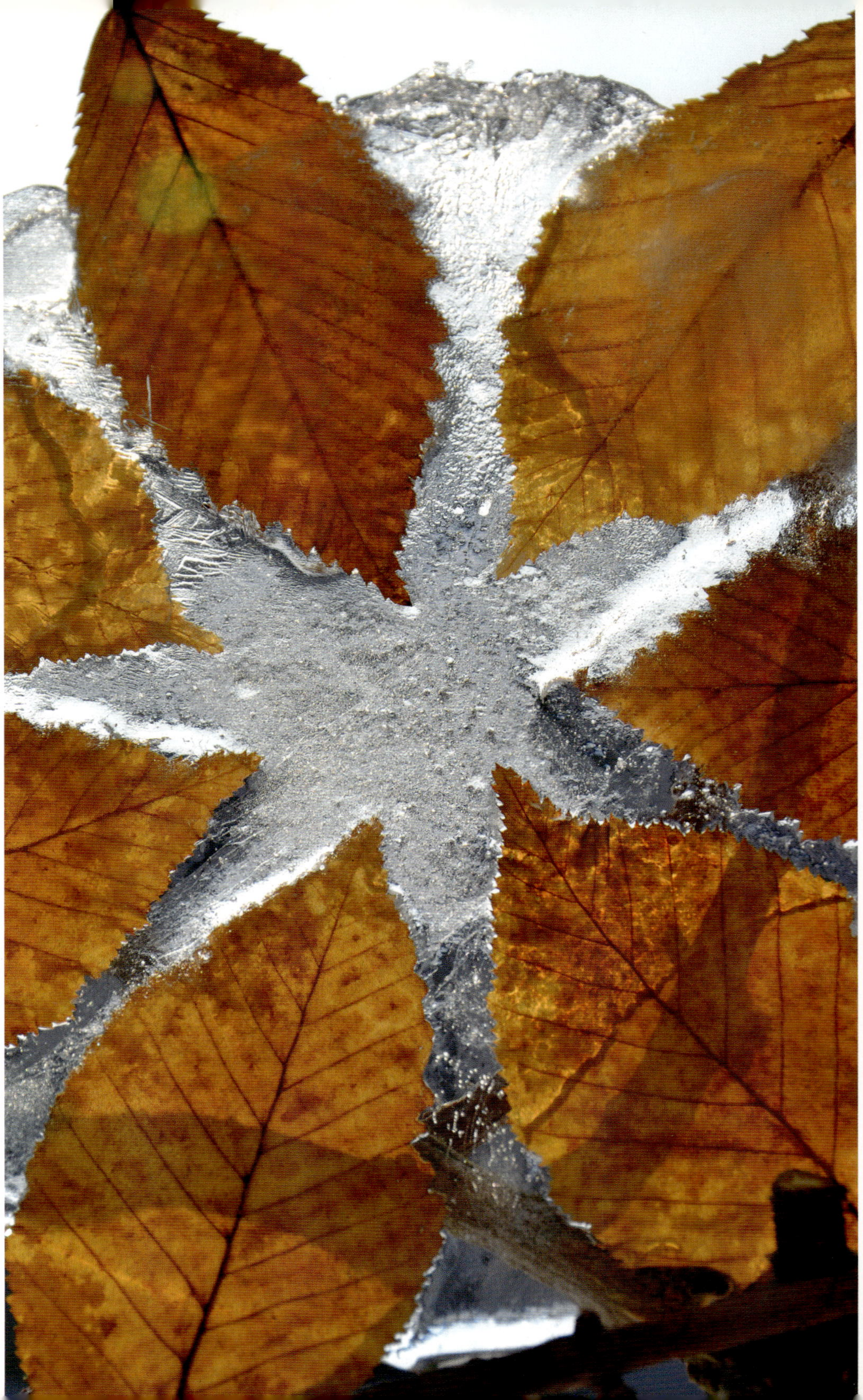

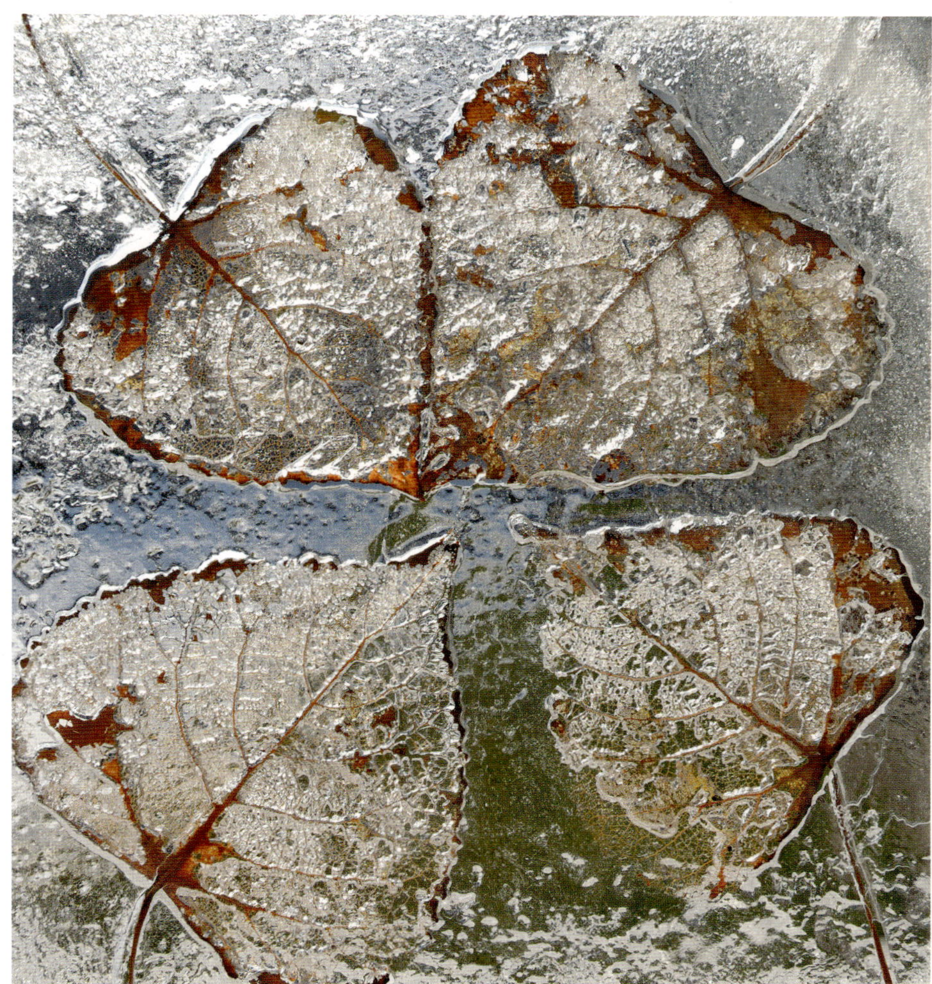

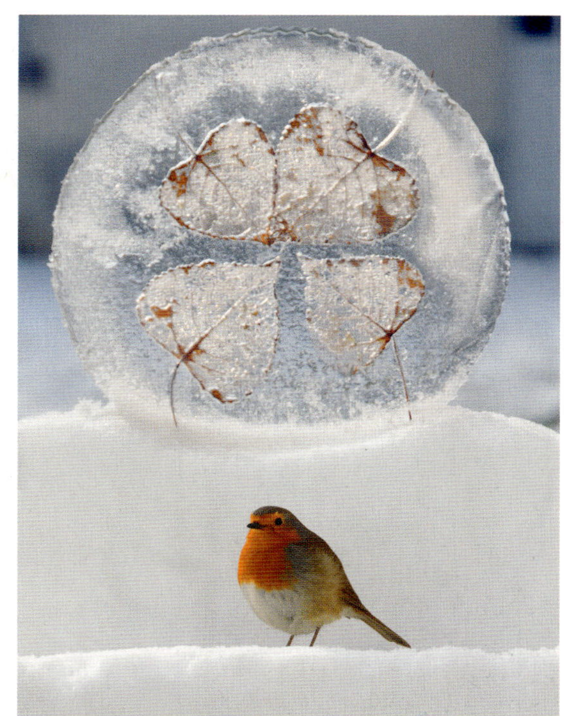

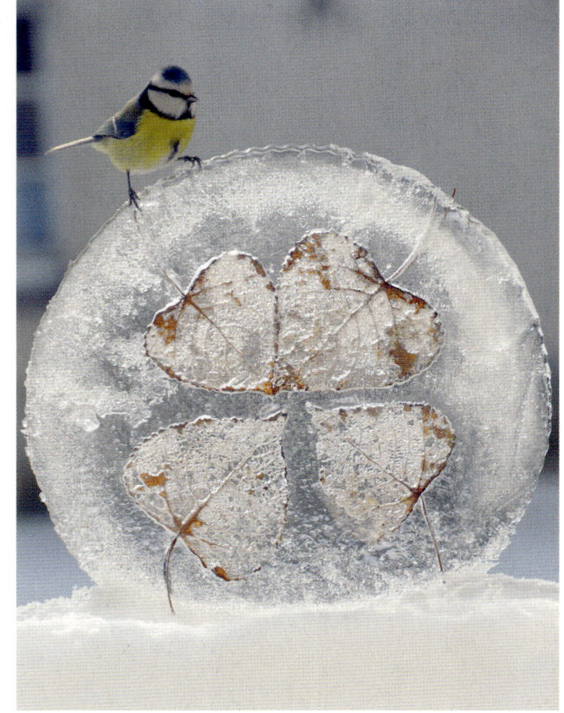

Frost, ice and snow are superb materials for land art enthusiasts, but a dose of good fortune helps too. I like to keep an eye on the birds, for they become much more curious and fearless when it gets colder, daring to approach closer to humans than usual. As soon as I have my back turned, a Robin pays a visit to my installation of ice and leaves, followed closely by a Great Tit.

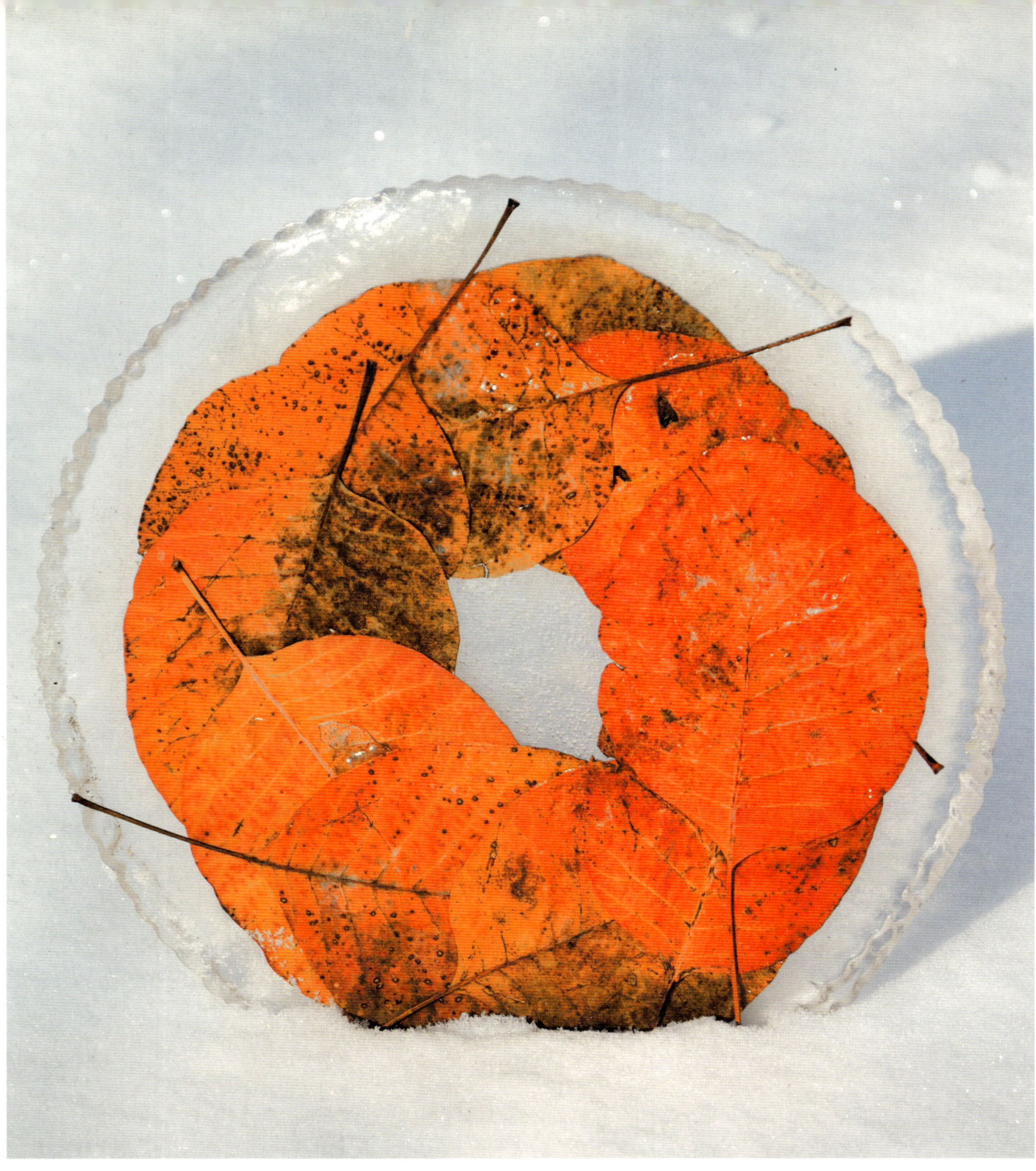

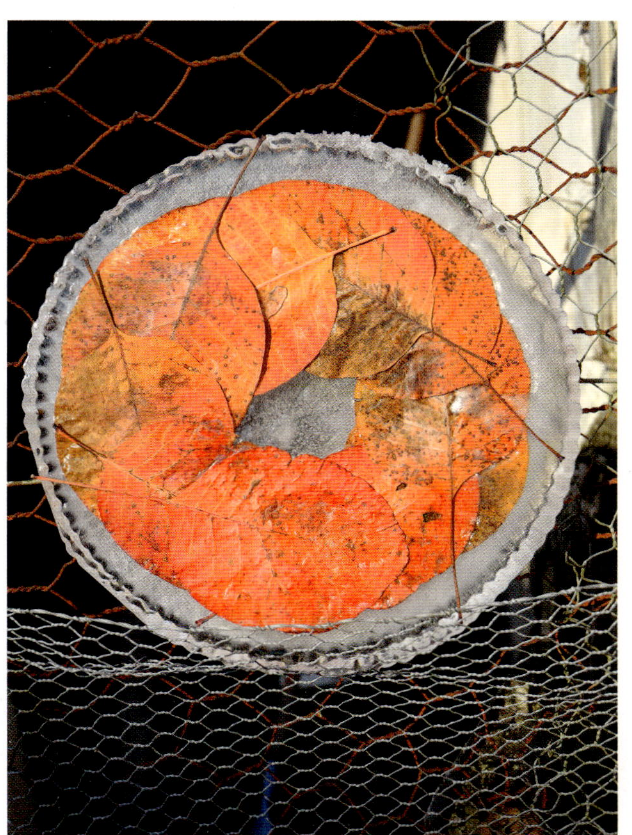

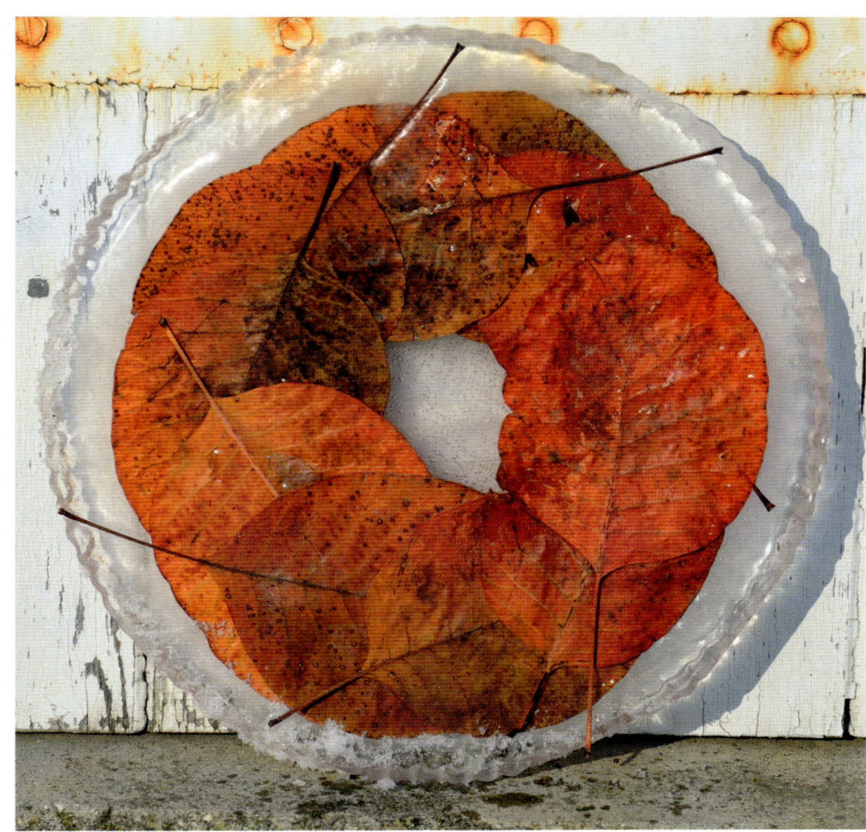

Fill a pie dish with water, place some leaves in it overnight and next morning you'll have a lovely frozen art piece.

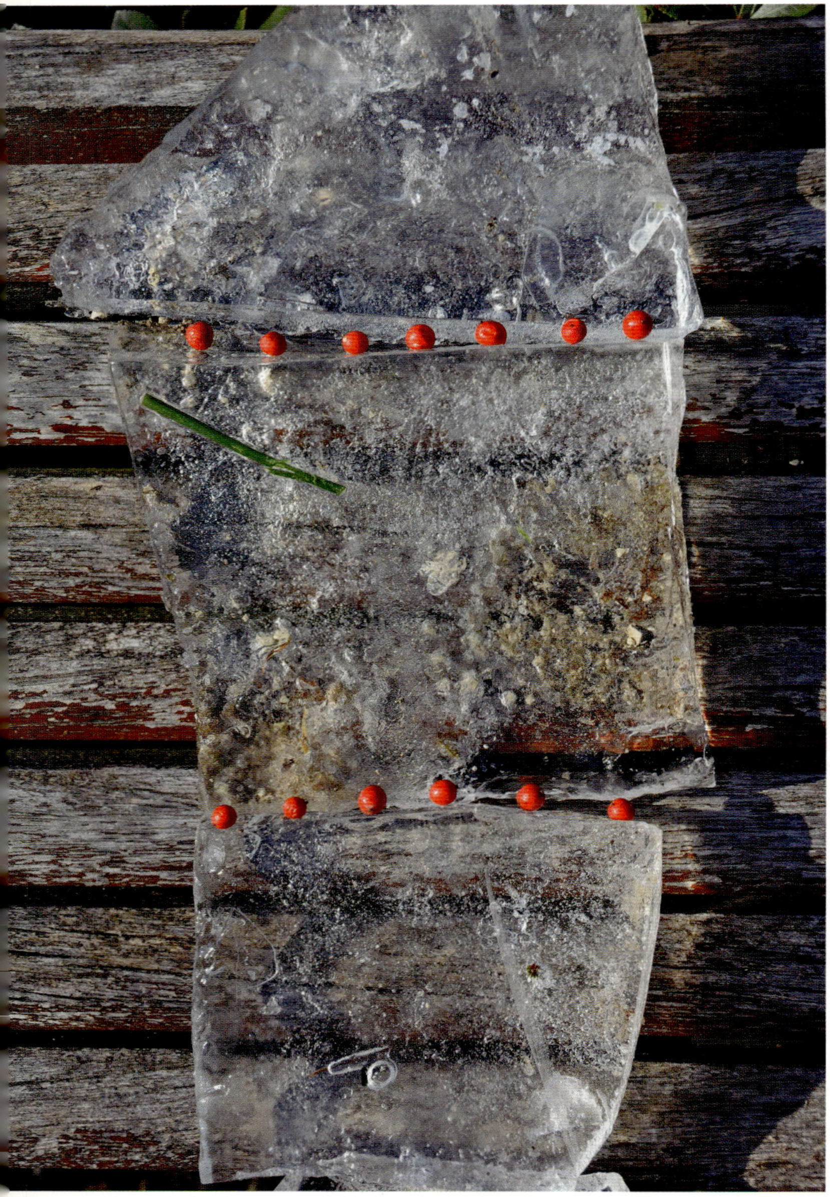

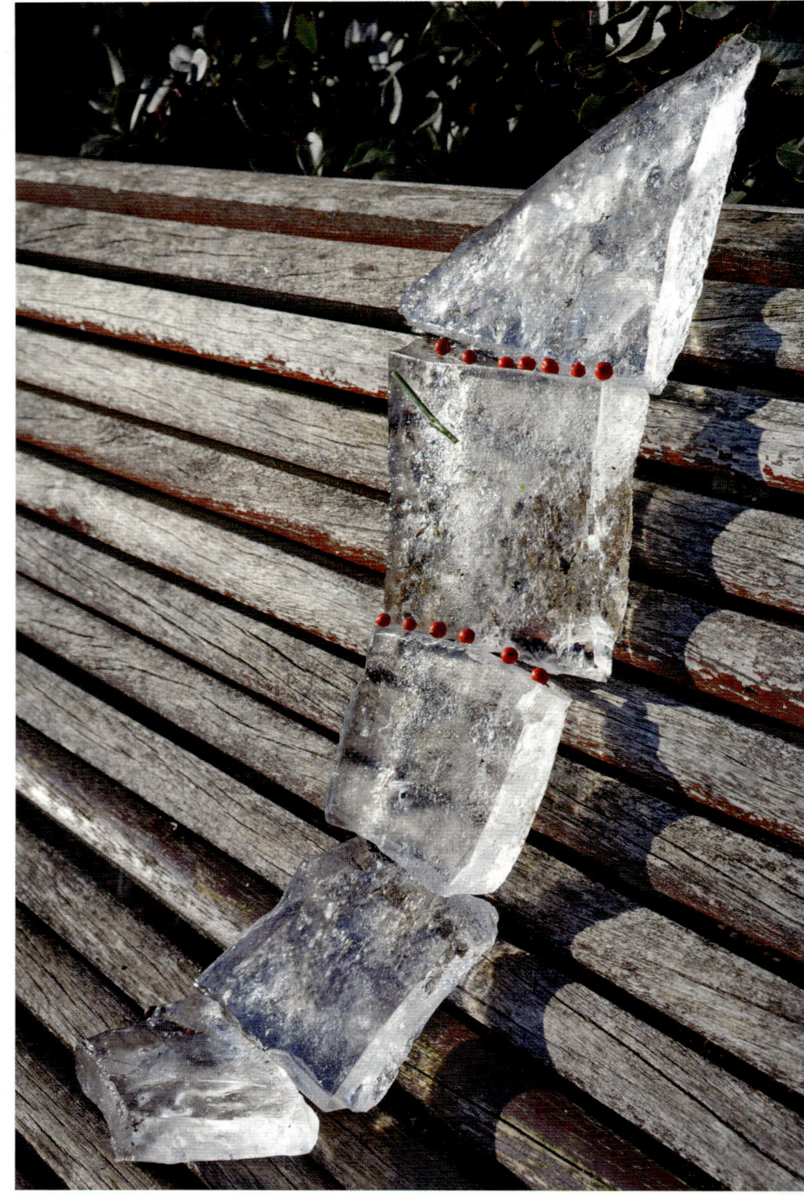

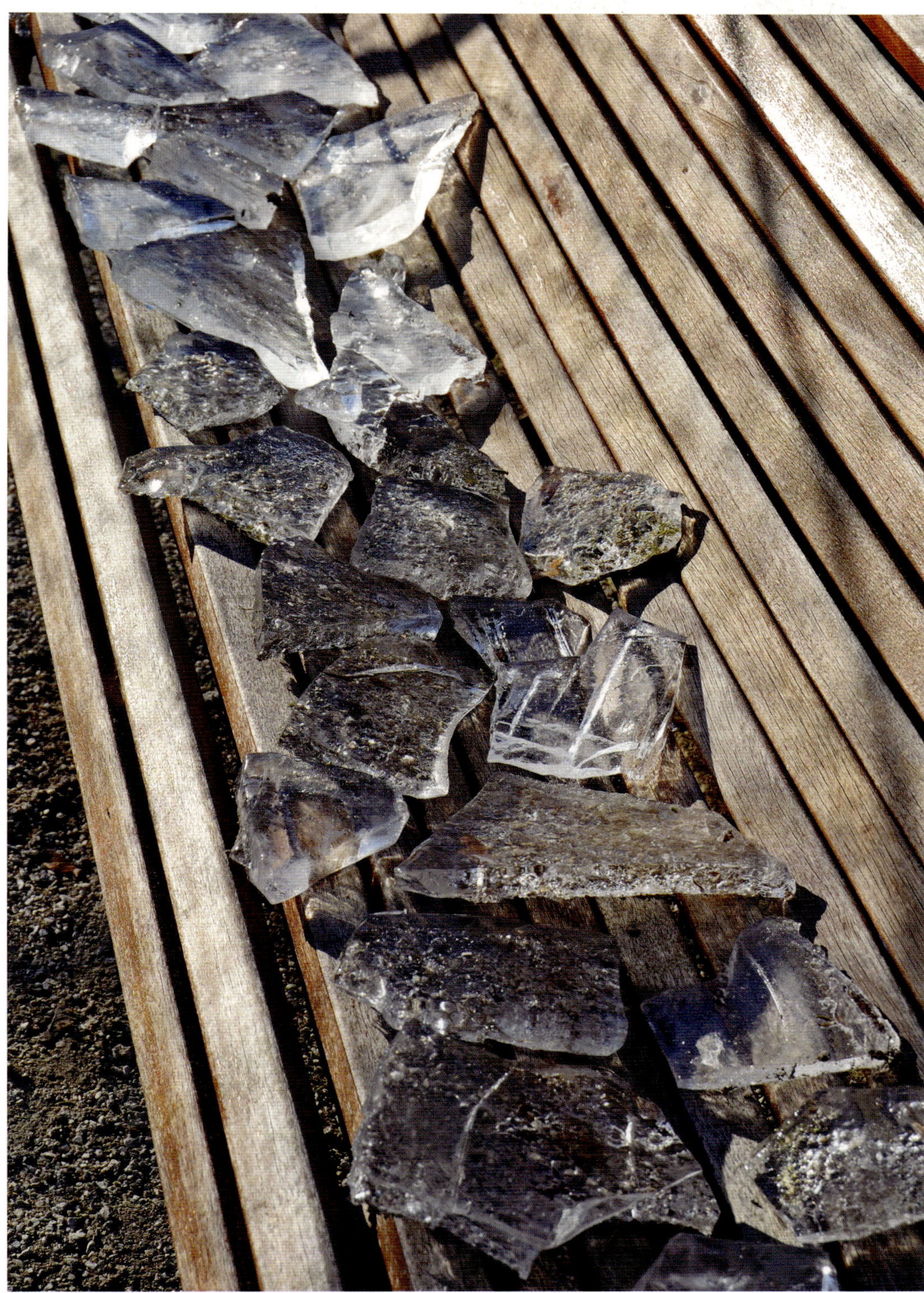

Ice is a great material to use for land art, since not only can you freeze things in it, but you can use found pieces in so many different ways.

Collect a number of pieces and arrange them to suit, or shape them as desired then fit them together in interesting ways. Use winter berries to add a splash of bright colour to your installation.

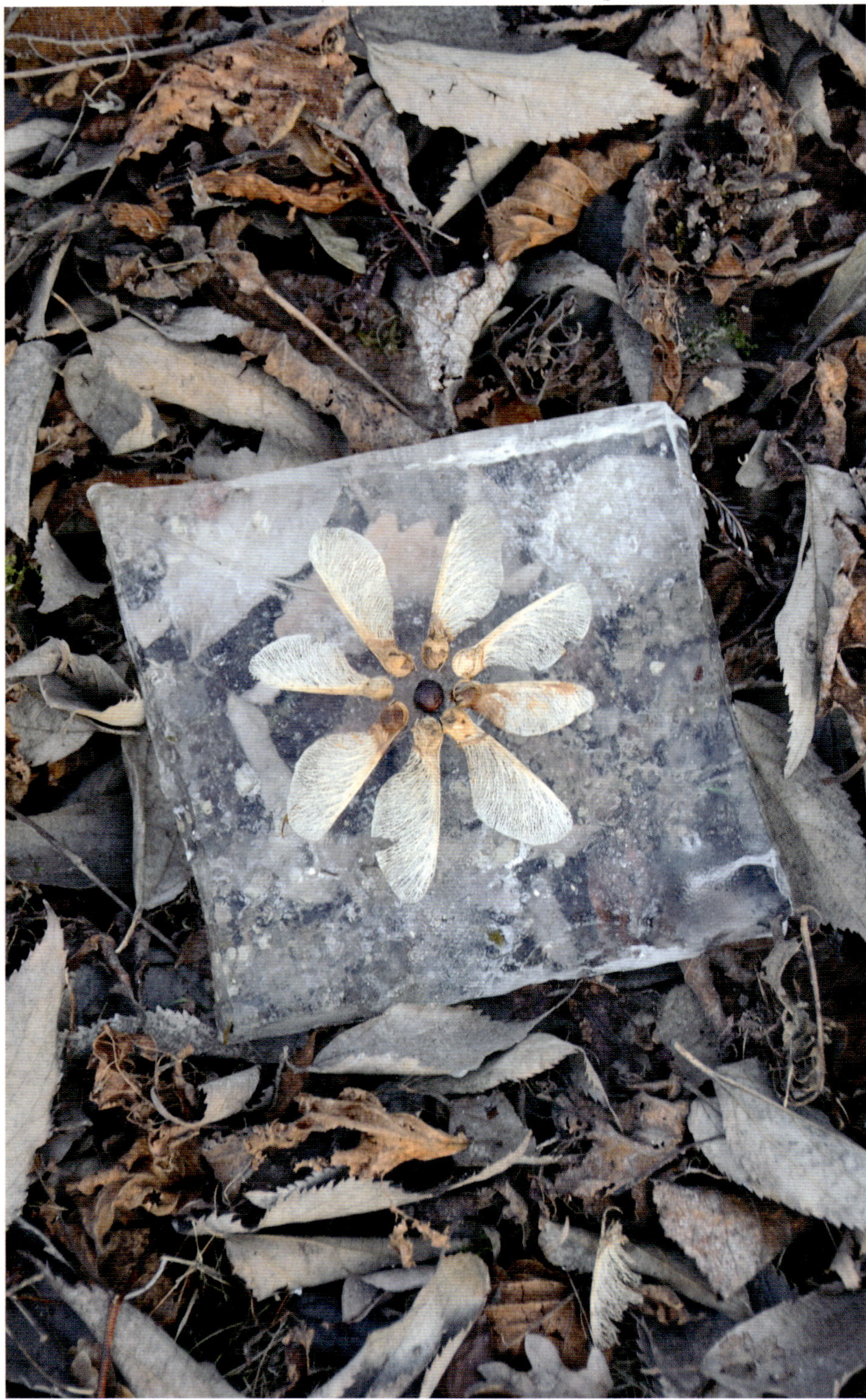

The colour of ice changes according to the light and the surface on which it is placed. Try different times of day, and place your piece on leaves, grass, earth or stones and see what different effects you can achieve.

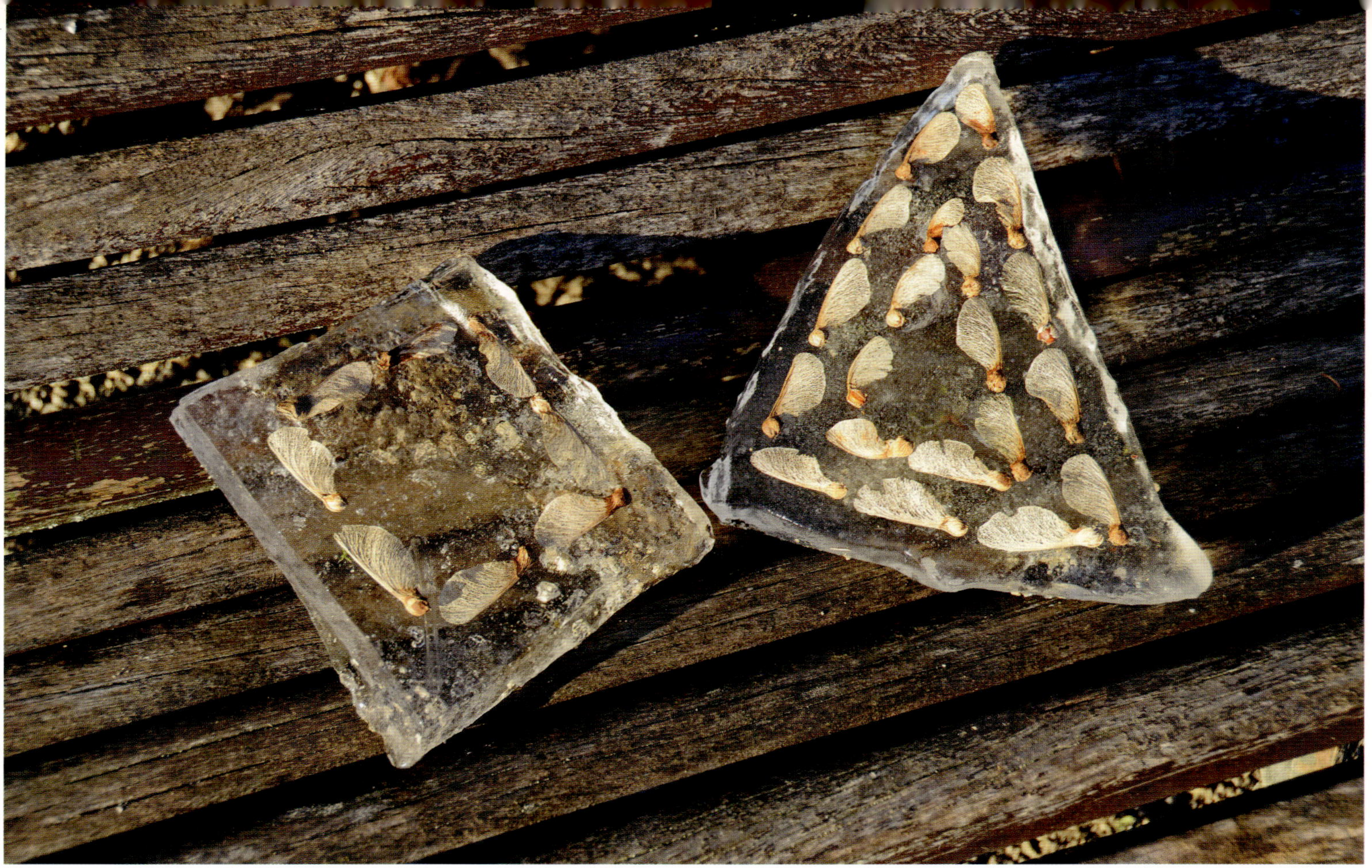

Like lovers cosying up together on a park bench.

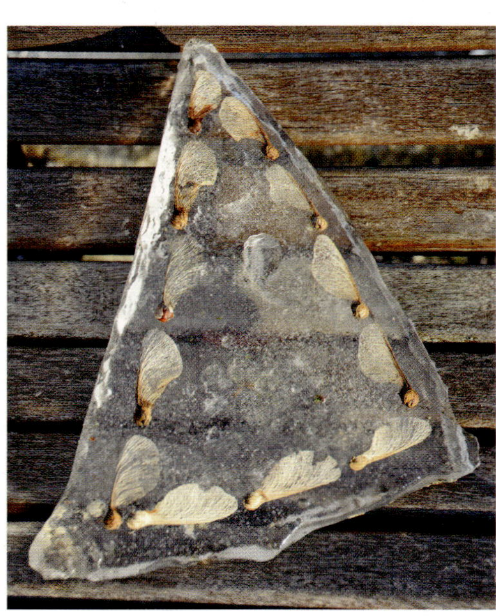

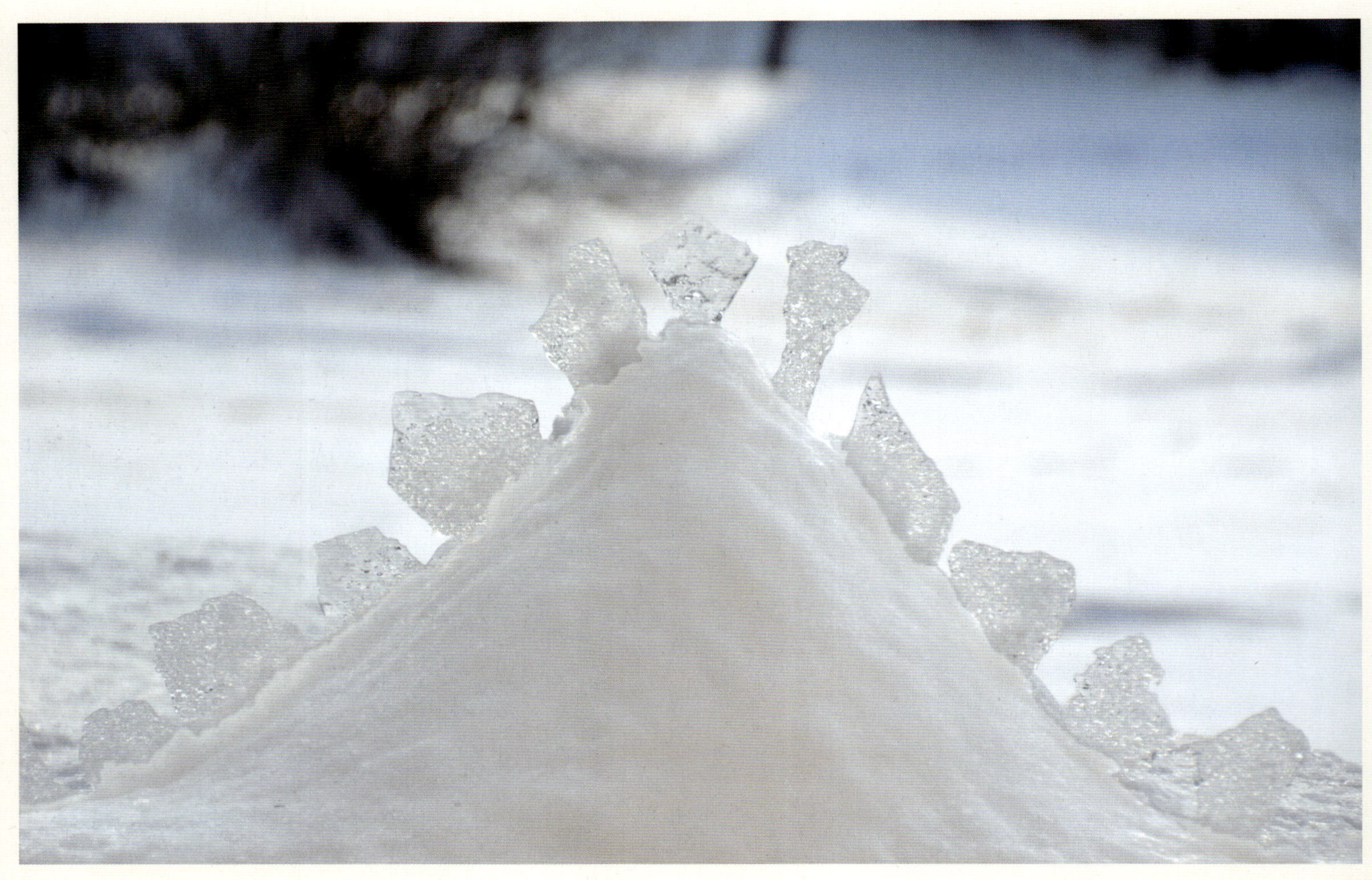

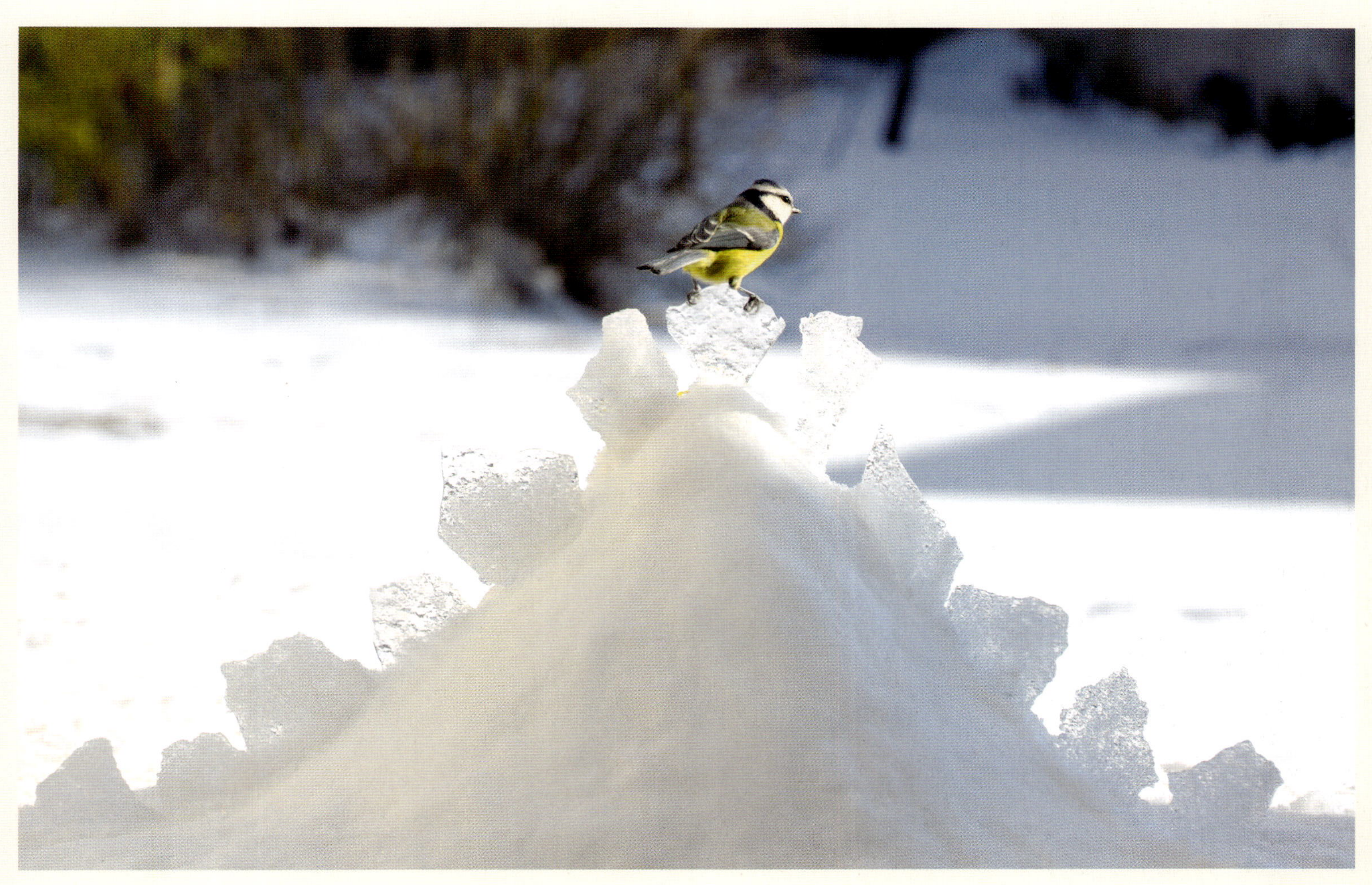

I'm the king of the castle!

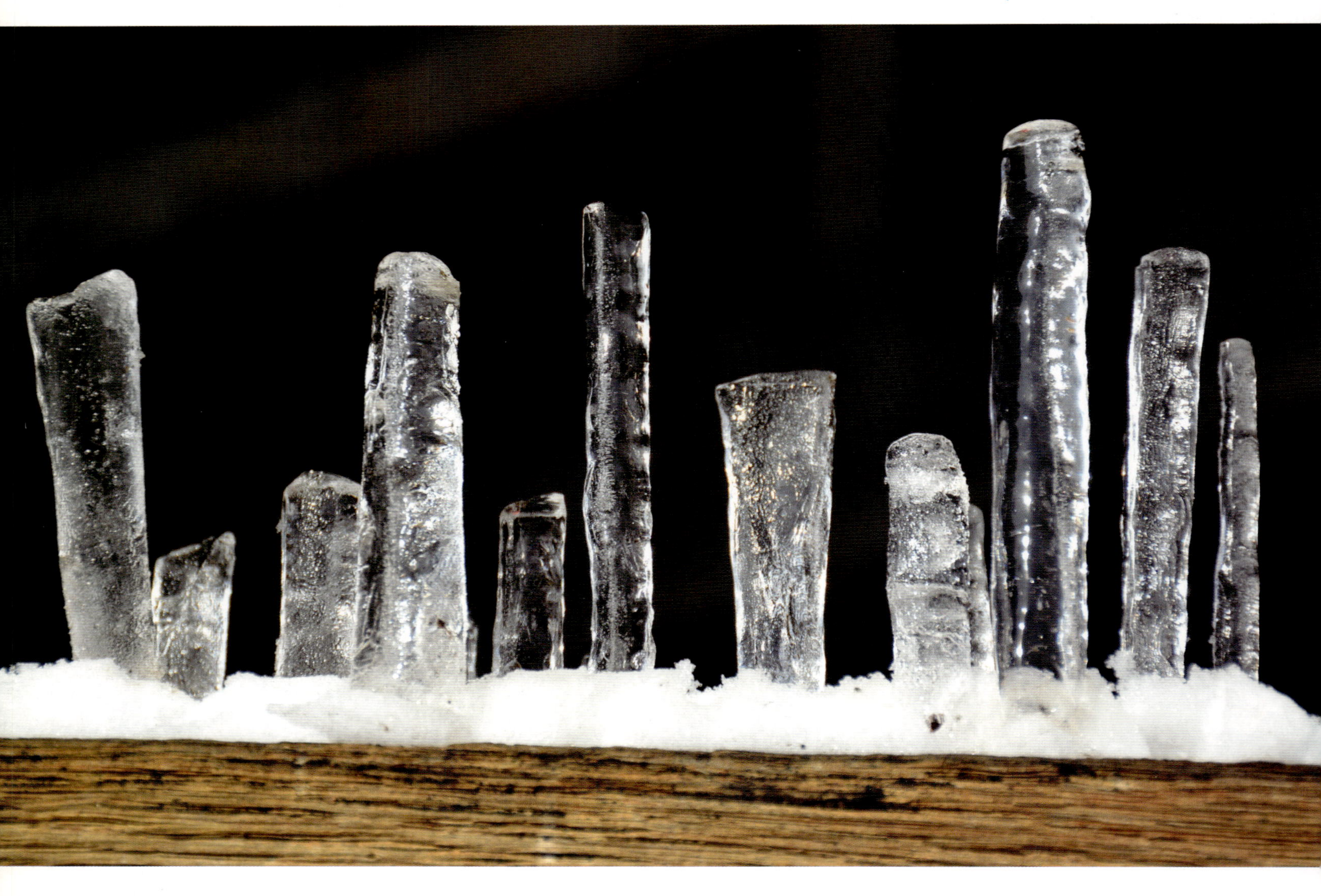

There is more to the urban environment than concrete, brick and tarmac.

Climatic conditions such as rain, frost, snow, wind and sun are still present, even though their effects are perhaps less noticeable than in the countryside.

A puddle of water offers a beautiful variety of reflections, while the wind sweeping round a street corner makes leaves dance in a swirling ballet of rustling colour.

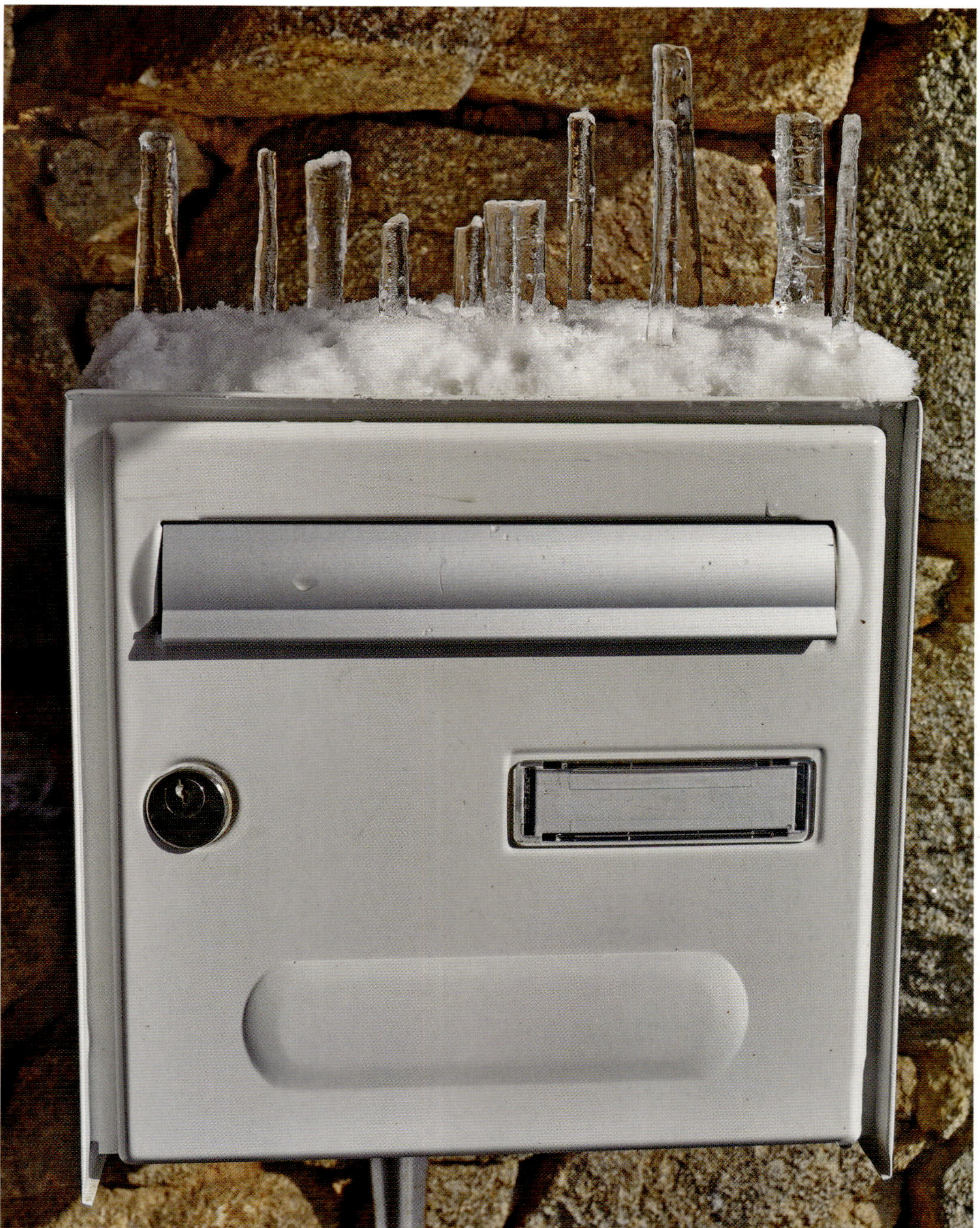

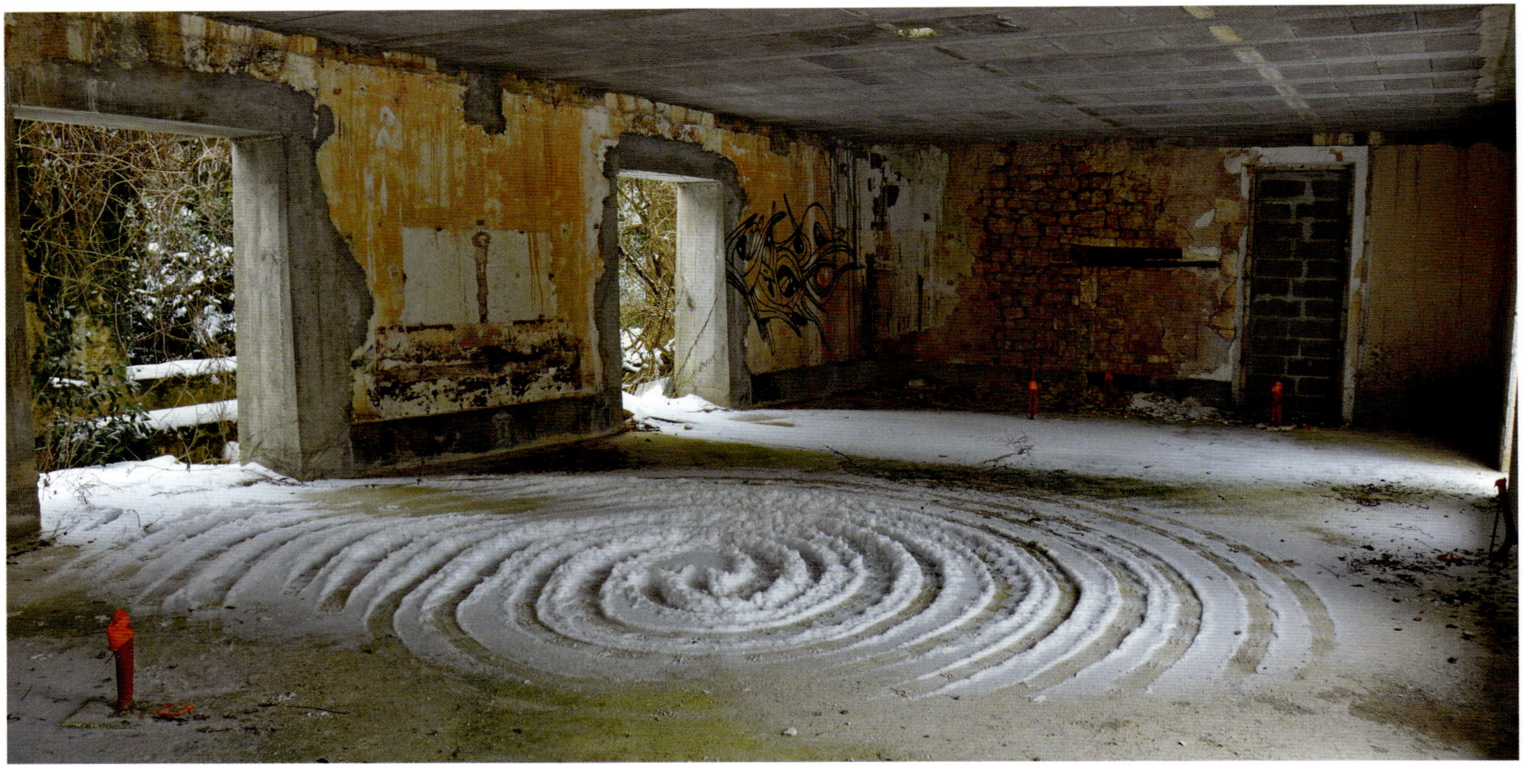

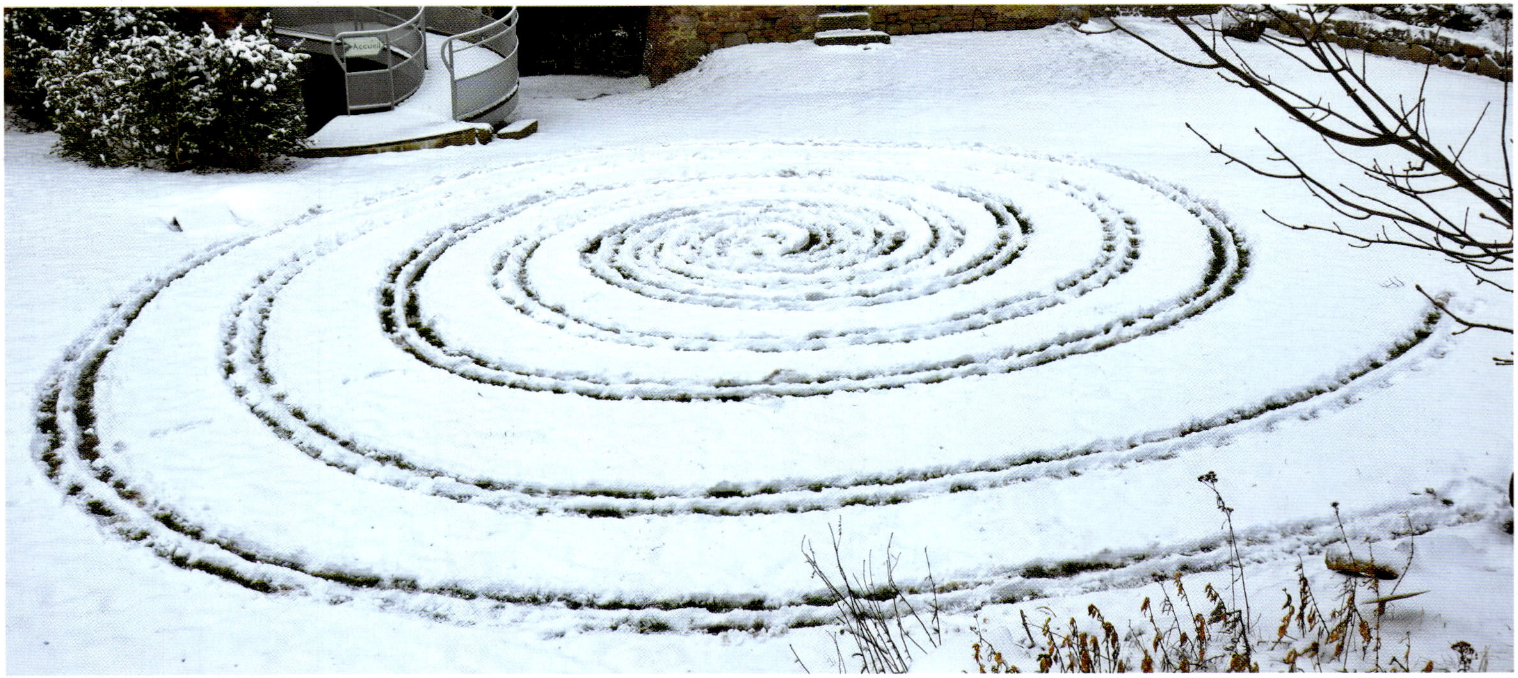

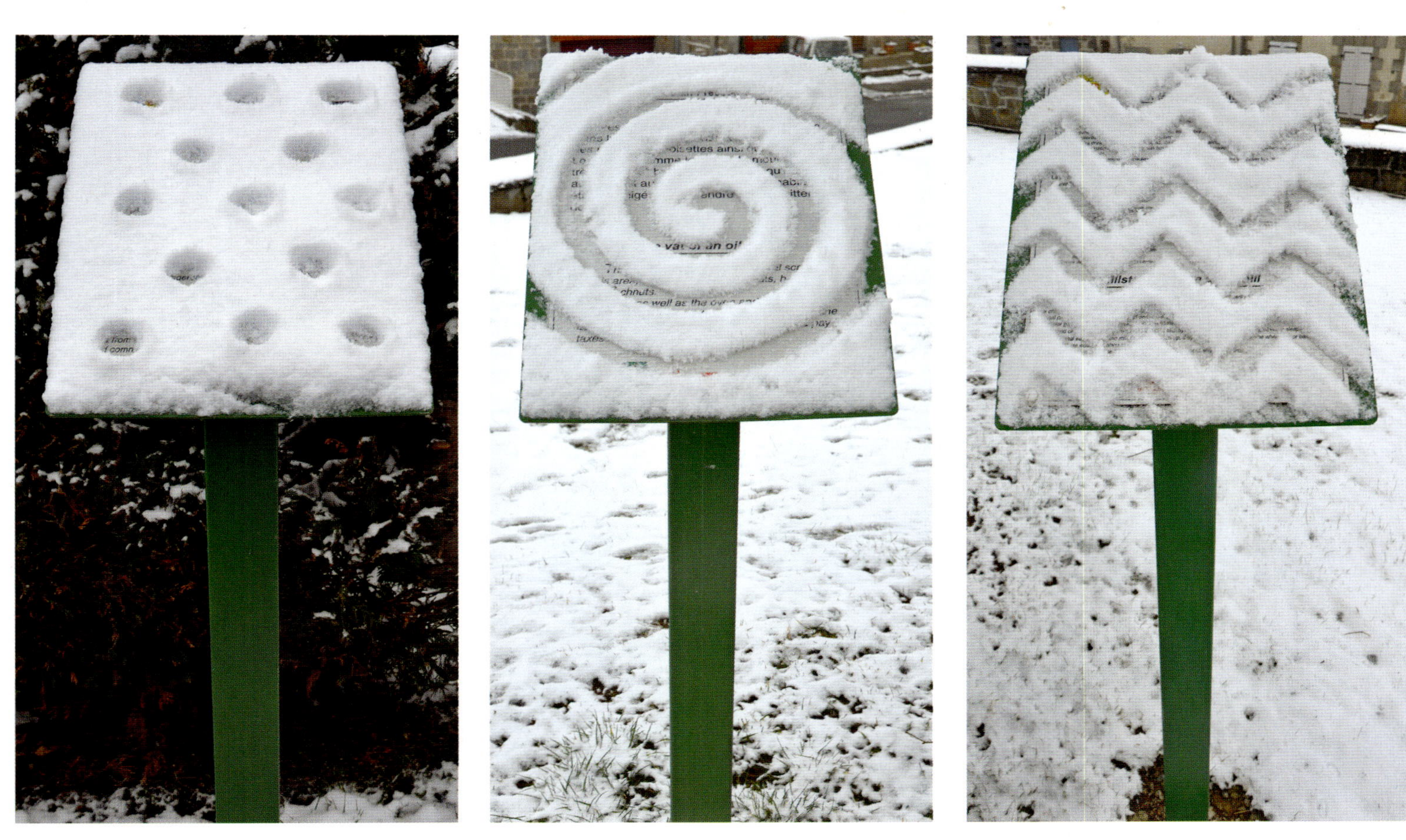

Doodling with snow is simplicity itself!

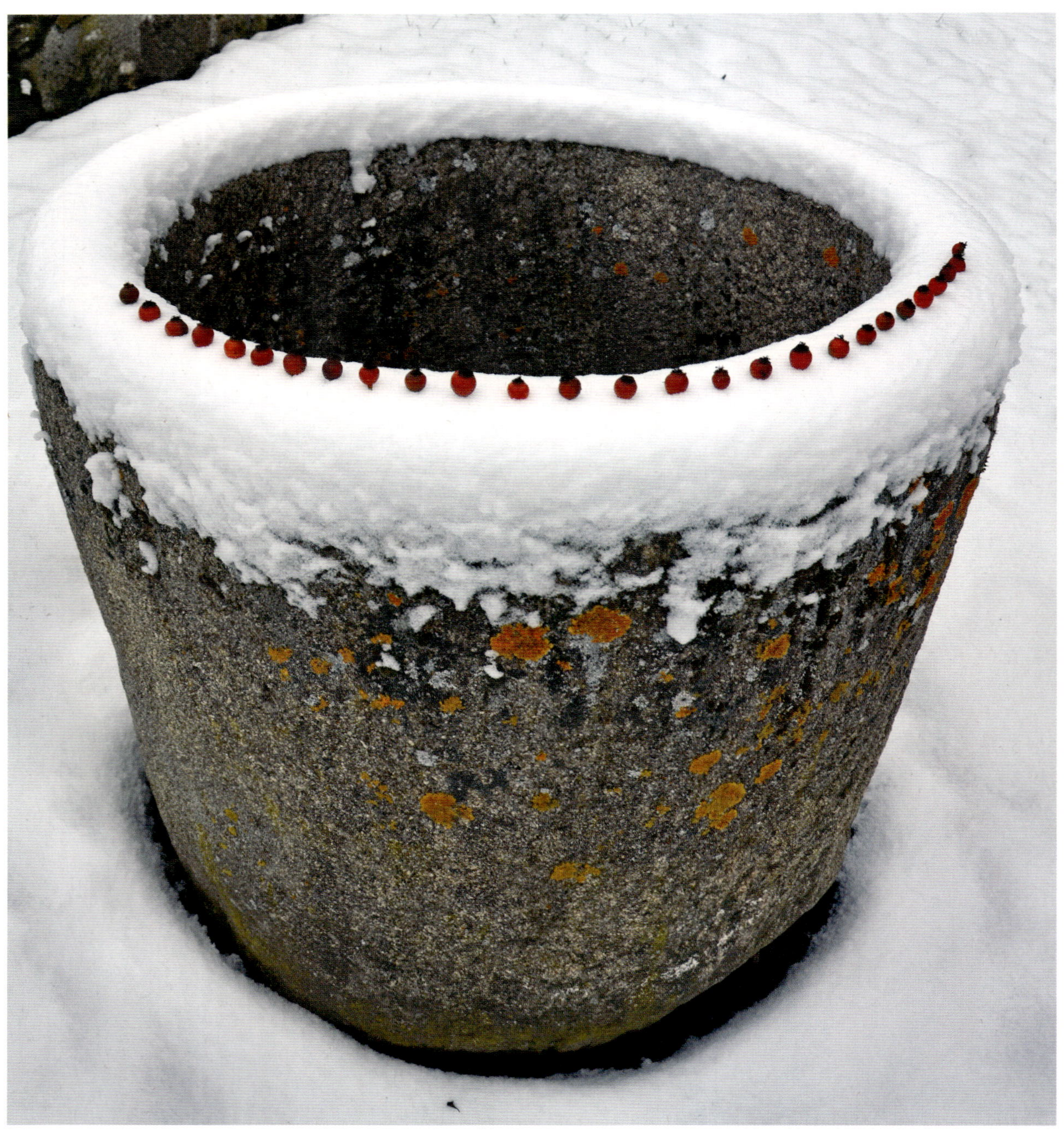

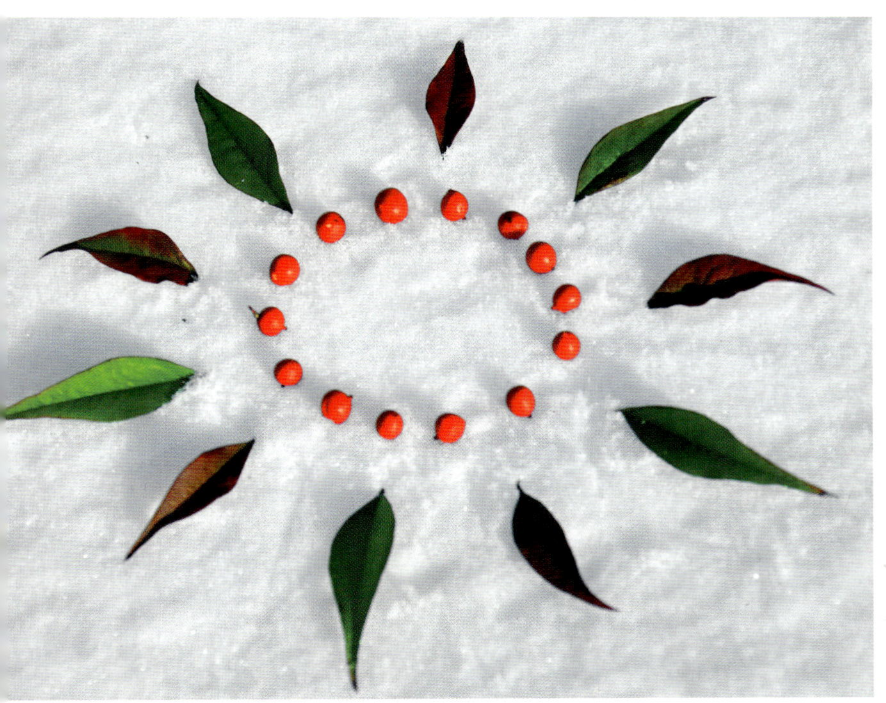

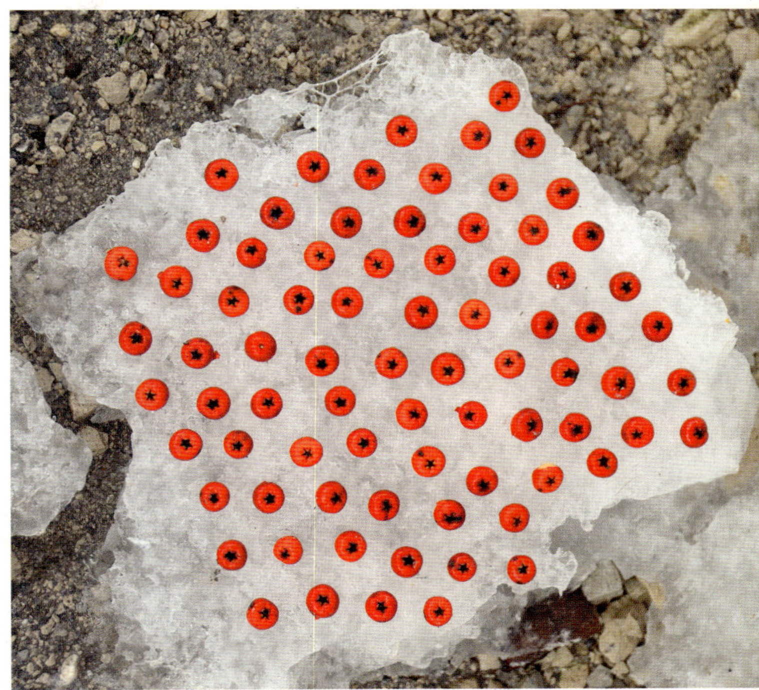

Bright red rosehip berries flourish in winter, so make the most of them.

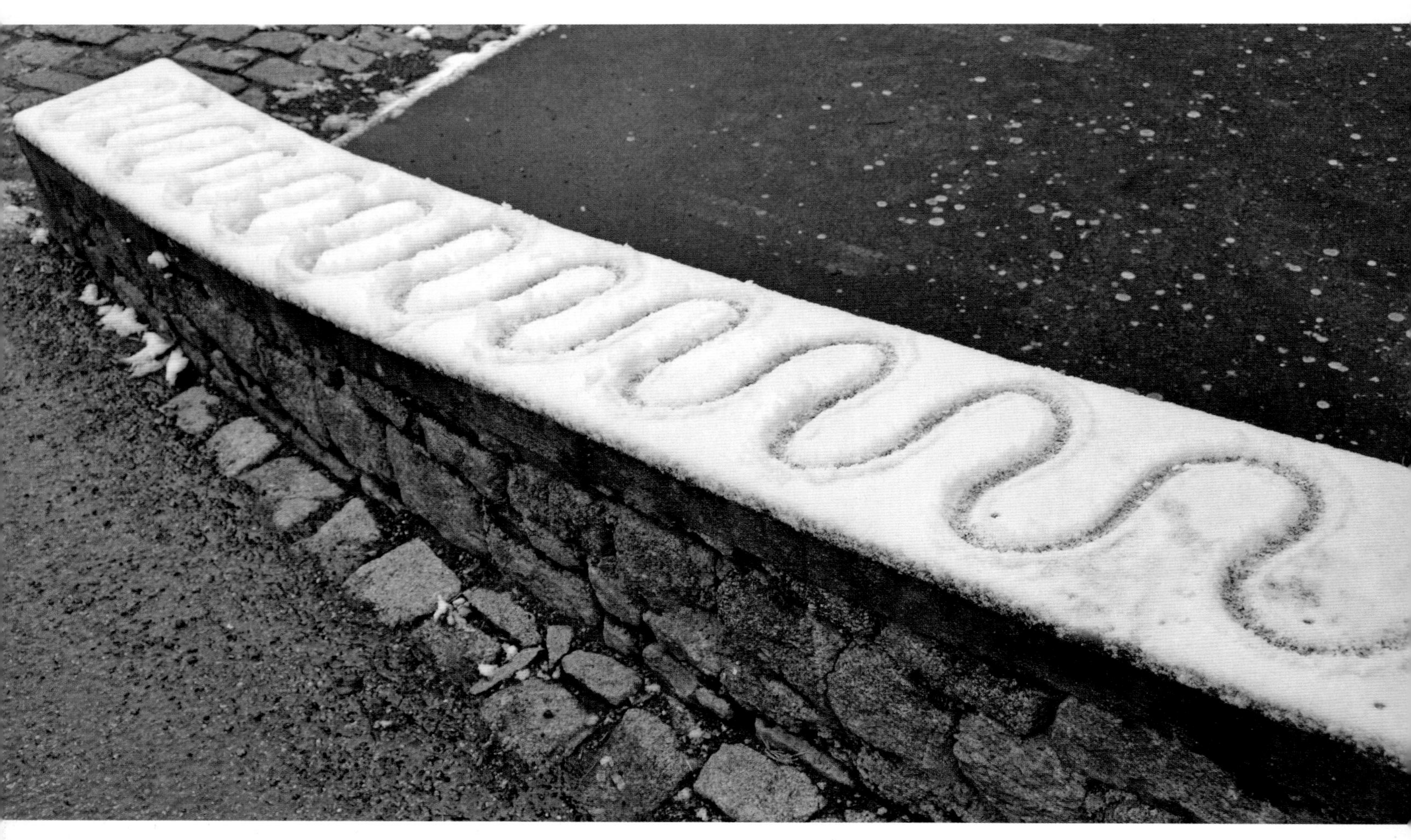

The long and winding road...

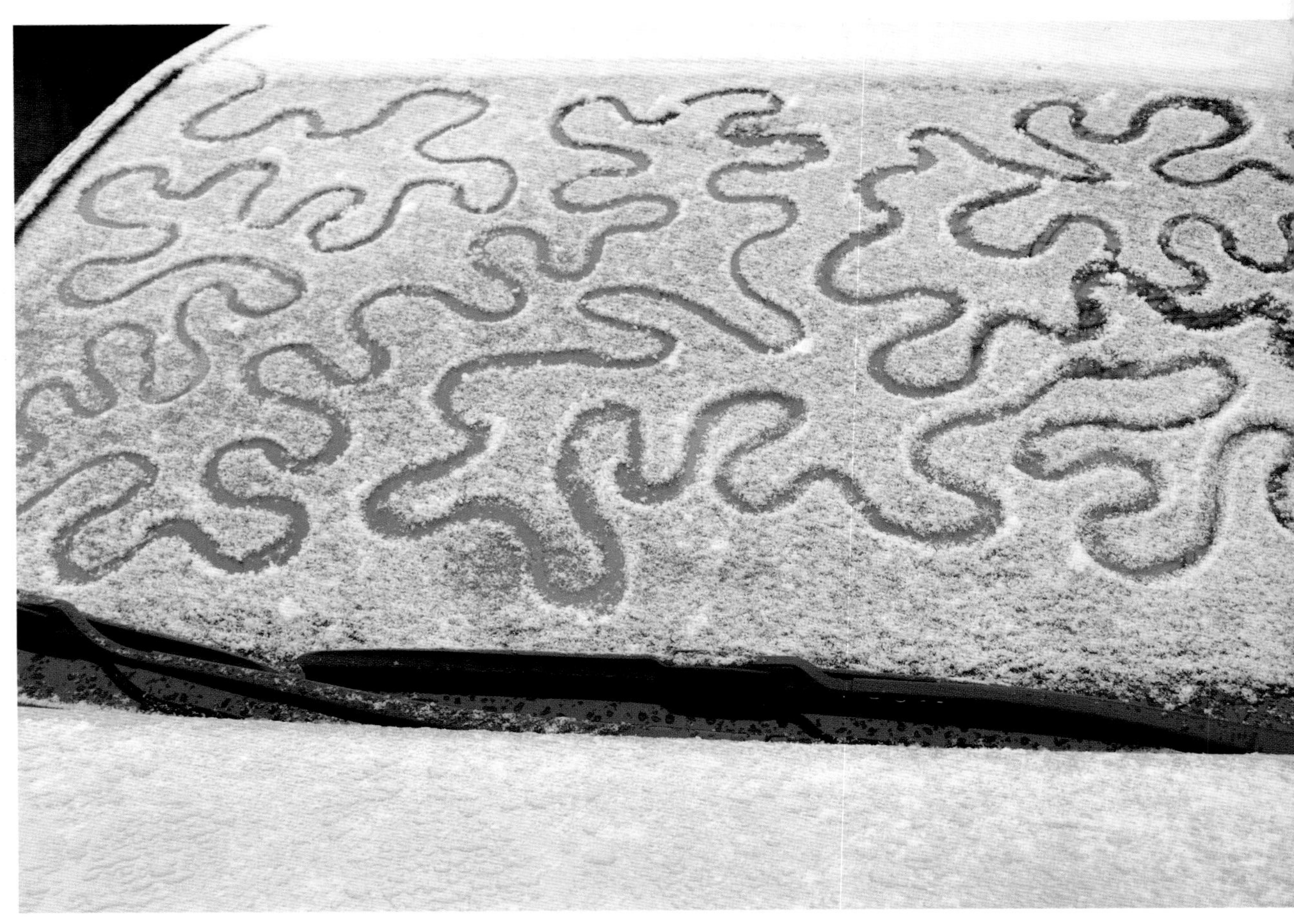

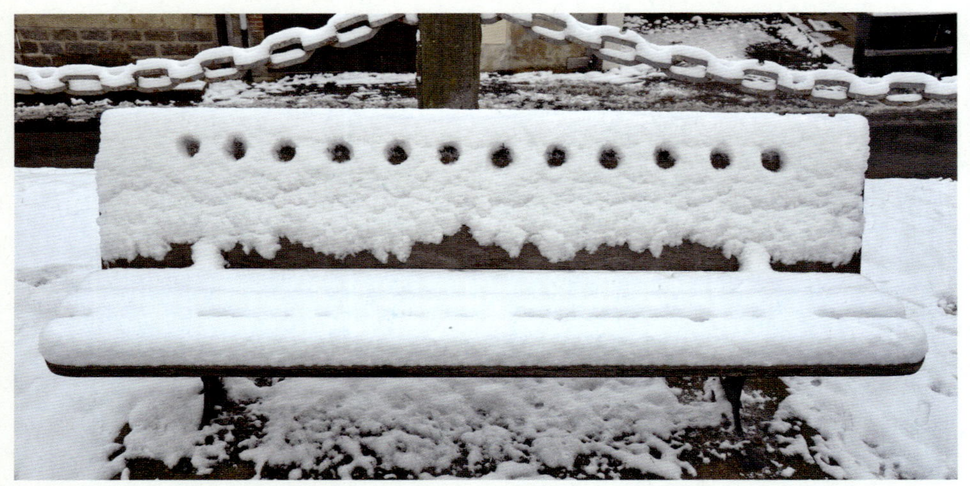

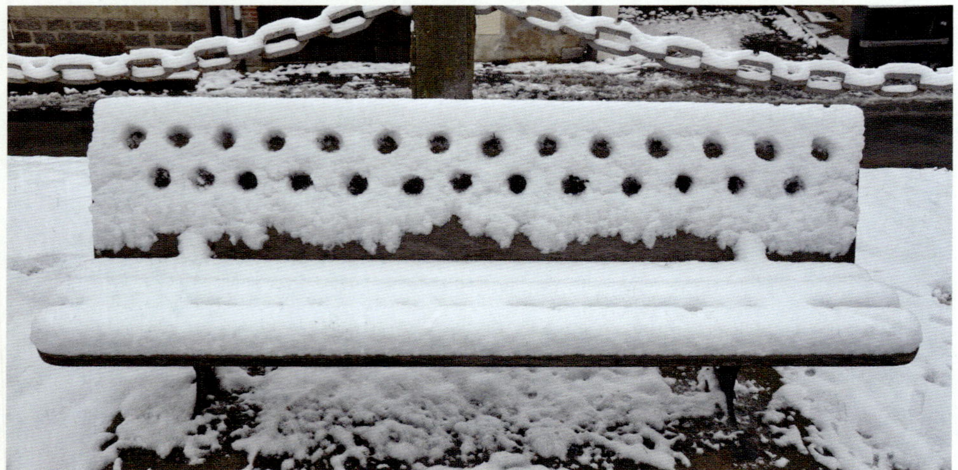

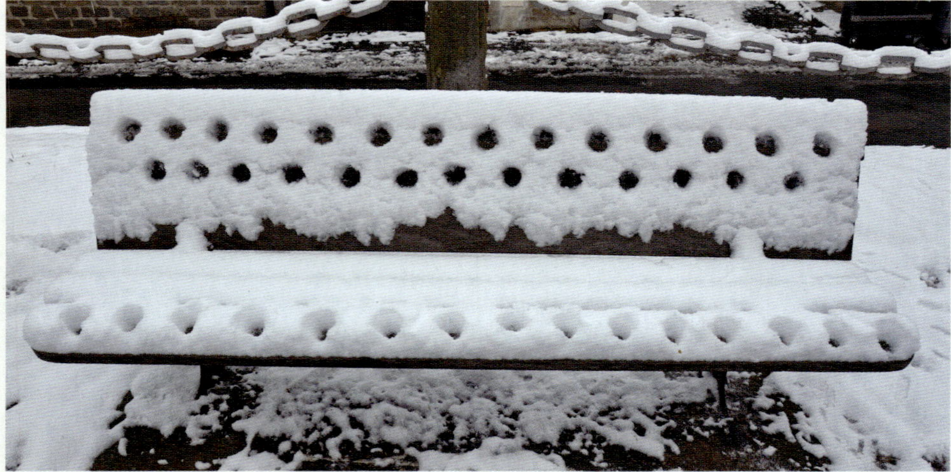

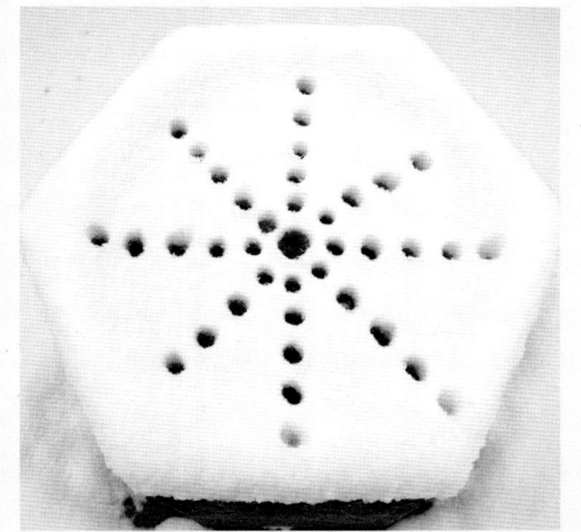

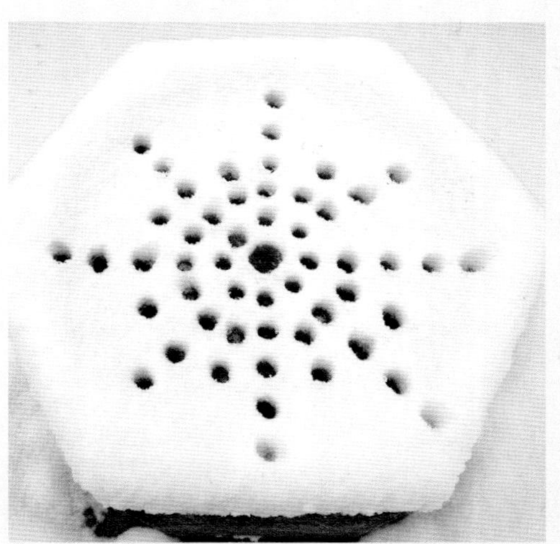

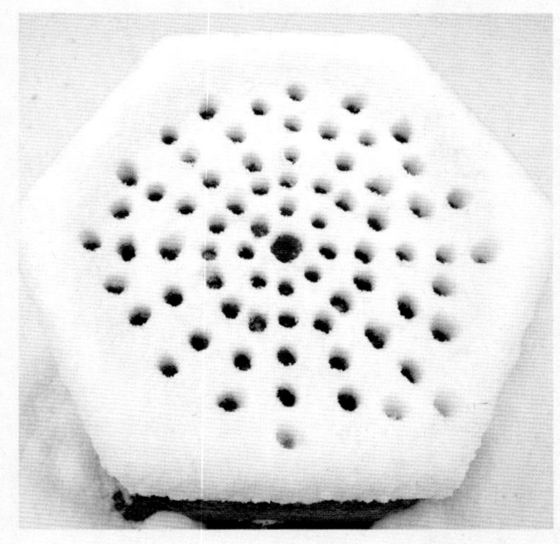

A whole lot of holes.

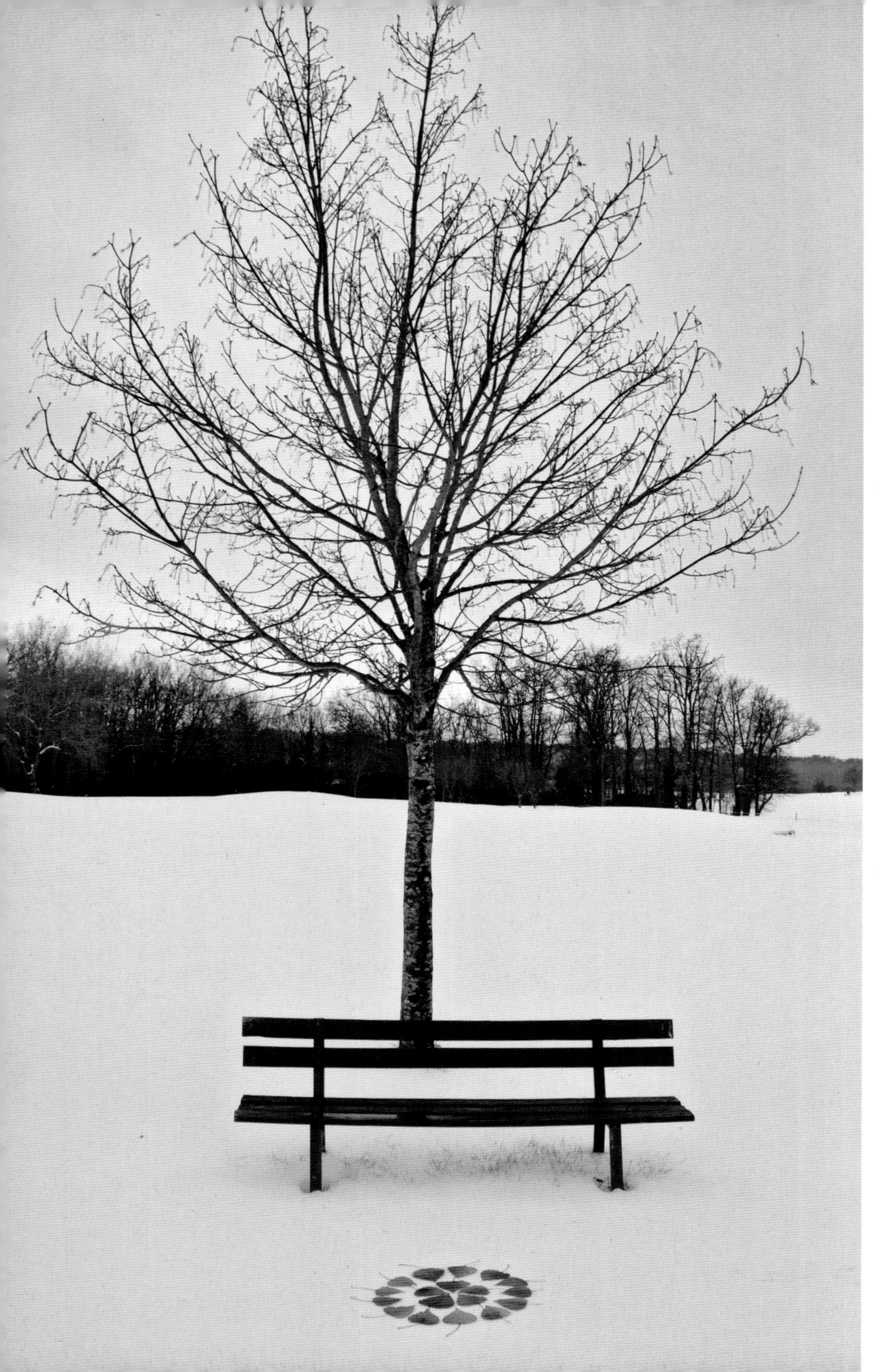

You might think it's more difficult to find a good choice of natural elements to collect in town, compared with the countryside. But that's rarely the case, although it depends on the neighbourhood. Indeed the opposite may be true, since town parks, public gardens and squares often contain treasures in the form of exotic trees, bushes and rare plants with leaves, berries and fruits that are magnificent in shape and colour.

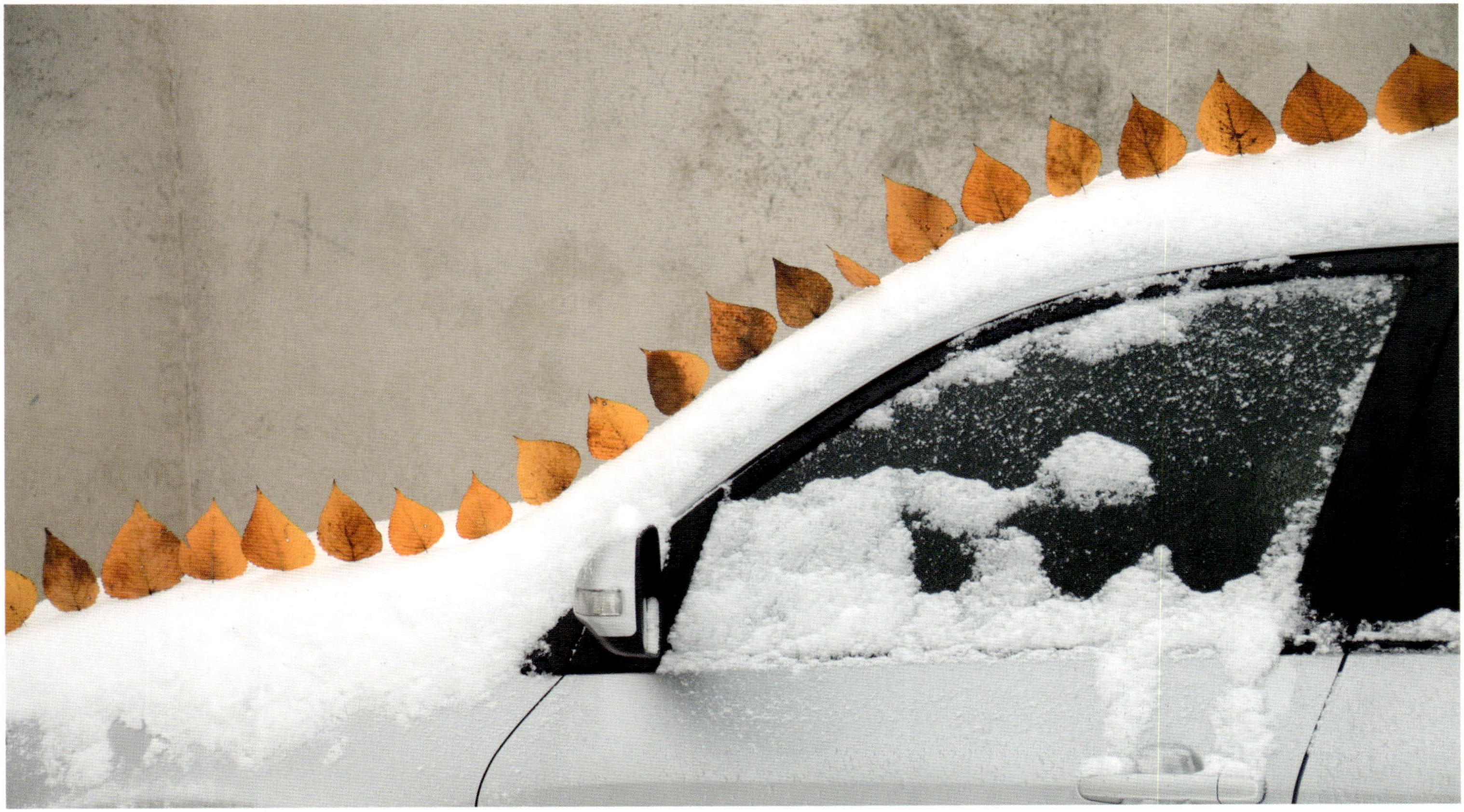

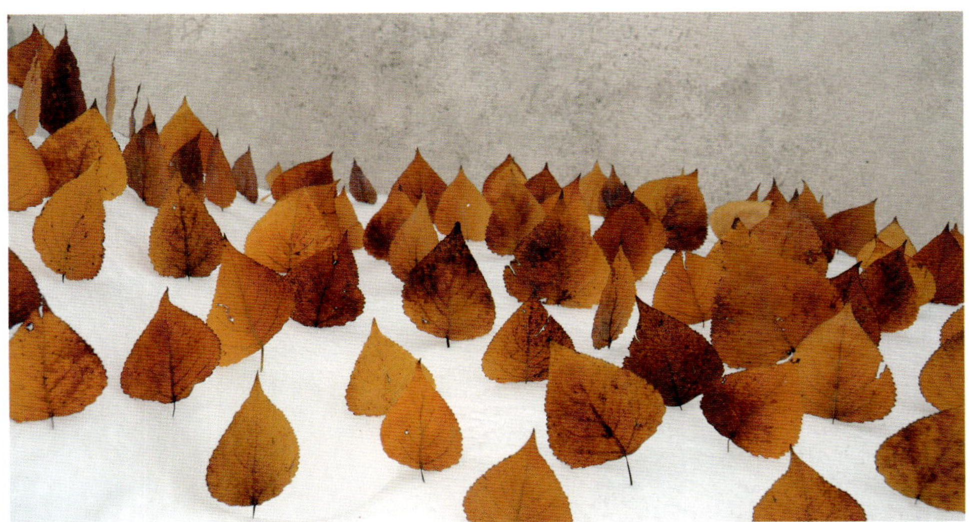

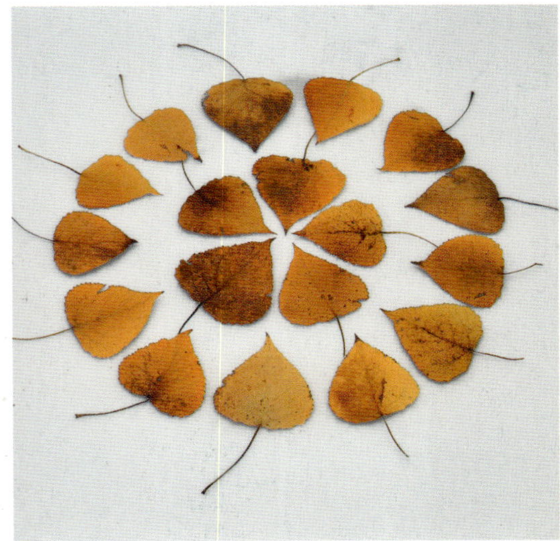

What would happen if a snowman tried to climb a tree?

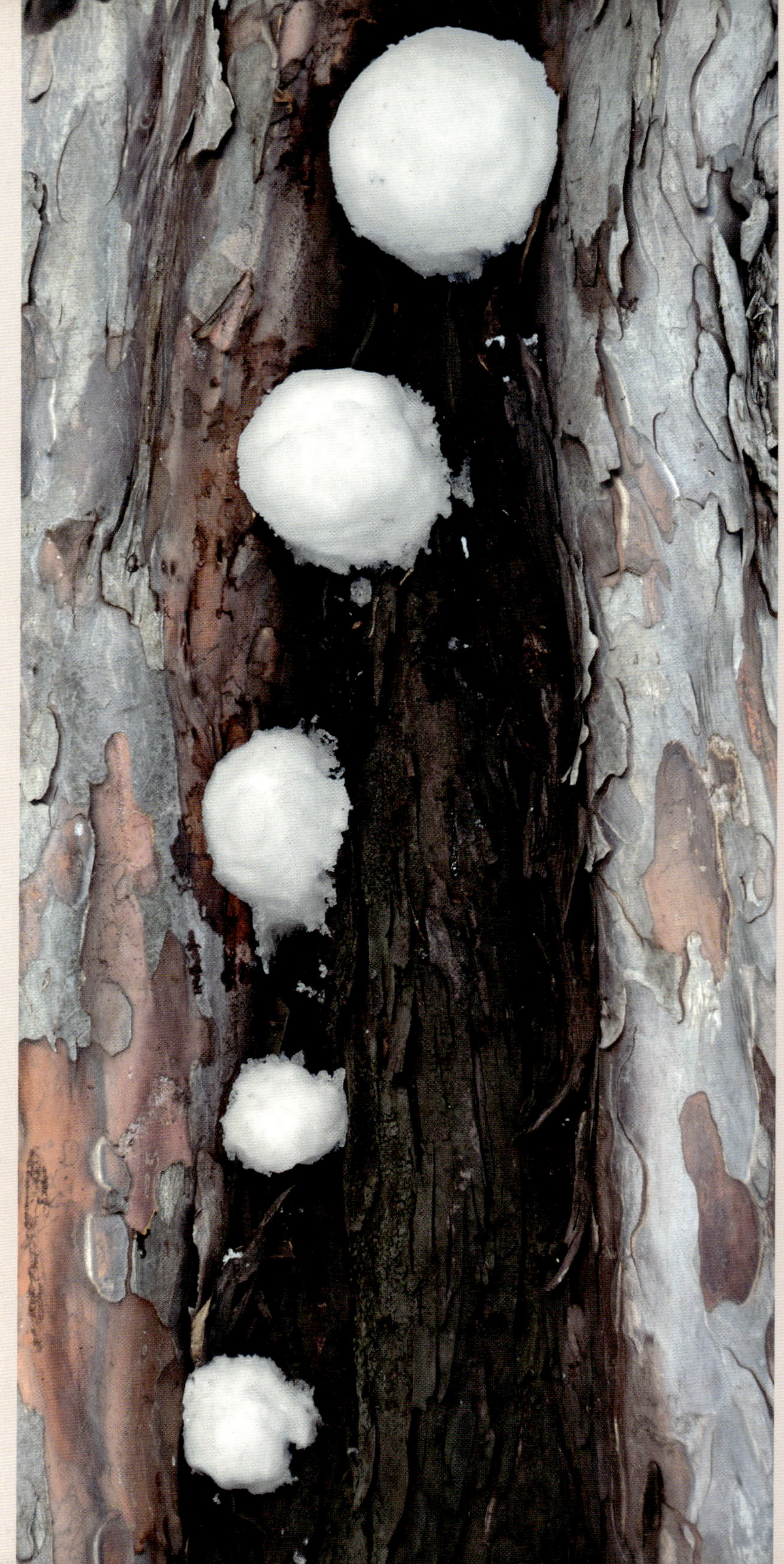

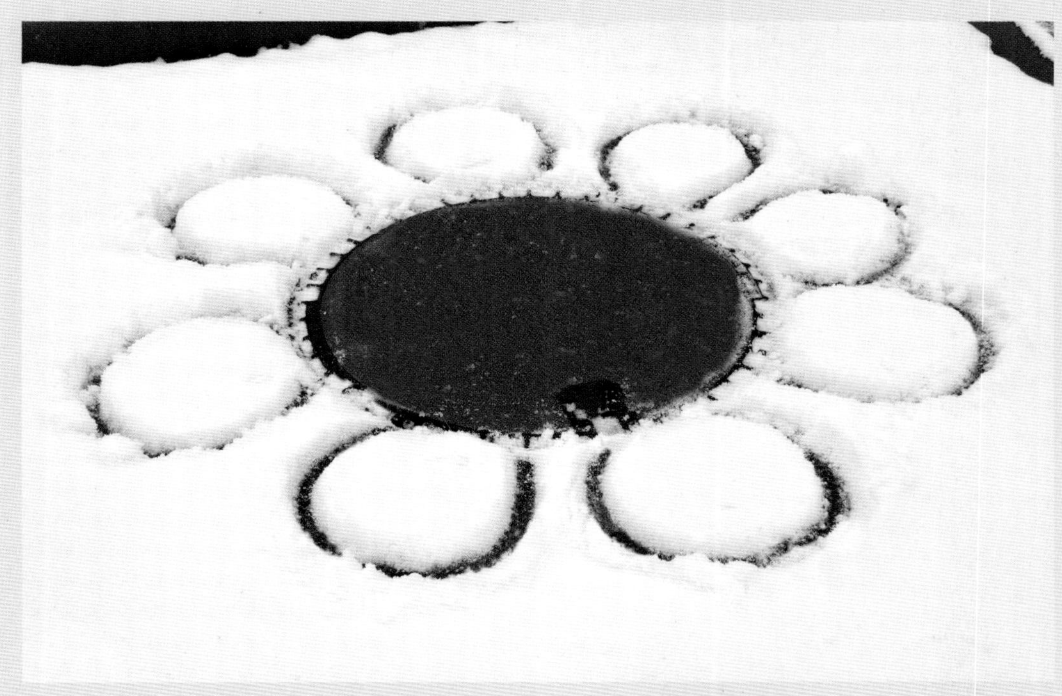

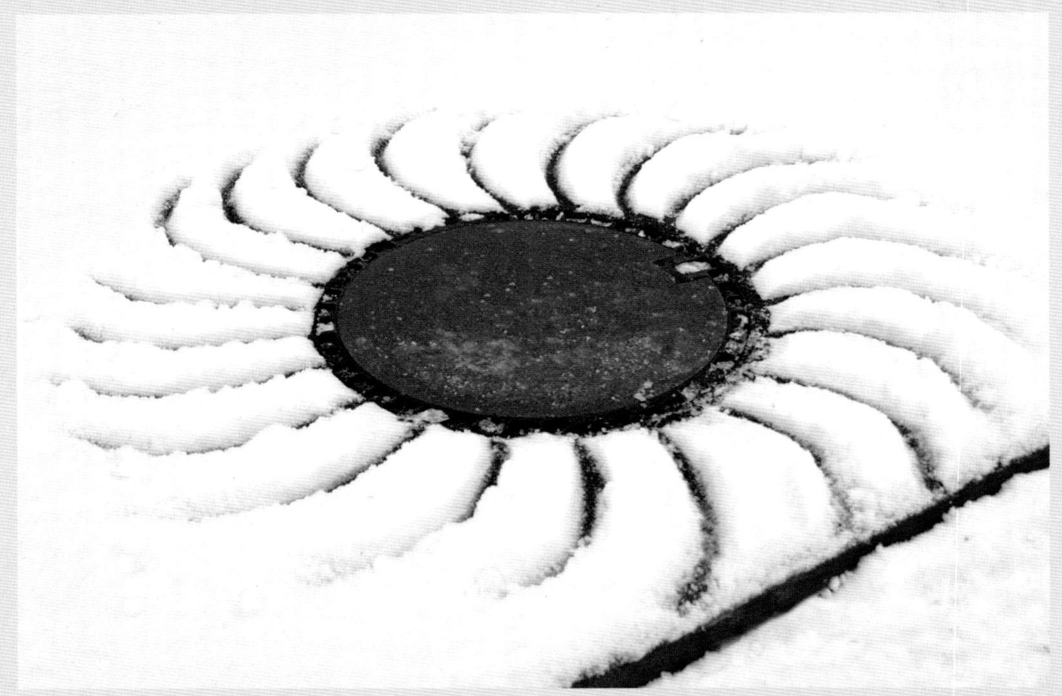

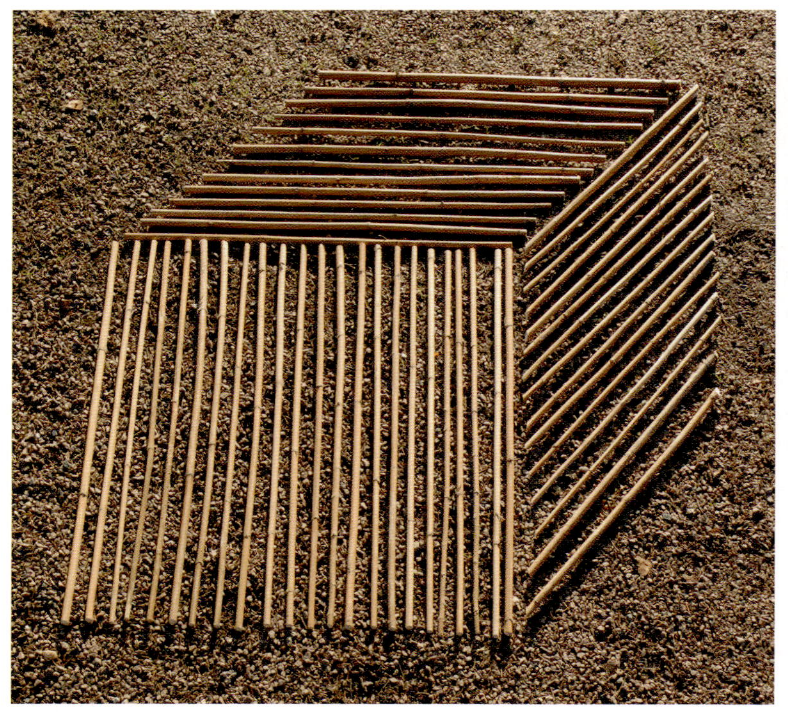

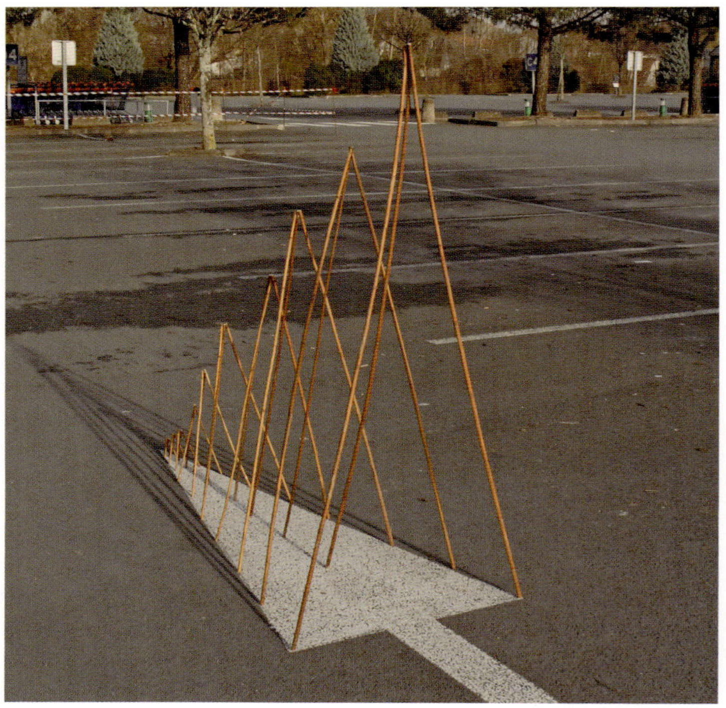

These installations are all about optical illusions.

Cube: really straight sunflower stems placed on the ground, although I have also used fern stems.

Arrows: made with the same sunflower stems placed together in threes to form self-supporting tripods.

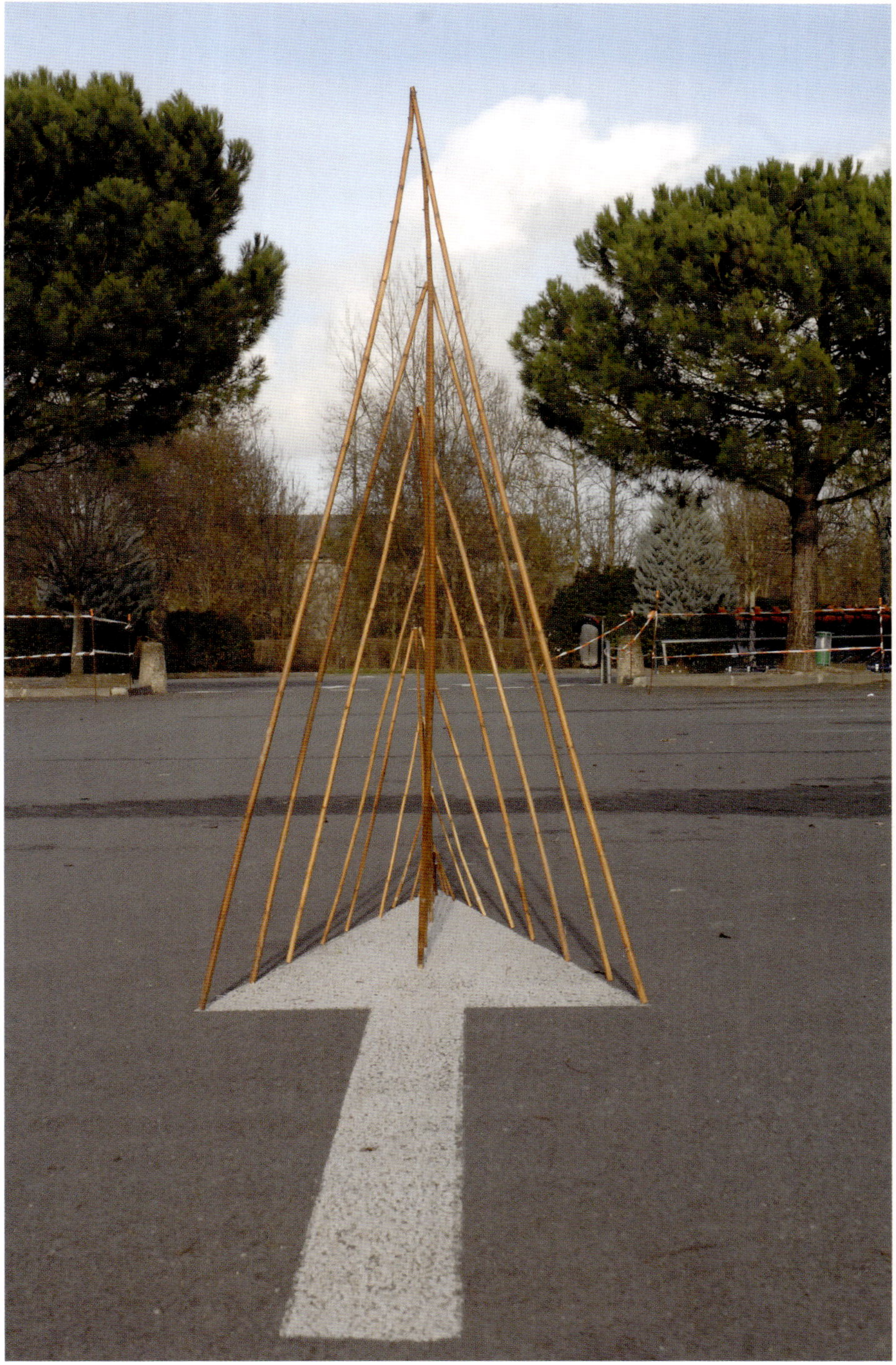

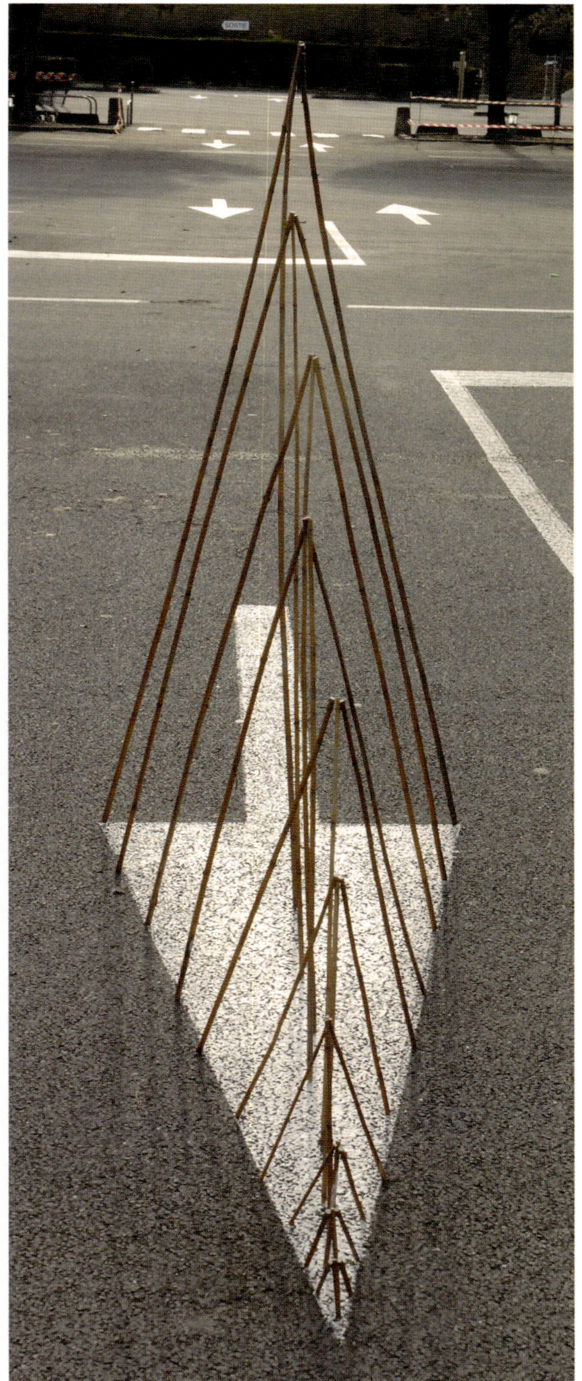

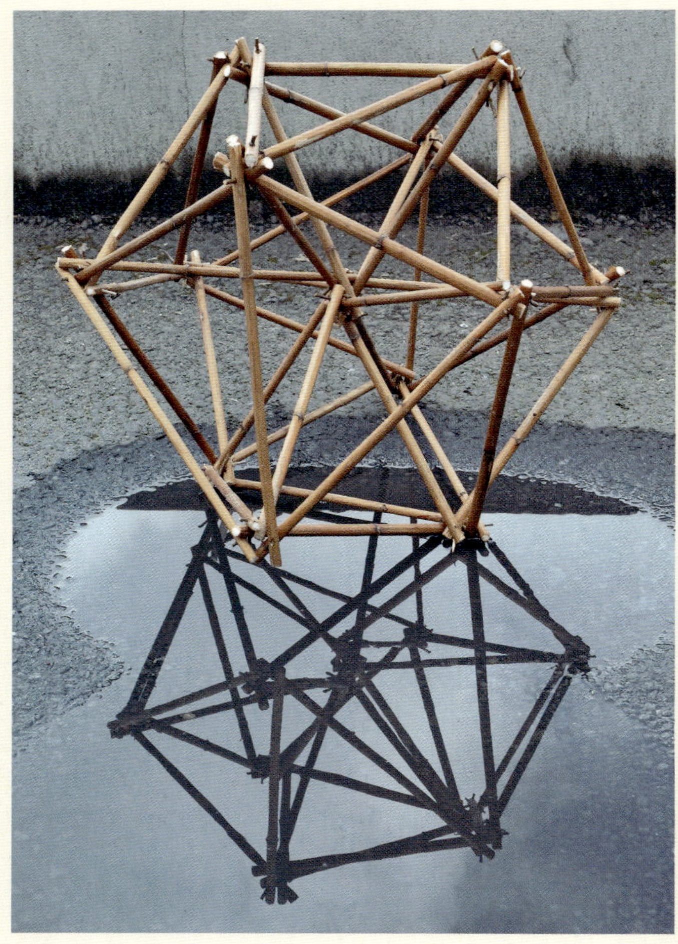

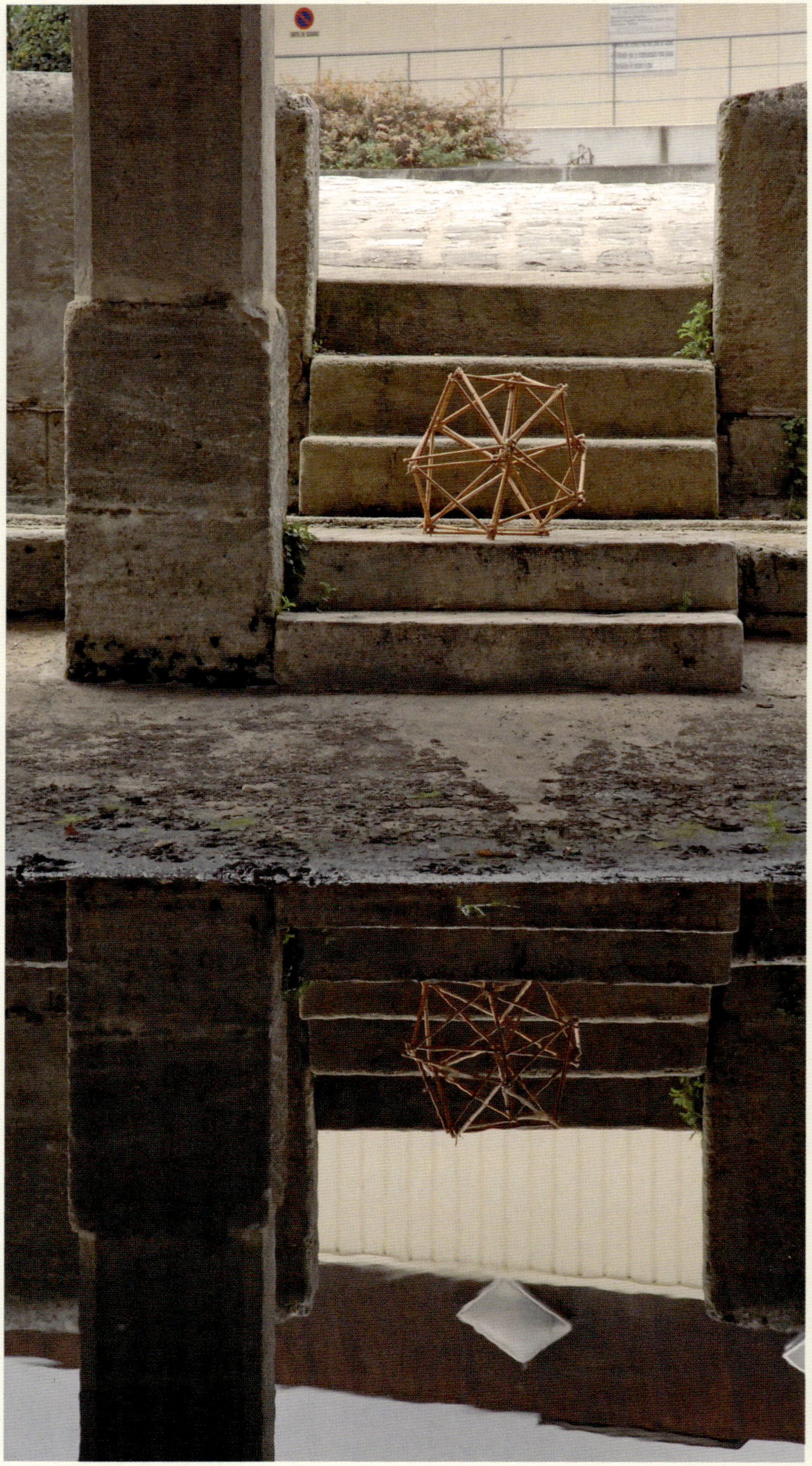

Sunflower stems fixed together with sloe thorns, the same elements and method used for the cube and feathers on page 107.

Remember that these installations remain very fragile, so it is better not to move them too much.

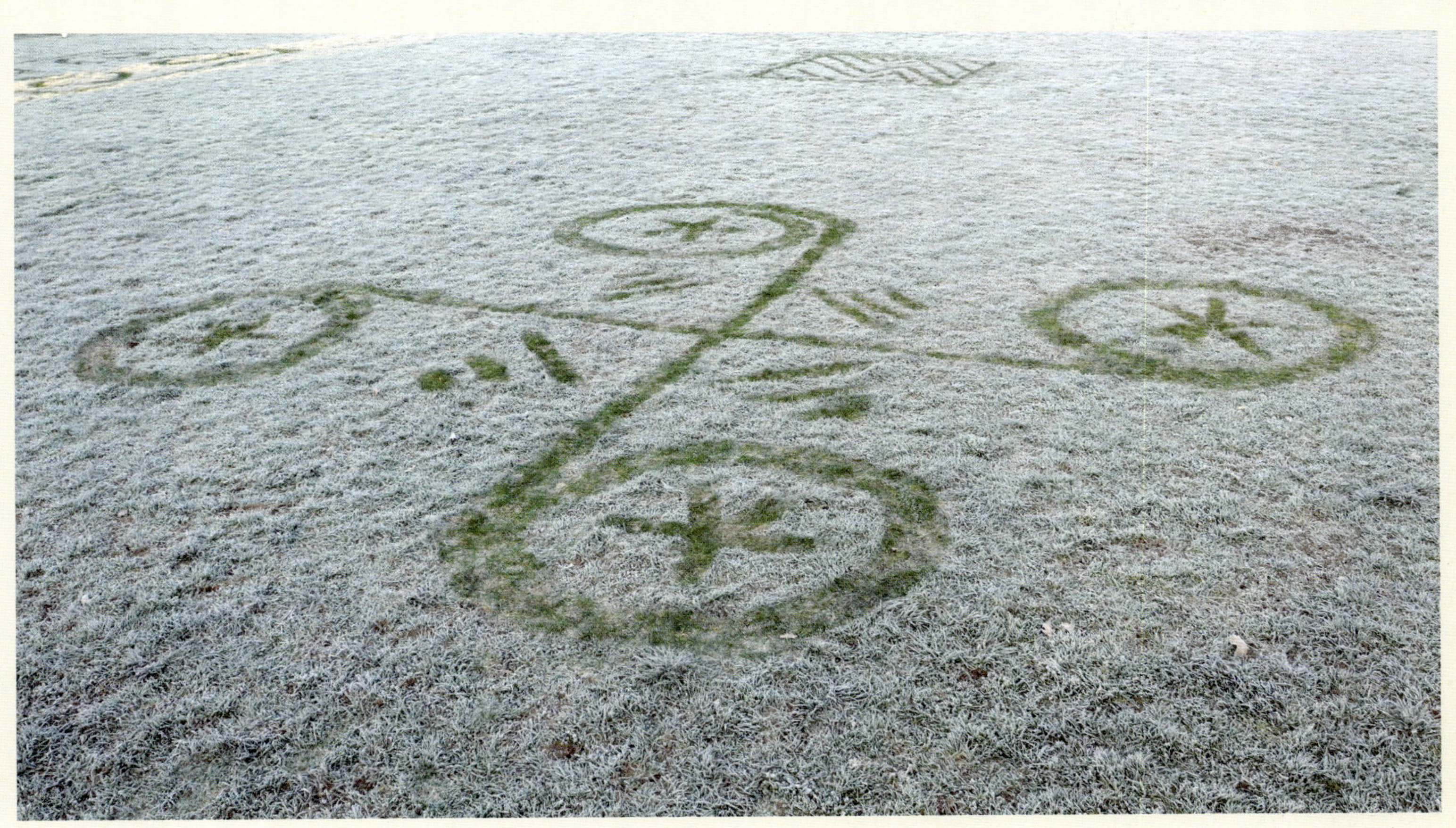

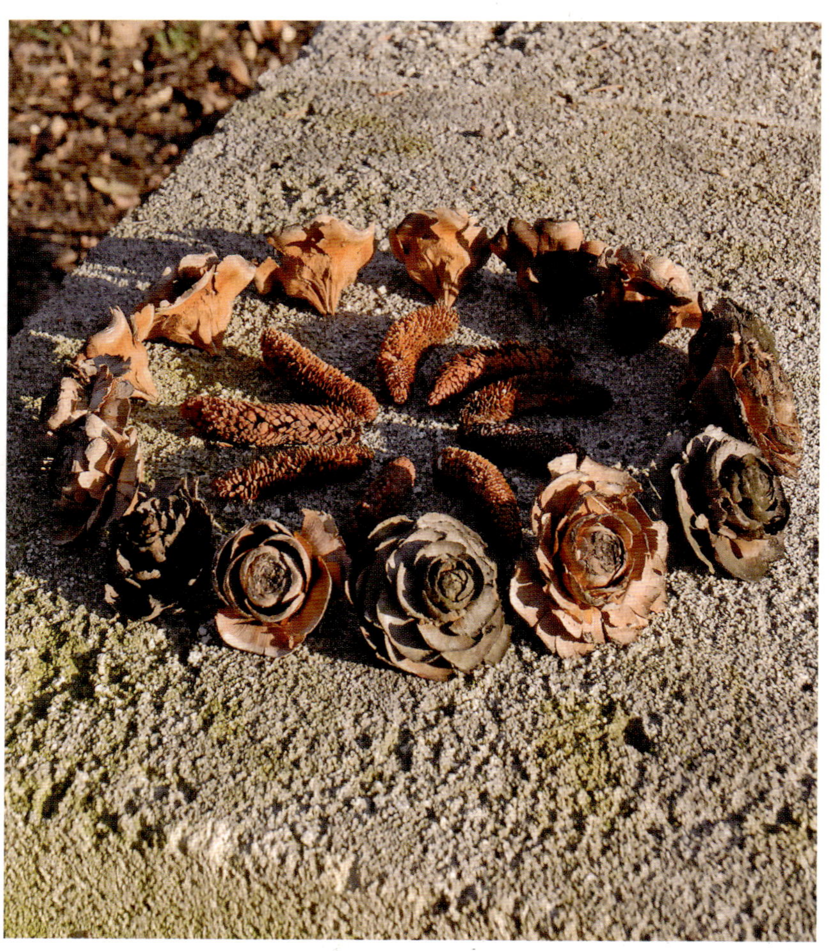

Catkins and cedar cones form a winter wreath in the afternoon sun.

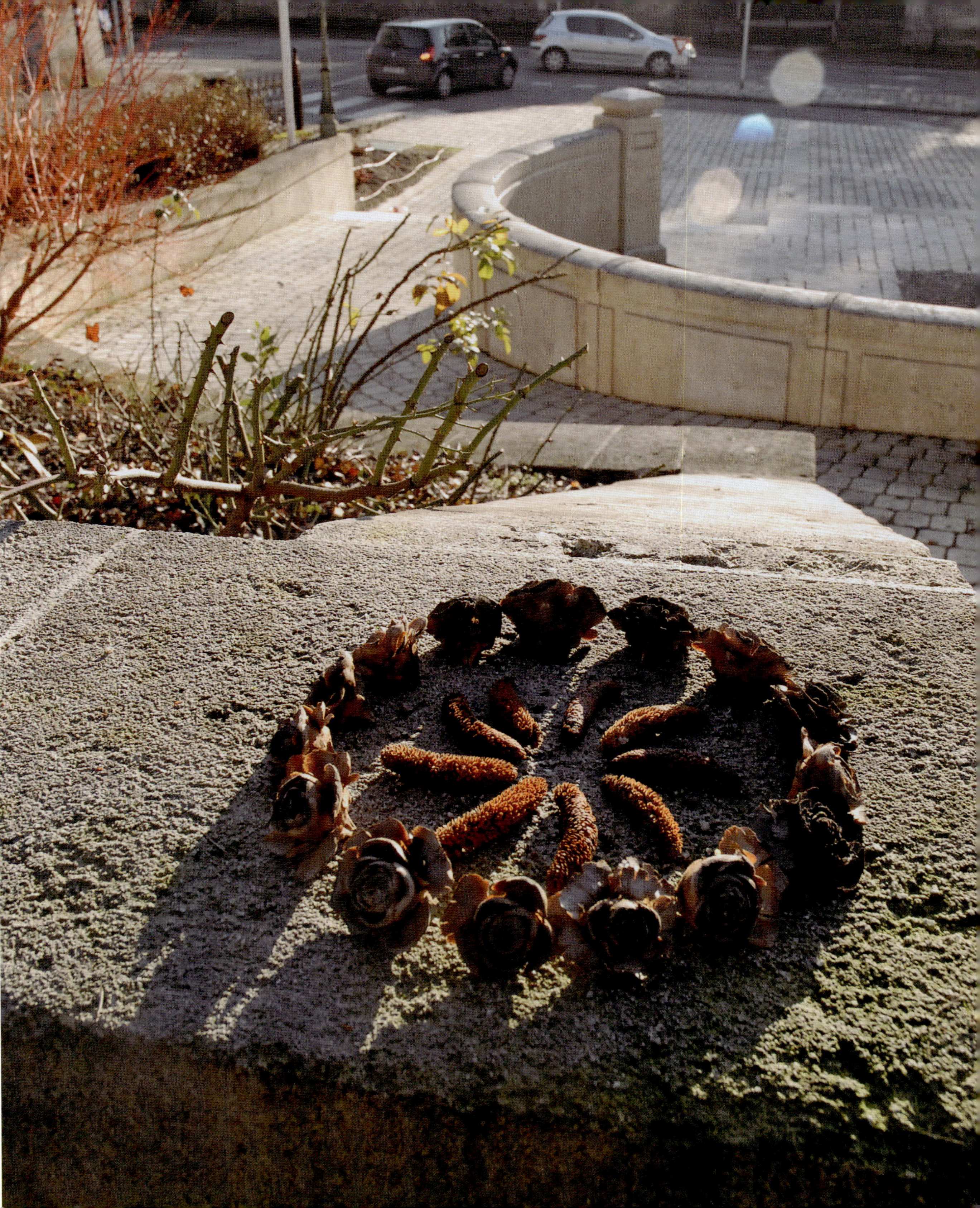

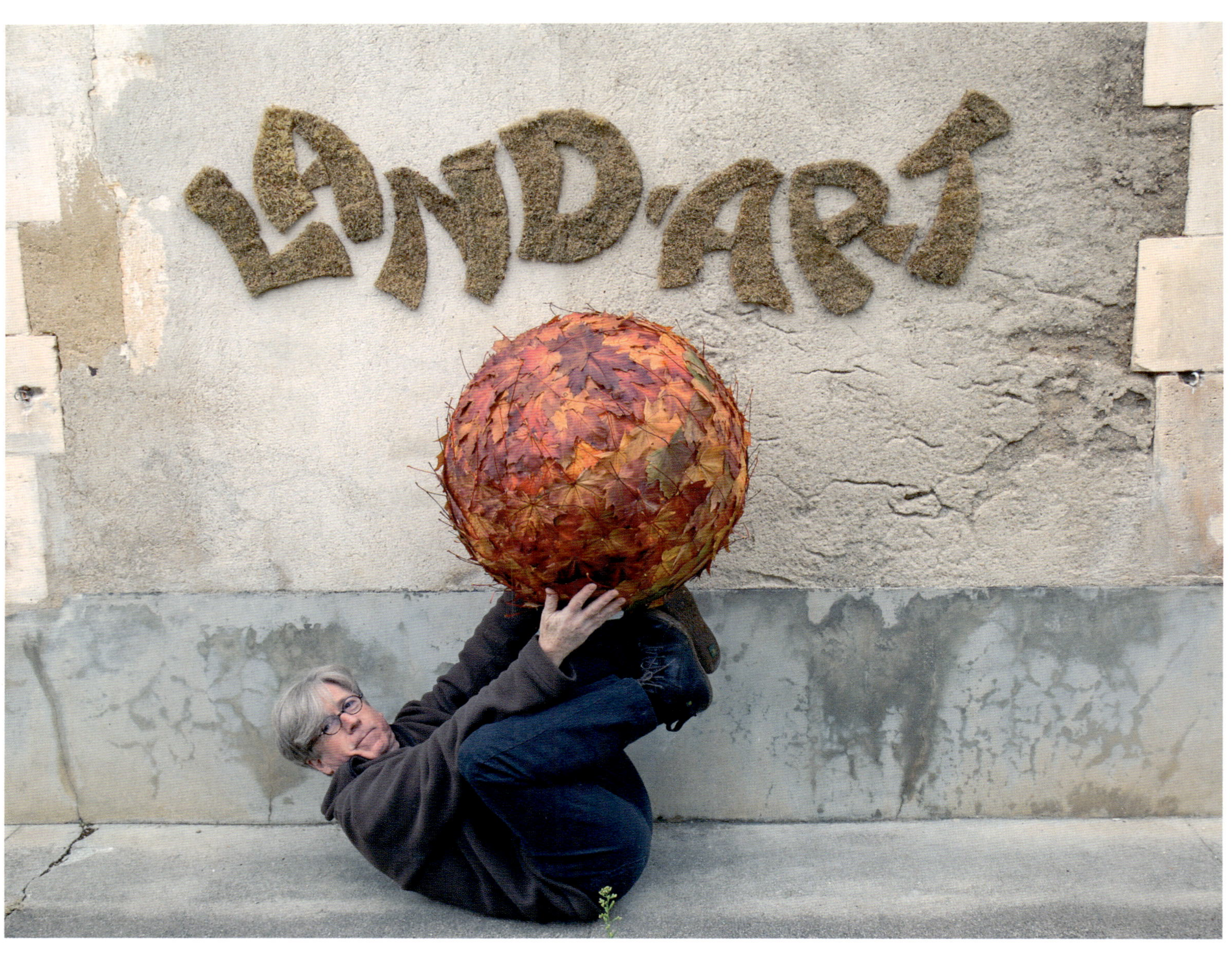
LAND'ART

ACKNOWLEDGEMENTS

The author would like to thank all the kind people he met by chance in the street while creating the images that appear in *Land Art in Town*. Thank you to everyone I met at workshops and courses, as well as my friends, for assisting me in making some of these installations. Thank you Maïté Milliéroux for her collaboration and her creative presence throughout the production of this book.

BIOGRAPHY

MARC POUYET trained as a graphic designer at the Corvisart School of Graphic Arts in Paris. He worked in advertising, then as a graphic designer and illustrator at the French publisher Nathan. He has illustrated several books for children, and leads Land Art workshops for children and adults. He is the author of NATURAL: SIMPLE LAND ART THROUGH THE SEASONS, also published by Frances Lincoln. www.marc-pouyet.net